UTOPIA'S GHOST

UTOPIA'S GHOST

Architecture and Postmodernism, Again

REINHOLD MARTIN

University of Minnesota Press

Minneapolis

London

For publication information on previously published material in this book, see Publication History on page 211.

Every effort was made to obtain permission to reproduce material in this book. If any proper acknowledgment has not been included, we encourage copyright holders to notify the publisher.

Published by the University of Minnesota Press
111 Third Avenue South, Suite 290
Minneapolis, MN 55401-2520
http://www.upress.umn.edu

Library of Congress Cataloging-in-Publication Data
Martin, Reinhold
Utopia's ghost : architecture and postmodernism, again / Reinhold Martin.
    p. cm.
Includes bibliographical references and index.
ISBN 978-0-8166-6963-9 (pb : alk. paper)
ISBN 978-0-8166-6962-2 (hc : alk. paper)
1. Architecture, Postmodern. I. Title.
NA682.P67M375 2010
724'.6—dc22

                                                2010011277

Printed in the United States of America on acid-free paper
The University of Minnesota is an equal-opportunity educator and employer.

17   16   15   14   13   12   11   10 9 8 7 6 5 4 3

FOR KADAMBARI AND NEELAN

CONTENTS

ACKNOWLEDGMENTS

The diversity of contexts in which much of this work first saw the light of day means that there are too many individuals to thank for their contribution to its realization. Some of these contributions were made knowingly, in the form of advice, criticism, or other direct support, and some were made unknowingly, in casual conversation or an invitation to consider a particular subject or a response to a presentation. Ultimately, this book would have been both impossible and inconceivable without the combination of audiences, readers, and interlocutors from whom it has thereby benefited.

Among these I must thank Felicity Scott, Brian Larkin, and Andreas Huyssen for uncounted conversations and collaborations from which I have learned a great deal. The intellectual context provided by *Grey Room*, in which some of this work first appeared, has, as always, been invaluable. There I also thank Branden Joseph, Karen Beckman, and Tom McDonough for making it what it is. In ways that remain largely intangible, this book also benefited significantly from the unique intellectual environment offered by the Institute for Comparative Literature and Society at Columbia University, especially in the persons of Gayatri Spivak and Rosalind Morris.

An important portion of the research for this book was completed while I was a visiting scholar at the Canadian Centre for Architecture (CCA). I warmly thank Phyllis Lambert, Mirko Zardini, and Alexis Sornin for a memorable and productive summer spent in their company at the CCA. Peter Sealy was an able research assistant during this time. The CCA generously allowed me to mount a collaborative research exhibition, "Utopia's Ghost: Postmodernism Reconsidered," cocurated with students from Columbia and based on two seminars at the Graduate School of

Architecture, Planning, and Preservation (GSAPP). At the CCA Giovanna Borasi, Howard Shubert, and Elspeth Cowell made significant contributions to the exhibition, which later traveled to the Arthur Ross Gallery at the GSAPP. There it was imaginatively reinstalled by Mark Wasiuta and his team. Cristina Goberna was an invaluable assistant on the exhibition in both venues, and the two groups of students in the seminars made the kinds of original contributions that only students can make. I am also grateful to Diana Martinez for her insight and assistance in assembling material for the illustrations for the book. At Columbia and at the CCA, the exhibition and related research benefited from the generous support of GSAPP dean Mark Wigley. Many other colleagues at Columbia and elsewhere also provided valuable input in a variety of ways.

Significant portions of this book were aided or provoked by invitations to speak or write in a wide variety of contexts. Their synthesis, which reflects tensions inherent in the book's subject, was among the most challenging and rewarding aspects of this work. Arindam Dutta and Aron Vinegar offered extremely thoughtful and productive critical readings of the resulting manuscript. At the University of Minnesota Press, Pieter Martin showed great care and professionalism in guiding this book through the editorial process. The text was ably copyedited by David Coen, and Andrea Rondoni and Laura Westlund graciously assisted with production.

Finally, I thank Kadambari Baxi for her modernism and Neelan Baxi Martin for the future.

INTRODUCTION

Architecture and Postmodernism, Again

WHY POSTMODERNISM, yet again? Is it not either too late or too early, too academic or too obvious, to return to that moment when architecture was taken up by so many thinkers for its evidentiary status, as marking a momentous interruption, or at least detour, in modernity's path? Today, when the conversation has turned in so many ways toward the prolongation, recovery, or multiplication of modernity itself, what would be the point of reactivating a term as vague and as apparently exhausted as *postmodernity* or its cultural accomplice, *postmodernism*?[1]

To speak of postmodernism today as anything other than a lapsed historical phenomenon or as a fait accompli may seem quaintly anachronistic or even parochial. But simply to historicize it, whether as a stage in the intensification of capitalist decadence, a coherent intellectual project, or a passing fashion, seems equally inadequate and, in many ways, premature. Exactly this untimeliness, this asynchronicity with respect to the concerns of the present and those of a more distant past, has defined the postmodern in its various guises and continues to require analysis and interpretation. This is especially true now, when watchwords of the modern like "crisis" have returned to the scene. In short, like the modernity to which it in many ways still belongs, the postmodern continues to pose historical and theoretical problems, which I address here through the refractory prism of architecture.

In this light, architecture appears as a cipher in which is encoded a virtual universe of production and consumption, as well as a material unit, a piece of that universe that helps to keep it going. At the very moment when so-called postmodern architecture jettisoned modernism's "machine aesthetic," it revealed itself to be part of a new machine as well as a representation of that machine. This book is therefore translated out of architecture, so to speak, with the conviction that disciplinary knowledge remains deeply relevant to understanding and interpreting such processes in more general terms. Read thusly, it is addressed to the multidisciplinary nexus in which the postmodern and its progeny continue to circulate, sometimes in barely recognizable form.

The place on the contemporary map occupied by the legacies of architectural modernism is hardly fixed, and architecture's postmodern turn has yet to be fully historicized. This book contributes to those tasks only secondarily. Instead, it emphasizes a set of concepts that were reworked as a consequence of that turn. By revisiting these in sequential but overlapping fashion, I have tried to open up new avenues for interpreting the period roughly from 1970 to the present, and with these, new possibilities for thinking the future. In essence, I argue that to retheorize postmodern architecture is to retheorize postmodernism as such, to the extent that architecture functioned as its avatar. By reactivating the term at the moment of its desuetude, I revisit the initial assumptions made regarding architecture's symptomatic status, in order to extract from the recent past new tools for new problems, without for a minute pretending that we are finished with the old ones.

So this is not a history of postmodernism; it is a historical reinterpretation of some of its major themes. Its subject is architectural *thought* (whether written, drawn, or built) as much as it is the architecture itself. Though accounts vary as to its tangible characteristics, and though the term had been used somewhat earlier, postmodern architecture is generally agreed to have emerged during the mid-1960s, in Europe and in the United States. It did so to the accompaniment of book-length manifestos that articulated its basic problematics and, later, a number of exhibitions that attempted to measure its scope.[2] Its benchmark year was arguably 1984, by which time a number of influential cultural theorists had adduced architectural examples to define the postmodern predicament more generally.[3] Beyond this, there is little agreement as to the characteristics that make a particular building or project "postmodern," only that such a designation is possible. My purpose, then, is not to sharpen the definition or to survey its contents. It is to rethink the problem from the beginning. And my point of departure is the simple fact that, by the mid-1980s, "postmodernism" had come to designate a discursive formation.

In architecture, this formation reorganized a number of key concepts, which I examine in successive chapters by connecting exemplary architectural texts and objects with events and phenomena in the political, social, and economic domains—not to contextualize the architecture but to *decontextualize* it with respect to existing narratives. In doing so, I take existing periodizations more or less for granted in order to show postmodernism's somewhat uncanny aperiodicity. Likewise for the generally canonical nature of the texts and objects I consider, which is a deliberate choice oriented toward this strategic decontextualization (and recontextualization) and toward the consequent reframing of concepts. My use of examples and case studies, which are drawn mainly from the United States and Europe, is intended to concretize certain abstractions and to problematize certain received interpretations. Inevitably there are many other, equally postmodern, architectures that I leave unexamined here, including but not limited to those of East Asia, of the Middle East, of Scandinavia, of Latin America, and of South Asia. Still, I hope that their resonance with the examples that I do take up will be evident to the reader. The same goes for the discursive frames, such as regionalism, in which many of these architectures were initially set. In their appeals to locality or to cultural specificity, such frames often seemed to brace themselves against the postmodern (and frequently, neocolonial) juggernaut; and yet, just as often, they reproduced its premises in their own statements.[4]

My method is comparative, though in a specific sense. I do not assume that the excerpts that I take up automatically run parallel to other excerpts from other contexts that could, ideally, be lined up side by side on a level playing field of cultural exchange. Instead, I attempt to show how hegemonic arrangements, many of which are represented by my examples, require and reproduce their own "outsides," the hazy, out-of-focus backdrops against which their projects operate. These outsides range from downtown Pittsburgh to Saigon to Bhopal. I do not necessarily take them into account on their own terms but, rather, as a sort of underarticulated reality against and through which postmodernist discourse was produced. The material abjection in which many actual lives are lived in these zones in order for the discourse in question to emerge is one measure of how postmodernism's power/knowledge nexus actually works.

It should also be clear that, in casting a backward glance, I do not attempt to reclaim postmodernism from its subsequent fate. Instead, I hope to reclaim for architectural thought a decisive role in the analysis, interpretation, and critique of *power*. In this, I mean to take advantage of architecture's immanence within widely ramified material and cultural networks that are interlaced with conflicting interests and ideological struggles. As they accumulate and repeat, the concrete practices through which these networks are configured help to shape nothing less than cognition itself, by differentiating what is thinkable from what is unthinkable and therefore remains unthought.

In architecture as elsewhere, the active "unthinking" of Utopia is among those practices that distinguish postmodernism from modernism.[5] This activity cannot be explained merely as a reaction to earlier, modernist excesses. Instead, under postmodernism, cultural production has been repositioned as a laboratory for auto-regulation, wherein power is redefined as control, and especially self-control. For a discourse caught in a net of double binds, structural transformation of the status quo becomes increasingly unthinkable, and not merely unrealistic. Thus appears another hallmark of postmodernism: the sullen withdrawal from engagement, or (what amounts to the same thing) the preemptive, exuberant embrace of the status quo.

To speak, as I do, of architecture's immanence is to identify an apparent paradox running through my argument. Namely, that architecture's participation in heterogeneous networks of power, including biopower, actually *increases* with its withdrawal into private games played in an esoteric language. As an example that exaggerates only a little, imagine an atomic physicist withdrawing daily into the laboratory to do science and only science, only to wake up one late-summer morning to discover that she had been working on the Manhattan Project. This is how to understand architecture's "autonomy." It is also how architecture makes power real, rather than the other way around. Conversely, with respect to well-intentioned efforts to expand or erase the discipline's inherited boundaries, remember that, as every ethnographer knows, fieldwork (i.e., work "out there") constructs both self and other at once. Either way, the interrelation of inside and outside, here and there, sits squarely in the crosshairs of my inquiry.

So postmodernism is not a style; it is a discursive formation. This is how I approach my object of study every step of the way. It is true whether we are speaking of postmodernism in the narrowly architectural sense, or in the sense of a generalized cultural assemblage. Here we are already revising the architectural narratives, since in the late 1970s and 1980s, in architecture, it seemed that you were either a postmodernist or you were not, a distinction that was most often expressed at a stylistic level. On its face, this was inconsistent with the possibility, much observed from the outside, that architecture offered the best indication of an across-the-board, epochal shift, a turn toward a generalized postmodernity, in which case it was hardly a matter of choosing sides. These opposite (though not mutually exclusive) scenarios added up to the ultimate postmodern impasse, in which the relation between cultural forms and historical truth was at stake.

To choose sides in the modern/postmodern game was to exercise a certain authorial freedom that echoed, however faintly, the chiliastic exertions of the historical avant-gardes and the life-or-death choices they proposed, whereas the emergent critique of representation suggested that all such choices were ultimately contingent upon forces to which the author/actor/agent had by definition only limited access, if any. It is no surprise, then, that the relation between cultural forms and historical truth was problematized in architecture largely by way of experiments with representation. This meant citing anachronistic visual codes, such as the classical orders, in a novel manner. Or it meant reproducing formal archetypes that dug deep into a supposed historical unconscious. Or it meant working rhetorically with the very same abstract geometries previously identified with modernism. Manifest stylistically but running much deeper, all such experiments implicitly conceded that the relation between architecture and historical truth could only be resolved willfully and, in that sense, arbitrarily—a decisive break from modernist master narratives. Indeed, what seemed most historically *true* was the contingent relation between cultural forms and historical truth. But this conclusion also demonstrated its proximity to the naturalized "truths" of advanced capitalism by serving as an alibi for the production of so much interchangeable raw material for the consumerist spectacle, if not emanating from it in the first place.

As it passes through architecture, the discursive formation that we call postmodernism therefore seems a cruel combination of freedom and servitude, truth and lies. As such, it does seem to mirror the shadow play that we may suspect is the defining characteristic of our time. But what if architecture offers something more than just material evidence of the "cultural logic of late capitalism," as Fredric Jameson has so forcefully put it? What if, as I have already intimated, architecture's most recent linguistic turn actually participated in the reorganization of life itself, as articulated and managed by power in its many forms? More specifically: What if postmodernism, in architecture and elsewhere, was *also* a matter of new biopolitical arrangements and protocols operating in the cultural imaginary as it intersected the real? Does such a hypothesis deepen architecture's capacity to serve as an interpretive guide in grasping a rearrangement of the terms governing the interaction of culture, politics, and capital in the latter part of the twentieth century? Does it refocus our attention on such questions in new and helpful ways? Or does it redirect it entirely?

As with *postmodernism,* the terms *biopolitics* and *biopower* cannot emerge from such an analysis unchanged. Though they generally refer to governmental techniques for the classification and administration of life that marked what Michel Foucault called a "threshold of modernity" for the West during the late eighteenth century, these practices can be followed forward into the twentieth century.[6] Seen in historically specific terms, biopower is at work not only in the spaces of "exception" explored by readers of Foucault such as Giorgio Agamben, or in the new, state-sanctioned privatized zones administered by multinational corporations. It is also at work in systems of representation like architecture. Such systems both enable and constrain thought, in ways that are no less concrete than the administrative protocols that organize life in a skyscraper or in a slum. To discern their effects, discourse analysis must take on an aesthetic or cultural dimension typically assumed to exist beyond or below the biopolitical horizon. At the threshold of postmodernity, aesthetic experience—including meaning, affect, and the representational codes they entail—is coterminal with the sphere of production and with the organization of everyday life. Here architecture, as a form of "immaterial production" fully materialized, stands at what we can call the crux of postmodernism, operating simultaneously along an axis of representation and an axis of production.[7]

I begin, in chapter 1, by tracing the interplay of these two axes with the help of key architectural texts, read against and across certain theses that guide Foucauldian biopolitical analysis, as well as certain claims made by postmodernist cultural theory. This builds on a long-standing tradition in which proto-architectural thematics, such as the thematic of space, migrate from one register to another. Here, I treat space largely as a territorial question that is staged simultaneously through two urban figures—networks and islands—while at another level I explore the reterritorialization of thought itself, in the sense of the redrawing of boundaries around what is knowable and what is thinkable, which in this case means Utopia's exile to a strange, inside-out center within the urban imaginary. In that sense, Utopia stands ultimately for an entire system of representation and production that is no longer available to architecture, rather than as an idol whose enchantments led modernism astray. And Utopia's ghost stands as the permanent possibility of its unexpected return, as ghosts tend to do.

Still missing from such an analysis, however, would be an explicit account of architecture's multiple functions within capitalist globalization. I use the latter term interchangeably with *late capitalism*, the designator for a third stage of capitalism developed by Ernest Mandel and taken up by Jameson. Though hardly limited to this, architecture's many, ongoing entanglements with capitalism are still best measured by the category of corporate architecture, loosely construed as buildings, design, and other work done for corporations, including both purpose-built and speculative works. These enter the cultural sphere as real estate, as corporate image, *and* as architecture. But given the penetration of corporate capital into nearly every aspect of the global marketplace, it would not be an exaggeration to suggest that under late capitalism virtually all architecture is, in effect, corporate architecture.

Mandel, writing in 1972, described the multinational corporation "as the main phenomenal form of capital."[8] In taking its architecture as a recurrent object of analysis, I will hence have implicit recourse to something like a phenomenology of capital: the corporation as the (partial) embodiment of capital, so to speak, and therefore the architecture of the corporation as something between body armor, armament, and adornment on the one hand and an inseparable, technical component of a cybernetic "organism" on the other.

Elsewhere, I have tried to capture this generalization of a corporate logic by analyzing architecture's role within an emergent "organizational complex" in the post–World War II United States.[9] Here, I want to direct attention toward the irreducibly *architectural* aspects of work that followed from this, much of which was at pains to assert a disciplinary autonomy in the face of commercializing threats from the outside. Largely as a result of this turn toward autonomy, the series of crises undergone by the discipline since 1945 remains at risk of being comfortably historicized, with its many unresolved internal dilemmas lined up as so many "themes" being debated and "concepts" being realized by various groups and splinter groups. These formations are susceptible in turn to scholarly representation in the metonymic form of charismatic personalities whose recollections, habits, quirks, and embarrassments both public and private seem destined to be assigned explanatory power, without any real explanation as to how or why. A theory of historical causality, or of the role and status of the discipline within a multidisciplinary nexus—to say nothing of a socioeconomic field—is hard to come by in the midst of all the new knowledge being accumulated about what is now known as the "postwar period," to which architectural postmodernism supplies a convenient coda.[10]

It is also well known that many initial, influential accounts of cultural postmodernism made reference to architecture. Jameson even acknowledges that his conception of postmodernism emerged out of architectural debates, while Andreas Huyssen credits architecture with helping to disseminate the term, which originated in literature. David Harvey offers a vividly reductive reading of Le Corbusier's unrealized tabula rasa Plan Voisin for central Paris as an opening backdrop from behind which the new regime of post-Fordist production emerges to leave its stamp on culture. While in the meantime, Jean-François Lyotard takes care to distance himself from postmodern architecture, reprimanding architects for "throwing out the baby of experimentation with the bathwater of functionalism."[11] Primarily, I engage these and other theorists by reading their arguments through reconstellated architectural and politico-economic phenomena. Architecture and architectural themes are the common denominator, which, I wager, is leverage enough to allow a modified picture of the entire postmodern discursive formation to come into view.

But is there a postmodern architecture? Fragmentation, disorientation, historical citation, signification without end: these ubiquitous properties seem to confirm that there was—and is—such a thing, to be duly distinguished from its modernist predecessors. However a second, less evident interpretative option also presents itself here, in the form of a question that might very well prove to be *the* question of postmodernism: Is there an *architecture*? Through the 1970s and 1980s, much of the work that we will encounter exhibited an almost neurotic preoccupation with the discipline's own history, as if to insist that this was *all* that it was about; it was architecture about architecture, and nothing else. But, like the censoring of Utopia, this collective neurosis and its corresponding fundamentalisms cannot be fully explained as a reaction to official modernism's antihistorical, activist bias. Instead, it may very well indicate a foundational insecurity that is far more revealing than are the ideological expressions of its protagonists.

So is there an architecture under postmodernity? There are any number of ways into this question, the most obvious of which begins with the presumed postmodern erasure of distinctions between high art and popular culture. Here, architecture threatens essentially to collapse into mass media. Exhibit A in this account would be the populism of Robert Venturi and Denise Scott Brown. However, this populism must be understood in dialectical interrelation with the historical connoisseurship underwriting the arguments of Venturi's *Complexity and Contradiction in Architecture*, as well as with all of the consequences that a refined "historicism" has had in the work of the Venturi/Scott Brown firm and many others. Venturi and Scott Brown's contribution to the 1978 exhibition *Roma Interrotta* (Rome Interrupted) installed at the American Academy in Rome stages this dialectic with diagrammatic clarity. A photograph of the Caesar's Palace casino in Las Vegas, with electric sign, is pasted onto a facsimile of the Nolli map of Rome from 1748. The message is ambiguous. Yes, we may be witnessing the popularization of classical iconography, but we may also be witnessing the classicizing of popular culture. There can be no Caesar's Palace and, indeed, no "learning from Las Vegas" without the earlier academic lessons learned from Rome and its monuments, particularly as these were brought into focus by then-recent revivals of formalist art-historical methods, a lineage that ran from Heinrich Wölfflin to Rudolf Wittkower to Colin Rowe.

A second, related way into the question concerning architecture's very existence under postmodernity is thus opened by what amount to neo-Kantian claims made on behalf of architecture as an autonomous art form.[12] This interpretative route appears more treacherous, since it goes straight to the heart of the architectural object's unstable status as an artwork, without taking a detour through the scope and demographic of its audience. Exhibit A in *this* account would be the range of objects collected together under the "Gray/White debate," both sides of which took architecture's aesthetic autonomy for granted, albeit in different and often circuitous ways. Here the fragment—the house as ruin (Eisenman, Graves), as collage (Stern), or as simply "one-half" of nothing (Hejduk)—seems to acquire a paradoxical autonomy in its own right. Increasingly less legible as an excerpt from a more "complete" totality, be it a lost historical object or a now-decomposed Platonic solid, the house-fragment stands, in effect, outside of all histories save its own. This is the meaning of Peter Eisenman's turn to irreversible, step-by-step process in his numbered series of house experiments. It is also the meaning of Robert

A. M. Stern's early, erudite formal quotations cut loose from historical narrative, prior to his turn to a more explicit and more "grounded" historicism that verified the metaphysical ambitions of his former teacher, Vincent Scully. And, for that matter, it is the meaning of the (again, only apparently populist) iconographic enthusiasms of Charles Moore, architect of the neon-lit, pseudo-Baroque Piazza d'Italia in New Orleans. In the autonomy of the disenchanted fragment, sitting on the shelf of the architect refashioned into Walter Benjamin's archetypal collector, we discern not only what Manfredo Tafuri called "the ashes of Jefferson" but also, the specters of Kant.[13]

But then what defines the horizon of architecture as autonomous artwork? As I have just indicated, postmodernist discourse bears the mark of neo-Kantian aesthetics as embodied, for example, in the historiographical chain of Wölfflin-Wittkower-Rowe. Consequently, we find the protagonists on all sides of the debates that characterize the neo-avant-garde and its exhaustions since the 1970s struggling with terms and concepts disseminated via such concatenations. Less remarked in the literature but still among these is architecture's "pure visibility," its potential reduction—or ascension—to a degree-zero of use value in favor of auto-referential formal experimentation or elaboration.[14] It is sometimes mistakenly thought that by stepping away from functionalism, which by the 1950s had been appropriated by the corporations, and into a renewed art for art's sake, architecture steps away from capital. This overlooks the fact that corporate capitalism had, by then, expanded into the aesthetic realm to such a degree that architecture's claims to formal autonomy played right into the demand for a maximum of spectacularization (in what is now called "signature architecture") that even Guy Debord might have had difficulty imagining. In a world in which each "signature" signs a private language in the attentive presence of the mass media, architecture reenters the culture industry through the back door, as autonomous form.

Still, even as certain architectural examples can be cited as the very image of what is meant by postmodern, many of those same examples can equally well be used to demonstrate continuities with modernism's technological, epistemological, and stylistic legacies. This ambivalence corresponds with the problematization of modernism as a unified category, which has gathered significant momentum in architectural scholarship since the 1970s, and which makes any effort to replace one hardly monolithic movement or period with another more than just ill-conceived or reductive.[15] Any inventory of discursive constructions that have emerged in the aftermath of programmatic, international modernism must therefore be compiled *around* architecture rather than just in it. Not only because this inventory construes the field of knowledge and production bracketed off as architecture to be permanently contestable but also because of the privileged position that the field has occupied in initial characterizations of postmodern practices more generally. With this in mind, I have selectively revisited the playing fields—and the battlefields—of postmodernism not to survey them but to discern their rules of engagement.

As I have already indicated, among these rules is a near-universal proscription against utopian thought and speculation. This, above all, is what puts the "post" in postmodernism. At times this proscription is explicit, while more frequently it is implicit. It is not unreasonable to believe that a quasi-consensual ban on utopian projection, particularly within the Euro-American architectural vanguard, stemmed from a generally unwritten (if misplaced) equation between social or technological utopias and political totalitarianism, especially of the Stalinist variety, whereas virtually every architectural endeavor that one way or another imbibed the utopian spirit was eventually assimilated into the juggernaut of capitalist development.[16] More than ideological illusion, however, the foreclosure of a particular category of thought—strictly *utopian* thought—capable of imagining that things could be otherwise, was and remains crucial to this assimilation. But like a ghost, what is repressed tends to return, transfigured. This logic of futurity, the eternal return of the repressed utopian future, haunts postmodernism and to some extent defines it, even as its architecture seems condemned to reproduce a world-historical status quo.

In this and other respects, postmodern architecture's aesthetic project is inseparable from the cold war and from the rise of Western consumerism, as well as from the intertwined sets of relationships gathered together under the term *globalization*. Introducing an issue of the journal *New German Critique* that reexamined the modern/postmodern conjuncture, Andreas Huyssen recently suggested that today's globalization debates have taken the place of yesterday's postmodernism debates.[17] A version of chapter 2 appeared in that issue, and in its revised form here it argues more directly for a friendly amendment to Huyssen's suggestion: that what we call globalization comes both before and after postmodernism. I do not mean this only in the historicizing sense about which much has already been written, which risks infinite regress into historical precedent for anything initially thought to be "new." I mean it in the sense of progressive circularity by which we can redefine something like a postmodern sense of history, which captures the homogenizing closure associated with globalization while still preserving the possibility of meaningful historical change.

To say it the other way around: Postmodernism comes after globalization, as well as before it. The reader would be correct here to hear an echo of Lyotard's well-known assertion that postmodernism *precedes* modernism, with which Huyssen also plays. But I am referring to it in a slightly different sense, since with "globalization" comes a host of problems that throw the self/other, inside/outside dyad into confusion if not outright crisis. This confusion, which thinkers like Gilles Deleuze and Félix Guattari as well as Jameson initially termed schizophrenic, can be tracked in architecture in relation to deterritorializing cycles of production and consumption, providing one also attends to the internal regularities that construct, reconstruct, and reterritorialize the discipline itself.

But I am unwilling to assign to the economic relations of globalization an irrevocable causality, however nuanced it may be and even "in the last instance." The sheer dialectical force and consistency of "late" or "postindustrial" or "post-Fordist" capitalism is clear enough. To comprehend it, I offer the feedback loop as a cognitive model that reintroduces causality into the postmodern equation in a manner that is capable of accounting for the nested character of power. In taking up this *dispositif* not only as a technical but also as an epistemic object, I have attempted to reveal its architectonics. Visible in the architecture itself, the architectonics of feedback is not purely superstructural or phantasmagoric. But neither is it by any stretch of the imagination purely structural. Architecture is among globalization's outputs, but it is also among its inputs.

By virtue of this dynamic circularity, feedback entails topological reversals and inversions that require other means by which to describe historical causality and to locate the different strata of cultural production within it. Such inversions and reversals are, to borrow an expression from the modernist architectural historian Sigfried Gideon, among the *constituent facts* of globalization. For whatever "global" might mean, it does not simply imply an extension outward from the centers of power, to the point where everything mirrors everything else in a nightmare of homogeneity. Nor can it be exhausted topologically by a center/periphery model of the sort initially employed by analysts of the "global city," wherein centralized administration and decentralized production coexist in an economy of mutual dependence. As has been demonstrated in any number of ways, what we call globalization is defined as much by exclusion as by inclusion. So to see capitalist technical and economic development as an ever-expanding, ever more inclusive promised land to be awaited eagerly by those on the "outside" and euphemized in the term *modernization,* is to remain indifferent to the fact that by definition every inclusion also excludes. Likewise, even in their most benign forms, every modernizing gesture, every translation, and every connection also incorporates while, conversely, every act of withdrawal into the "home" or the "homeland" cannot help but connect back out into the networks from which it seeks refuge.

In short, the further inside you go, the further outside you get, and vice versa. In interrelated sections of several chapters, I have attempted to construct a partial genealogy of this axiom, which I take to summarize the discursive conditions from which postmodernism initially emerged, and under which it continues to operate. This is not to say that there is no outside to the networks of power and knowledge that shape social and economic relations under late capitalism. With feedback loops also come multiple, if uncertain, sites of intervention for countering and redirecting history's apparently inexorable endgames. It is, however, to insist on their status *as networks,* the most decisive properties of which are discernible at a topological level. Basic to this level are problems of connectivity and of inside and outside, which I argue architectural analysis is especially capable of revealing. Indeed, this may even be the secret of its semiprivileged status within postmodernist discourse to begin with. The chapters below therefore move in and out of architecture, in an irregular rhythm or pulse that reflects the local conditions of the subject at hand.

Like other forms of cultural production, architecture needs continuously to be explained and interpreted, while also serving to interpret that which seems to explain it. Such is the case with the various examples and episodes I take up. Whether the visits paid are long and detailed or short and sweet, the ghosts never arrive via a one-way street. The economic never simply precedes the cultural (or the social for that matter), nor does it simply follow it. Instead, the different levels reflect and refract one another, along the axes of representation and of production with which I began. In retrospect, it is impossible to say for sure that the postmodern turn in architecture represented or prefigured a shift in a more fundamental, underlying socioeconomic arrangement. It is only possible to say that what we call postmodern architecture helped to build a particular socioeconomic arrangement, even as that arrangement helped to build it.

The chapters that follow are written as essays that can be read independently or in sequence, as elements in a larger, somewhat recursive narrative. In recognition of this, and in place of chapter summaries, I conclude here with a list of major issues and themes that the reader is likely to encounter as she or he goes. This list also serves as a road map of sorts; it is intended to alert the reader in advance to what might occasionally seem like counterintuitive or abrupt juxtapositions and to give fair warning of upcoming intersections, exits, and forks in the road. The chapters themselves are arranged under the headings of Territory, History, Language, Image, Materiality, Subjects, and Architecture. In keeping with the pattern of feedback outlined above, however, particular issues taken up in one chapter often reverberate through others as well, sometimes predictably, sometimes not.

To begin with, there is the problem of inside and outside, captured (and rearranged) in the figure of the mirror, as well as in the actual mirrors that lined both the interiors and the exteriors of many postmodern buildings. Chapter 1 sets out this topology as a spatial/territorial imaginary that both brackets and reproduces the real; chapter 3 extends it into relations between environmentalism and language; chapters 5 and 6 pick it up again by looking at two different sides of the mirror as an architectural device, including what it makes visible and what it obscures. And chapter 7 replies with the figure of the ghost as a boundary problem.

There is also the problem of history, both in the sense of a return to historical citation in architecture, which took as its master discourse Mediterranean classicism, and in the sense of various historical eruptions or disturbances, such as the war in Vietnam, the environmental movement, or the economic transformations visible in the none-too-deep surfaces of the architecture itself. These are taken up in chapters 2 through 6 in a series of case studies that reposition architecture relative to specific political-economic developments. Corollary to this is the problem of historical change, condensed into the figure of Utopia, vanishing. For this, see chapters 1 and 7.

There is the problem of language, which was used during this period to distinguish and even to seal off architecture from external factors.

Building on the epistemological and historiographical frameworks sketched in chapter 2, chapter 3 follows this move in the opposite direction, which leads from language to politics. From there, in chapter 4, images and signs commingle with ecologies and economies. Chapters 5 and 6 follow architectural examples into more tangible economies organized around material production. These, in turn, support "immaterial" language-based economies rather than simply make way for them.

There is also the thematic of the island, in the form of new enclosures, paradigmatic enclaves, as well as in the spectral presence of the island of Utopia itself. Chapter 1 maps inside/outside in terms of this figure by comparing, as inverted mirror images, the camp-as-island with Utopia. Figures of enclosure echo through subsequent chapters, to which chapter 7 responds by inviting Utopia's ghost back into architectural and political thought, in place of paranoid postmodern exorcisms.

There is the unequivocal fact of real images, the existence of which continues to challenge interpretive grids premised on hierarchies (or dialectics) of surface and depth, real and unreal, material and immaterial. Chapter 4 thematizes this most explicitly, by considering the scientific laboratory as a site for the intersection of imaginaries in a kind of architectural science fiction. This interplay of image and truth, representation and production, returns to the virtual economies that are explored in chapter 1 and developed at the level of signification and communication in chapter 3.

There are the objects, the buildings themselves but also the materials from which they are assembled, the material complexes through which they circulate, and the cities that are assembled from them. These appear and disappear in irregular movements through the chapters. Never invoked as ends in themselves, architecture's objects accumulate, building a case for their own conceptual porosity, as they often inadvertently make visible the very worlds that they seem to close off. Again, their accumulation is not intended as an exhaustive inventory of "postmodern" designs. It is only meant to underscore a plainly visible repetition of patterns that lends them their discursive coherence.

There are the subjects, the actual humans but also the historical constructions that we call "human." And there is the ever-sharper divide that a fetishization of the "human" as a universal value paradoxically imposes upon these actual humans, increasing numbers of whom are forced to struggle for their right to be represented as such. Evidence of this eversion, which is both spatial and political, is to be found most directly in chapter 6, though the previous chapters (notably chapter 3) help set the stage, onto which walks a parade of inhuman ghosts in chapter 7.

There is the concept of work, both in the sense of the ever-problematic status of the "work" of architecture, and of the work that it and those who labor on it and in it perform—a type of work or labor that is only "immaterial" to the degree that it takes on new material forms. Chapters 2 and 3 are the main vehicles for developing this concept by reframing it in linguistic terms. This is connected with new modes of technical production in chapters 5 and 6.

In general, chapter 1 and chapter 7 (on Territory, and on Architecture, respectively), mark the poles between which the intervening case studies circulate. Like two mirrors standing face-to-face, the book's beginning and its end are set in an open-ended dialogue that is mediated by the concepts developed in its middle portion. Historical narrative is therefore not so much forsaken as it is amplified, as each chapter restates, in miniature, the arc that is followed by the book itself. If the result is a certain disorientation, wherein objects, names, and moments that we may have forgotten, or that we may have thought over and done with, reappear in barely recognizable form, then the analysis has been partially successful. If this, in turn, brings with it a reorientation toward a different sense of the past but also toward a different sense of the future, then it is even more likely that the effort has not been entirely in vain.

1 TERRITORY

From the Inside, Out

"THINK." By 1911 this had already become a corporate command. By the 1930s, as the slogan of International Business Machines (IBM), it announced the formalization of what would come to be known by the early 1970s, as immaterial or post-Fordist production.[1] In 1997, in belated recognition of a countercultural, affective engine driving the neoliberal "global" economy this command was translated by IBM's competitor, Apple Computer, into the slogan "Think different." The state of affairs to which these events belong has over time acquired a variety of names. In 1973, Daniel Bell enthusiastically announced the "coming of post-industrial society." In the late 1980s, Gilles Deleuze called it the "society of control." More recently, Alain Badiou has called it the "second Restoration." And in a related, Deleuzo-Foucauldian vein, Antonio Negri and Michael Hardt have called it Empire.[2] But in the cultural sphere, the term that continues to haunt all of these others, whether as consequence or as precursor, is the one favored by many other theorists beginning in the late 1970s and running through the 1990s: simply, *postmodernism.*

With postmodernism, what was in fact thinkable was subject to new epistemic limitations on which architecture provides a unique perspective. In particular, architectural discourse reproduces the resulting boundary problem, in which what is thinkable is divided from what is not. This is especially true for architectural discourse on the city. I therefore begin with the term *territory,* instead of the more resonant and more modern *space,* to mark an oscillation between the territoriality of thought—its epistemic delimitations—and thought concerned with the city and its territories, especially as translated into architecture.[3] More specifically, in postmodernism Utopia is not only a special kind of territory; it is also another name for the unthinkable.

. . .

Although accounts vary as to its makeup and scope, in architecture post-modernism is the term generally used to denote the discourse and production that dominated the international scene roughly from 1970 to 1990, coming mainly but not exclusively out of the United States and Western Europe. Riven with inconsistencies and incoherence from the start, the coordinates of an institutionalized postmodernism—a new "international style"—can nevertheless be gauged in the 1980 Venice Biennale or alternatively, in the 1984 *Post-Modern Visions* exhibition at the new Deutsches Architekturmuseum, to name just two significant events. Of greater importance, however, were the publications that followed from these and other exhibitions, which must be read alongside the first polemical synthesis of any real impact: *The Language of Post-Modern Architecture* (1977) by Charles Jencks. Reading further back, the year 1966 stands as another marker. This was the year in which both Aldo Rossi's *Architettura della Città* and Robert Venturi's *Complexity and Contradiction in Architecture* were published. In very different ways, these two books registered problematics that would become central to post-modernist debates. The same can be said to an even greater degree for *Learning from Las Vegas,* the collaborative work that Venturi and his partner Denise Scott Brown produced with their associate Steven Izenour, which was based on research conducted with students at Yale University in 1968 and appeared in 1972.[4]

Jürgen Habermas was probably the first to connect architectural discourse to the nascent philosophical debates regarding the eclipse of modernism, in a brief evaluation of the 1980 Venice Biennale that opened his Adorno Prize lecture of that same year, titled "Modernity—An Incomplete Project." There, he implies that architecture's new "historicism" correlates with a more general abandonment of the Enlightenment project for "the rational organization of everyday social life."[5] Habermas followed this a year later with a more sustained reflection on architectural developments, in a lecture on "modern and postmodern architecture" given in response to an exhibition of modern architecture in Munich.[6] Subsequently, many other theorists, including Fredric Jameson, Andreas Huyssen, Seyla Benhabib, David Harvey, Ihab Hassan, Jean-François Lyotard, Terry Eagleton, and Alex Callinicos, made reference to architecture as a signal instance of the postmodern, mainly as evidence of a perceived populist turn, a mixing of messages derived from high and commercial culture, and/or pastiche of historical elements in place of modernist teleology.[7]

The countercultural urban uprisings of the 1960s in Europe and North America, and especially the racially charged riots that occurred in many American cities, were more than mere background or context for all of this.[8] Equally important, that decade also saw a decisive turn—in the United States in particular—toward the virtualization of both production and circulation. The accompanying rise of a neoliberal economic regime was marked symbolically and practically by the dissolution, in 1973, of the monetary controls put in place by the Bretton Woods Accord of 1944. As many accounts have emphasized, in addition to ever more speculative financial markets, this economic regime has been characterized by the productivity of intellectual, affective, and other "post-Fordist" forms of labor and exchange. A plausible homology can therefore be constructed between what David Harvey has called "flexible accumulation" and the economy of interchangeable images in which postmodern architecture certainly partook.[9] Less widely observed, however, was an accompanying reterritorialization of the urban imaginary, for which the unthinking of Utopia served as a test case.

In architecture, theoretical arguments such as those formulated by Venturi and Scott Brown or Rossi were initially offered as guides to the amelioration of modernity's most disruptive effects. This makes later readings in terms of postmodernist disaggregation all the more puzzling; these theoretical moves were essentially stabilizing ones. They were moves toward a "re-semanticization" (to borrow Manfredo Tafuri's expression) that, however polysemous, complex, or contradictory it may have seemed, was in the main a *rappel à l'ordre* directed against the far more destabilizing forces of modernization that modernism had failed to master, rather than toward a disruption or dispersal of the signifying field as such. This was the lasting legacy of the diverse theoretical lines that developed within the architectural discipline during the 1960s: a return to meaning and to various *architectures parlantes,* whether in the form of McLuhanesque dreams (or nightmares) of universal communication (Reyner Banham, Archigram, megastructures, but also Venturi), narrative or mnemonic critiques thereof (oddly enough, both *architettura radicale* and the Tendenza group in Italy, with Rossi counted among the latter), the new monumentality of Louis Kahn and his followers, or the syntactical and figural coherence attempted, with primitivist overtones, by former members of Team X such as Herman Hertzberger or Aldo Van Eyck, or by Christopher Alexander.

To acknowledge this *rappel à l'ordre* is to complicate the prevailing sense among theorists of cultural postmodernism that architecture's primary contribution to this complex formation was a sort of spatial or visual map of its foundational instabilities. But even more, I want to suggest that the reterritorialization or regrounding that lay behind even the most hermetic and obtuse architectural efforts of the period bespeaks not the *withdrawal* of architectural discourse into a self-imposed exile that asymptotically approaches (and borrows from) the intertextual playing field of "theory" at large but the construction of a new type of immanence. In other words, what might be most postmodern about architectural thought since 1966 is not its verifiability in practice, but its status as a mode of production in its own right.

Hence the need for an interpretive model that is capable of explaining the interplay between discursive constructions, urban imaginaries, and new politico-economic configurations. Such a model must move along two distinct but related axes: an axis of representation and an axis of production. Consistent with the materialities of post-Fordism, I offer the feedback loop, and the complex topologies that it entails, as a diagram for thinking the relation between these axes. Though treated in more detail in subsequent chapters, this model requires minimally that we concentrate on the back-and-forth movements between levels (or axes), rather than presuppose mechanical jumps from one level to the other. In the latter portion of this chapter, I will track these movements across two urban topologies that are often seen to be in opposition: the network and the island.

The reference to topology is not accidental.[10] It formalizes a boundary problem that is central to postmodernism, the problem of distinguishing the real from the unreal, including the problem of distinguishing between real and unreal boundaries. As we will see in subsequent chapters, postmodernism has a way of doubling up and folding together such distinctions. Learning to think topologically means, therefore, learning to think our way into the starkness of what is real by way of what, apparently, is unreal. Thus is representation enfolded into production, including the networked production of urban territories and their populations and the lives that are lived inside (and outside) their boundaries.

To begin with, the problem of representation can be approached via the much-cited populism of Venturi and Scott Brown. But in lieu of understanding populism as an ideological refusal of the dialectic of high art and mass culture, I want to suggest that we consider it as a measurement or calibration in relation to a perceived norm. Seen from this perspective, populism forms the basis of Venturi and Scott Brown's entire argument but in a way that is oblique to Jameson's formulation in particular.[11] The ornamental, communicative model advocated in *Learning from Las Vegas* is based on a recalibration of architectural communication toward the aesthetic norms documented in the book's analysis of the Las Vegas strip and, by extension, of megalopolitan sprawl more generally. As Venturi and Scott Brown put it, "To find our symbolism we must go to the suburban edges of the existing city that are symbolically rather than formalistically attractive and represent the aspirations of almost all, including most ghetto dwellers and most of the silent white majority."[12]

A redistribution of the population, already well documented in nonracial terms in such works as Jean Gottmann's *Megalopolis* (1961), is ultimately what is at stake in the controversy that accompanied (and determined) the use of this last phrase—"silent white majority"—both in the text and as a subheading. Fending off accusations that they had thereby acceded to the racist sloganeering of the Nixon presidency, Venturi and Scott Brown refer to the accumulating sociological literature on suburbanization as precedent, including the classic study of Levittown by Herbert Gans, which for them suggests that "Levittown-type aesthetics are shared by most members of the middle-middle class, black as well as white, liberal as well as conservative."[13] But in many ways this is not a question of ideological preferences or even of the penetration of right-wing politics into architectural discourse. Instead, it entails a reorganization of the discursive field according to the imperatives of *normalization*.

This means that architectural populism can be understood here, even at the aesthetic level, as a biopolitical practice in which territories are inscribed. However, developing such a proposition requires addressing the theses on biopolitics outlined by Michel Foucault in his lectures at the Collège de France in the late 1970s with a question, central to architecture, that Foucault's work left largely unanswered—the question of cultural representation. Biopower and biopolitics are the categories by which Foucault characterizes security as a dimension of governmentality that emerges in the late eighteenth century. Its basic unit is the population, described statistically as an object from which technological and administrative protocols are extrapolated. Securing the territory, then, is linked with deducing populational norms.[14] Adjusted for the historical passage to the other end of modernity, which includes, by the late twentieth century, the privatization of security as states and corporations mix, as well as its displacement onto the psychosocial plane, normalization comes increasingly to be associated with aesthetic populism.

In this case, the term "majority" as used by both Venturi and Scott Brown and Nixon carries within it a specific set of techniques for reproducing what *Learning from Las Vegas* disingenuously called (in the book's second edition) "the aspirations of almost all Americans." As demonstrated by analyses of advertising by thinkers as diverse as Horkheimer and Adorno or McLuhan, by the mid-twentieth century techniques for the normalization of aesthetic judgment had been transferred or extended into the "culture industry," or what had symptomatically come to be called "popular culture."[15] Thus deployed as an indicator of the popular will, by the late 1960s the force and the menace of the term "majority," used in a cultural sense, lay as much in the implicit a priori division of the population into quanta, and the identification of the aesthetic preferences of a particular quantum (white, suburban, etc.) as "normal," as it did in the implication that the signs and symbols of the predominantly white, middle-class suburb captured in some ideological way and through aesthetic mediation the values of the general population. From this perspective, to characterize such gestures as populist is somewhat misleading, in that such a characterization implicitly naturalizes the very distribution of the population that they enact.

Learning from Las Vegas can therefore be read as a kind of technical instrument that, using the social-scientific methods of urban planning in which Scott Brown in particular had been schooled, differentiates between the apparently modest, everyday (i.e., "normal") symbolic language of the suburban strip and the eccentricities of modernism. Rather than recommend complete reversal to secure the city against such threats, the book recommends readjustment, whereby the ex nihilo utopianism of the Corbusian "radiant city" is recalibrated according to the norms suggested by Levittown and Las Vegas. And architectural modernism, rather than being taken up as the opposite of the popular or the vernacular, is recast as an extreme, a sort of statistical aberration.

But can something similar be said of Venturi's earlier work, *Complexity and Contradiction in Architecture,* or of Rossi's *Architettura della Città,* both of which did so much to reintroduce the problem of symbolism and meaning that was central to postmodernism's self-understanding? Neither can be considered populist in quite the same sense that *Learning from Las Vegas* can, and so their respective contributions to the postmodern turn must be gauged differently. For Rossi, the city itself is to be considered as a work of architecture, with the cultural memories and political priorities of its inhabitants, figured as a collective, condensed into singular urban monuments. While for Venturi (and this surely does reflect ideological differences between the two), renewed attention to architectural symbolism is required to overcome the "puritanically moral language of orthodox Modern architecture" by confronting it with the "difficult unity" of multiple references and meanings, many of which draw their semantic resources by historical association.[16] So where for Rossi the question is one of figuring the many in the one, in the city as a work of architecture as well as the work of architecture as a work of the collective, for Venturi it is a question of confronting the one with the many.

In a disarming climax to his book that draws on the work of Maurice Halbwachs on expropriation of property in large cities and on that of Hans Bernouilli on land ownership, Rossi offers the "urban artifact," understood as a cultural unit, as an alternative to deterministic narratives of urban development based on industrialization. For Rossi, the urban artifact, in its formal and typological particularity, condenses the irreducibly political choices that have led to its construction, including those influenced by economic factors. Thus, Rossi avers that "Athens, Rome, and Paris are the form of their politics, the signs of their collective will," and further, "it is through the natural tendencies of the many groups dispersed throughout the different parts of the city that we must explain the modifications in the city's structure," and finally, on a note that emphasizes the psychological dimensions of Rossi's overall thesis that "[t]he city is as irrational as any work of art, and its mystery is perhaps above all to be found in the secret and ceaseless will of its collective manifestations."[17]

David Harvey has found Rossi's argument out of tune with the pace of change in (post)modernity in a way that renders the relative permanence of architectural meaning inherently mythological.[18] In this respect, the question is whether Rossi's closing statements merely fetishize the aesthetic artifact at the expense of a lucid grasp of its political-economic determinants or, rather, renegotiate architecture's role as an actor within the politico-economic field. In *Architecture of the City*, Rossi is working out a project for architecture's autonomy that would steer much of his later work and writings. This project is premised on the transhistorical (and, in Rossi's later "analogous city" drawings, transcultural) persistence of certain architectural types. But as posed at this relatively early point, this is not merely a question of substituting a typologically embedded memory for the teleologies that guided architectural modernism, as was suggested by Peter Eisenman in his introduction to the English translation of Rossi's book in 1982.[19] For this apparent substitution carries a history of its own, which Eisenman reproduces even as he rightly assigns to Rossi a "latent humanism":

> To propose [as Rossi does] that the same relationship between individual subject (man) and individual object (house) which existed in the Renaissance now obtains between the collective psychological subject (the population of the modern city) and its singular object (the city, but seen as a house at a different scale) is to imply that nothing has changed, that the city of humanist man is the same place as the city of psychological man.[20]

By "psychological man" Eisenman means the subject of psychoanalysis and the inhabitant of the industrial city, whom he opposes to the "mythic hero-architect of humanism, the inventor of the house," whose inner life, born of the house, was correlated to that of the city in Alberti's formula: "The city is like a large house, and the house in turn is like a small city."[21]

But the problem that Eisenman finds in Rossi, that of representing the collective unconscious of the entire city by analogy to the artist-architect's unique psychic reserve, is a deceptive one. The problem is not one of scale, or even of the universal versus the particular; it is that for Rossi, as for Alberti, both house and city mark a territory with a strictly delimited interior. But what Eisenman calls a "personal text" (extrapolated from Rossi's *Scientific Autobiography* of 1981) that "nostalgically evokes the individual subject" in the face of the anonymous masses is not, in fact, opposed to the actual historical experience of this "population," as inside is to outside. Nor is the historical experience of the population simply mystified through Rossi's dreamlike autobiographical reconstruction, in which "memory begins where history ends," as Eisenman claims.[22] Instead, it is revealed, since the inner life of this "population" was at that very moment being displaced onto *and constructed through* the signifying fields of the postmodern city, behind which there was nothing—in the singular *or* in the plural—but more signs.

Already by the late 1970s, Foucault had sensed that biopolitics was mutating into what he tentatively called "environmentality," which entailed a reorganization of inner and outer life under the sign of such practices as environmental psychology.[23] Reversing the Albertian formula of the house-as-city, as well as the domestic bias of Freudian psychoanalysis, this would be to see subjectivization taking place largely *on the outside,* out in the city or in the communications media rather than inside the house, with the guidance of a behaviorism from which the American culture industry in particular had long drawn sustenance. Or better: with such environmental technologies as television, house and city, living room and cinema, are effectively turned inside out, to become overexposed nodes in a generalized urban-exurban field, *without* losing their apparent interiority.[24]

So whether they asserted humanist or posthumanist versions of architecture's autonomy (Eisenman found Rossi oscillating between the two), Rossi and later Eisenman were not just fighting lost battles; in many ways they were fighting the wrong war, by failing to take into account the unfolding (and enfolding) of inside and outside, house and city, individual and population, into a dispersive, networked "environment" made up of apparently discrete units. Instead, they offered two different structuralisms, at either end of architecture's postmodern turn. For Rossi, writing in 1966, architecture's deep structures were still to be found in the political enactments of the "collective will" that it indirectly commemorated; for Eisenman reading Rossi's book sixteen years later and in a milieu that had already undergone its decisive neoliberal conversion, these were to be found in architecture itself.

Whereas Venturi's path toward architecture's autonomy—and autonomy it is—runs through very different terrain. If there is something like memory at work in *Complexity and Contradiction,* it is not collective, historical memory. It is technological memory on the order of a computer database. This is what Venturi ultimately means by complexity, a premise that would be carried forward in more clearly cybernetic terms in the visual data sets compiled in *Learning from Las Vegas* and later in Venturi's explicitly McLuhanesque *Iconography and Electronics upon a Generic Architecture* (1996). Here, in *Complexity and Contradiction,* it is stated only indirectly, when in conclusion Venturi returns to the problem of the "difficult whole." He understands the latter as a "complex system," as defined by the political scientist and systems theorist Herbert Simon in an article on cybernetics, systems theory, and the behavioral sciences titled "The Architecture of Complexity," from which Venturi quotes: "a large number of parts that interact in a non-simple way."[25]

Venturi's "complexity and contradiction" thus construes the work of architecture as an ensemble of interacting parts that achieves organic unity through ambiguous relationships that accrue circumstantially as heterogeneous formal elements are assembled, rather than through conventional formal mechanisms like symmetry or hierarchy. And although most of its pages are devoted to demonstrating how assorted canonical works exhibit these characteristics, Venturi's book does take what seems to be a manifestly populist turn at the very end. There, discussing architecture's "obligation" to this type of internally differentiated formal unity, he notoriously asks, in response to Peter Blake's condemnation of the commercial Main Street common in American small towns, "is not Main Street almost all right?" To this rhetorical question Venturi adds his sympathies for other depositions of consumer culture, such as the commercial stretches of Route 66, where "[t]he seemingly chaotic juxtapositions of honky-tonk elements express an intriguing kind of vitality and validity, and they produce an unexpected approach to unity as well."[26] So all along, what appears to have been a series of informed (if dilettantish) musings on the formal properties of architectural works selected from the random-access memory of the historical canon has in fact been a direct response to megalopolitan commercialization. It is a tentative embrace, to be sure (Main Street is "almost" all right), but it is an embrace nonetheless. Or possibly a capture, since what Blake had termed "God's own junkyard"—what we can call the *informe* of consumerism—has been recycled by Venturi into a perfectly serviceable and coherent syntactical repertoire capable of extracting vital unity out of "chaos," a repertoire that could subsequently be overlaid onto Las Vegas rather than "learned" from it.

Thus the problem of representation is ultimately the same for Rossi and Venturi, though they resolve it in different and even opposite ways. It is not so much a question of restoring to architecture its symbolic or communicative capacities as it is a question of *how to represent unity.* This is understood, respectively, as the lost organic unity of the body politic that biopolitics has converted into an amnesiac population to whom memory must be restored (Rossi), or the recovery of a "vital" unity from within the disaggregated landscapes of the market and the mass media (Venturi). Moreover, the representation of organic unity has been renewed here as a problem for architecture even as—or more likely, *because*—architectural modernism, as an avatar of modernization, seems decisively to have replaced the mythically vital, social body with a collection of empty shells, which have now been expelled from the city like so much junk gathered along the commercial strip, or empty automobiles lined up in

A&P parking lots. Again and again Venturi and Scott Brown will refer to the authentic "life" of the commodity sphere that Blake had represented as a junkyard, as in their "Signs of Life" exhibition of 1976, which was dedicated to the communicative protocols of suburban domesticity. Either way, for so-called postmodern architecture, the problem of representation, far from being a referendum on cultural meaning that was ambiguously decided by dissolving the boundaries between high culture and popular taste, was a question of life and death. That this question was not merely symbolic becomes clearer still when these representations are reinserted into the productive circuitry of capital.

Here we move from architecture's axis of representation to its axis of production, specifically, the production of new inside-outsides to secure the unity of the biopolitical body. These include the "new segmentations" characterized by the "close proximity of extremely unequal populations" that Hardt and Negri associate with a postimperial empire organized around the networks of multinational capital.[27] They also include Giorgio Agamben's topologies of exception, which are exhibited vividly in this passage from *Homo Sacer*:

> The state of nature and the state of exception are nothing but two sides of a single topological process in which what was presupposed as external (the state of nature) now reappears, as in a Möbius strip or a Leyden jar, in the inside (as state of exception), and the sovereign power is this very impossibility of distinguishing between outside and inside, nature and exception, *physis* and *nomos*. The state of exception is not so much a spatiotemporal suspension as a complex topological figure in which not only the exception and the rule but also the state of nature and law, outside and inside, pass through one another.[28]

Referring to the Nazi death camp as the paradigmatic instance of this inclusive exclusion produced and occupied by power, Agamben calls its space a "zone of indistinction" (after Deleuze), in which sense "[t]he camp is a piece of land placed outside the normal juridical order, but it is nevertheless not simply an external space."[29]

In comparison, consider an aphorism from Rossi's *Scientific Autobiography* (1981). In his introduction to *The Architecture of the City*, Eisenman cites Rossi's statement that "cities are in reality great camps of the living and the dead where many elements remain like signals, symbols, cautions."[30] Despite Eisenman's mysterious conclusion that Rossi's city is therefore a "house of the dead," it may seem easy to see here a variation on Agamben's insight, whereby the camp is indeed the urban paradigm par excellence, for it is unclear whether its inhabitants (or its architectural elements) are alive or dead. Thus too, does Harvey's insinuation that Rossi's architecture is "fascist" acquire a different cast.[31] At one level, Rossi's invocation of the camp (by which he actually means a holiday camp) to describe a diffuse urban field outwardly constituted by empty or ruined "signals, symbols, cautions" recalls the necropolitan urbanism of Ludwig Hilberseimer, in which scattered, anonymous humans dart about like so many postapocalyptic survivors. Unlike his modernist predecessor, however, Rossi proposes that architecture, as a bearer of historical and political substance, be reconstructed to contain this diffusion. Only, such a reconstruction of meaning entails the erection, both on the ground and in the mind, of a wall dividing those on the inside of architecture's polis and its myths from those on the outside.

Whence comes this wall? Hardt and Negri assimilate cultural postmodernism (including postmodern architecture) into a mode-of-production narrative that correlates postindustrial labor (including extraterritorial industrial labor) with the distributed networks of biopower that are responsible for the diffusion against which Rossi reacts. Urbanists might also find in Agamben's cartographies of exclusion the basic diagram of a splintered or "splintering" urbanism associated primarily with the uneven distribution of, and access to, infrastructures and services.[32] In cities like São Paulo or Mumbai, stark, cheek-by-jowl juxtapositions of gated, luxury high-rise residential towers with walled-in favelas, or slums, subterraneously connected and separated by social, technological, and economic networks, might serve as paradigmatic instances of simultaneous isolation and proximity.[33] However, the materialist (and historicist) association of such spatial patterns with networked (or telematic) production or with a refractory postmodern culture industry does not find much support with Agamben. Rather than identifying the period 1945–75 as roughly transitional (as many theorists of postmodernity, including Hardt and Negri, do), Agamben locates the historical rupture (following Carl Schmitt) at or around the First World War, at which time he argues the sovereign exception, which has its origins in classical times, was first deployed in the modern era.[34]

From an architectural standpoint, there is nothing particularly new in Agamben's periodization. At around this time, for example, the rationalization of everyday life in large-scale and primarily state-sponsored housing estates in many ways defined architectural modernism across Europe and later in the United States. Similar developments followed later still across the newly urbanizing, recently decolonized Third World. The strictly bounded, tabula rasa spatial configuration of so many of these new housing enclaves, often imagined for the proletariat but realized for the middle classes (as in the German *Siedlungen*), followed the Corbusian model of large swaths of open space at ground level accessible to the surrounding city but at the same time distinctly set off from it. We can also think here of Le Corbusier's own long-standing identification of the housing block with the ocean liner. Territorially open and enclosed at once, these great modern housing estates were surely instruments for the rational management of a population, as well as instruments of corporeal discipline; but they were also diagrams of inclusive exclusion (or exclusive inclusion) on the order of Agamben's biopolitical topology.

Stretched further, we might also want to see the postwar French *banlieux* (similarly addressed by the Situationists) or Italian exurban housing estates such as the Corviale in Agamben's assertion that "[t]he camp as dislocating localization is the hidden matrix of the politics in which we are still living, and it is this structure of the camp that we must learn to recognize in all its metamorphoses into the *zones d'attentes* of our airports and certain outskirts of our cities."[35] Such readings are further encouraged by an earlier and less careful version of the same passage, in which Agamben goes so far as to suggest that "the gated communities of the United States are beginning to look like camps," in the sense of the indeterminate sovereignties that they, too, entail, a proposition that has since been reinforced by certain of his interpreters.[36]

Although there is much to object to in associating the violence of the camp with the languor of the gated community, this proposition has the virtue of testing the limits of Agamben's camp-as-paradigm thesis at a theoretical rather than at an empirical level. For it suggests obliquely that, if the Nazi death camps stand at one pole of an inside-outside paradox as a limit case—"the most absolute biopolitical space that has ever been realized"[37]—something like Utopia stands at the other: a self-contained space absolutely exterior to the modern order of things, on which that order was nevertheless founded. Far from existing in a state of nature, however, the inhabitants of Utopia are typically governed and protected by a distinctive set of laws and rights, as is characteristic of many literary utopias with their lengthy explications of constitutional detail. In the gated community, with its fundamentally defensive and securitized posture, these rights, beginning with the rights of access, are not suspended but fetishized as a kind of class privilege rather than as a universal human value. As a private sphere extrapolated from the enclave to the city or even the nation as a whole, the gated community paradigmatically limits the rights of those on the outside in defense of the rights of those on the inside.

In that sense, the American-style gated community is integrated into the body politic—and into capitalist economic relations and the networks that carry them—*by virtue of its exceptionality* rather than despite it, in an inversion of the nineteenth-century utopian enclave that realizes a distinctive type of sovereignty over a delimited space. Invented to protect the property of the new urban bourgeoisie (an early example would be Llewellyn Park in New Jersey), the gated community's postmodern variant is built around "laws" and covenants that secure its privacy. These intensely privatized zones nevertheless remain genealogically linked to the public housing estates of the interwar period, with both types sharing a common source in the European Garden City movement.[38] But to appreciate the stakes of this hidden connection, the suburban gated community must also be reconnected with the products of postwar American "urban renewal" from which it was effectively extracted.

Urban renewal internalized already-reified racial and class divides to the degree that, again paradoxically, a regime of desegregation was overlaid to compensate for the very partitioning of urban space on which many of these large housing complexes were founded in the first place.[39] Among the latter, perhaps the most infamous was the Pruitt-Igoe housing development in St. Louis (Leinweber, Yamasaki & Hellmuth, 1950–54), the double name of which reflects the racially segregated nature of its original plan (the Pruitt section was intended for black inhabitants and Igoe for whites). Though before being built the two were joined under desegregation laws, the vast majority of the development's inhabitants were impoverished African-Americans who had either been relocated from the slums that the new housing complex replaced or had migrated to the city from the rural South.

Even before demolition began in 1972, Pruitt-Igoe had become an icon of modern architecture's presumed failures in the area of social reform. The fetishization of its architecture as a bad object has been so intense and unremitting that it has since inspired counterclaims that emphasize political-economic factors such as underfunding, administrative neglect,

Partial demolition of Pruitt-Igoe housing complex (Leinweber, Yamasaki & Hellmuth, 1950–54), St. Louis, Missouri, 1972. Photograph by Lee Balterman.

and the de-urbanization of the largely white middle class to account for the project's ultimate demise.[40] Still, Pruitt-Igoe continues to haunt architectural discourse in the United States and beyond, as its demolition is replayed in the urban imaginary again and again, as if to confirm the ruination, several degrees removed, of the modernist utopian enterprise more generally. As a historical actuality and as a still-vivid afterimage, Pruitt-Igoe brings together several important elements: discourses and practices of environmental reform, where the (modern) normalization of the physical environment is turned toward the (postmodern) normalization of the psychic environment; the biopolitical reshaping of the city along new lines of inclusion-exclusion through such mechanisms as "slum clearance"; and the becoming-spectral of a utopian future that, by the time the project was completed, was already identified with the past.

As an instrument of environmental reform, Pruitt-Igoe sits on the threshold of a mutation, where the normalization of the biophysical environment, which was given deterministic force by the parascientific, functionalist discourse on "light and air" still visible in Pruitt-Igoe's architecture, is internalized within a new functionalism of the mind. A key marker of such a shift was the publication, in 1972, of Oscar Newman's

Defensible Space: Crime Prevention through Urban Design, the title of which refers to "a model for residential environments which inhibits crime by creating the physical expression of a social fabric that defends itself."[41] On the back cover of its dust jacket was the same photograph of the partial demolition of Pruitt-Igoe that Charles Jencks reproduced five years later (with reference to Newman) in *The Language of Post-Modern Architecture* to commemorate the "death of modern architecture."[42] Throughout Newman's analysis, which integrates the territorial with the affective, Pruitt-Igoe stands as a representative example of a *terrain vague* possessed of an indefensible porosity and figural indeterminacy, inside and out. That what is physical here is equally psychical is reinforced by Newman's accounting of less tangible characteristics of a building like "image and milieu" alongside the more tangible construction of physical boundaries to encourage what he called "territoriality." Further, *Defensible Space* interweaves micro-opportunities for postpanoptic, "natural surveillance" in order that architecture might "[allow] mutually benefitting attitudes to surface," if not exactly determine them directly.[43]

As a particularly telling instance, Newman offers an anecdote from Pruitt-Igoe's history. A temporary construction fence had been erected around one of the eleven-story slabs for the installation of playground equipment. Tenants requested that the fence remain, which it did. Newman reports:

> [T]he crime and vandalism rate in this building is 80 percent below the Pruitt-Igoe norm. This building, like others in Pruitt-Igoe, has no security guard. It is the only building in which residents themselves have begun to show signs of concern about the maintenance of the interior: picking up litter, sweeping the corridors, and replacing light bulbs. The vacancy rate in this building varies from 2 percent to 5 percent, in contrast with the overall vacancy rate for Pruitt-Igoe of 70 percent.

On the basis of these rates, Newman concludes:

> This is an extreme example of territorial definition and is certainly not one which we are advocating. But its accomplishments are significant in light of the Pruitt-Igoe failure. The question to be asked is how does one initially achieve thoughtful building groupings rather than having to resort to barbed-wire fences and locks after the fact.[44]

In other words, how to *sublimate* the fence into an architectural language that does its biopolitical work at the level of the spatial imaginary ("thoughtful building groupings" that inscribe a *virtual* territoriality) rather than through the raw power of barbed wire? While admitting that it may be "premature," Newman avers that "it is possible that an inadvertent result of a socially mobile and open society is its required segregation into physically separate subclusters which are inviolable and uniform, both socially and economically."[45] Neither here nor anywhere else in the book does he discourage the association of "social mobility" with the "openness" of metropolitan capitalism, citing, for instance, rural-to-urban migrations as a factor in social inadaptability to high-rise, high-density living. In response, and with apologies all the while for its authoritarian implications, *Defensible Space* offers a formula of territorial definition plus diffuse, microphysical surveillance, both on the ground and in the mind. We would seem to be, then, at the other end of the historical arc sketched by Foucault, where the functions of the police, which have extended through the infrastructures of governmentality since the eighteenth century, gradually migrate into the interstices of the city's nongovernmental spatial and social fabrics, in correspondence with what Deleuze called a generalized "society of control."

Though attributing to it less direct influence, Newman returns throughout to the problem of density as the crux of the issue, since it opens onto economic considerations to which federal and local agencies are subject. Associating the relatively high densities of many urban public housing developments (Pruitt-Igoe in this case excepted) with fiscal pressures brought to bear on housing agencies by the speculative urban real estate market, he cites data for New York City that suggest that above fifty units per acre "crime rate increases proportionately with density." Further, and with a note of caution: "Crime rate may not correlate specifically with density, but it *does* correlate with building height and type."[46] Consequently, normalization of the crime rate requires adjustments to the apparatuses of security, which in this case include architecture. In New York, high density generally means high-rise, elevator buildings with double-loaded corridors, a building type that Newman's data target as an efficient if not final cause of criminality and thus subject to reform. Recognizing, however, that incorporating defensible space into high-density buildings will lead to higher construction costs, Newman summarizes the encounter between a reformist state and expansionist capital in a succinct formula: "more costly high-density buildings, or less expensive, lower-density buildings."[47] The reconciliation he proposes, of territorial and psychic management within an economics in which the state is logically (rather than merely practically) subordinated to the "open" market, indicates that we are also witnessing here strategies for the dissipation of social risk within or *inside* the city, rather than the heterotopic exclusion of the sort analyzed by Foucault in the nineteenth century in buildings like prisons or asylums.

Faced with this spatial paradox, Newman declares: "Defensible space may be the last stand of the urban man committed to an open society."[48] But troubled by the implication that this only means displacing crime to other, less well defended areas, he goes on to ask: "If, for the sake of argument, one accepts as a proposition that the total amount of crime cannot be diminished, only displaced, this then offers a new question: is a pattern of uniformly distributed crime preferable to one in which crime is concentrated in particular areas?" Having thereby reformulated urban crime as essentially a problem of risk management which is economic before it is social, Newman can only repeat his conclusion: that pockets of refuge in the form of residential enclaves remain preferable, since they have the side effect of displacing "danger" to those nonresidential areas (shopping, institutional, business, etc.) that "are inherently more easily served by police protection."[49]

This reformulation summarizes a historical process in which the economic does not so much replace the social as absorb it. Thus also, we arrive at a segmentation of urban space comparable to that of the gated community. On one side of the line, the residential or domestic realm, a space *without police* that must therefore be protected by other, more intimate means; while on the other side of the line, the nonresidential civic or public realm, which remains subject to police control and to the older forms of governmental rationality with which that has long been attended.[50]

As a resolution of the risk management problem posed by urban economics, defensible space is therefore a correlate of neoliberalism rather than a retreat or a refuge from its deterritorializing winds. What Newman calls "the urban man committed to an open society," whose psychic and physical well-being must be defended, is also neoliberalism's new and improved *homo œconomicus*.[51] It is no accident that the crime rate is the privileged index in Newman's analysis, where it is made to stand on the one hand for such intangibles as "quality of life" to which the urban real estate market attaches economic value, and on the other hand, for the whole racialized dynamic of white-collar production, which since the 1950s had been fleeing the city for the suburbs. Thus (implicitly white) "urban man," secure in his domicile, was productive man, a form of "human capital."[52] He is also the opposite of Agamben's *homo sacer*, who has been internally exiled from the city and its productive/reproductive circuits, or rather incorporated into the civic body as a profoundly external (yet still productive) unit. But is there yet a space that connects *homo œconomicus* with *homo sacer*?

Consider a set of diagrams from Agamben, in which he aims to show the transition from something like a temporary state of emergency (1), figured as external to the normal political system, to a proper "state of exception" (2) in which the ability to suspend the law is a condition of sovereign power rather than external to it. Here, the outside enters deep within, as an island-like space in which the law does not apply. This space is the violent inverse of a utopia, with which it nevertheless shares certain properties, including a radical rearrangement of the prevailing economic order. The Utopian abolition of money, figured in Thomas More's account as the use of gold for chamber pots, is perversely replicated upon entry into the "naked life" of the camps, as in the Nazi practice of expropriating the material belongings of prisoners for recirculation on the outside. That the border between inside and outside can never be absolute is verified in both cases, however, as the economic function of the island is displaced onto another level: in the camp, in the primitive accumulation of capital attached to the expropriated belongings as well as to the inmates' forced labor, and in Utopia, in the use of gold to pay external mercenaries to defend the sovereignty of the Utopian island itself.[53]

The island-space diagrammed by Agamben is also the territorial inverse of a capital city, where the rights of citizenship are represented symbolically and protected through political representation. The state of

Diagrams showing movement toward "state of exception." From Giorgio Agamben, *Homo Sacer: Sovereign Power and Bare Life*, trans. Daniel Heller-Roazen (Stanford: Stanford University Press, 1998). Copyright 1998 by the Board of Trustees of the Leland Stanford Jr. University.

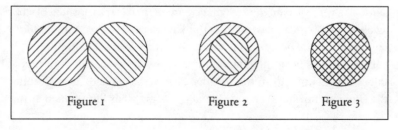

Figure 1   Figure 2   Figure 3

exception, on the other hand, refers to the gradual withholding of rights and other instruments of law, as well as to the withholding of access to the symbolic order in which these rights are represented and secured. Recall that the capital city—"Athens, Rome, Paris"—is a privileged site for Rossi's collective memory, the gradual exclusion from which can be understood as the aesthetic equivalent of the withholding of rights of representation in the political sphere. But in Agamben's account the governing paradox is that, increasingly through the twentieth century, state sovereignty (as figured, we can add, in Speer's Berlin) seems to be *built on* the state of exception, whereby power accrues to those who assume the sovereign right to suspend the rights of others—an "exception" that, as Agamben's third diagram warns, is fast becoming the rule.

How, then, are we to understand the state-sponsored, modernist housing complex in these terms? As a utopian urban island, which finds a weak echo in Pruitt-Igoe (the project's evident failures notwithstanding)? Or as a biopolitical "camp," a space in which rights are slowly, imperceptibly suspended, including—eventually—the right to public housing itself, which has been systematically eroded by the narratives emanating out of Pruitt-Igoe's demolition? The underlying oscillation is strictly undecidable, in which sense Pruitt-Igoe figures in the postmodern imaginary as Rossi's city of the living dead. On the one hand, we have the utopian project of light and air, of hygiene and of rationally managed productivity but also of proletarian awakening to historical consciousness and immanent critique of the welfare state; while on the other hand, we have a barbed wire fence and with it exclusion from the symbolic order and the consequent exhaustion of history.

To the extent that such urban artifacts as the gated community reproduce the Utopian diagram, they resolve this oscillation by incorporating Utopia's critical function within extant economic relations: Utopia as norm. So if Agamben is right, Utopia, too, died in the camps, only to be monstrously reborn in archipelagoes of defense and exclusion based on the normalization of Utopian exceptionality. Thus for postmodernism, Utopia is not a representation of an ideal city. It is a topos, in the sense of a very specific *thought* that circulates and is transformed discursively in biopolitical networks. Its thinking depends on certain material conditions *in the present,* of which architecture forms a part. As such, it can be and has been integrated into the productive machinery of capital as a regulating norm that divides inside from outside by absorbing the Utopian "nowhere" into the banalities of everyday life, typified by the gated community. Actively *unthought* by postmodernism through this appropriation, Utopia nevertheless remains a latent or repressed threat to the machinery itself.

For Fredric Jameson, the postmodern inability to think a truly utopian thought corresponds to the much proclaimed end of ideology and end of history at the hands of late capitalism or neoliberalism. Though Jameson generally focuses his critical attention on what he vaguely defines as "the power network of multinational capitalism" rather than on biopower proper, Hardt and Negri have helped to show the connections between the two.[54] Jameson has also vividly analyzed expressions of late capitalism's cultural and spatial logic in architecture, be it Frank Gehry's house in Santa Monica or John Portman's Westin Bonaventure Hotel in downtown Los Angeles.[55] Whereas, writing on utopian science fiction, he has analyzed Utopia's island form as it is sublimated into a range of literary figures: moon, Mars, spaceship, colonial outpost, and so on.[56] And though we can agree with Jameson that Utopia's consequent and absolute exteriority is a necessary condition for the island as "determinate negation" or critical reflection of the status quo, we return to our spatial paradox when we note again that the island or enclave is also a basic unit of the postmodern city: not only gated communities but also self-contained shopping malls, manicured corporate campuses, weather-sealed atriums, barricaded office buildings, golf courses, and spaceship-like towers. The slums, prisons, and refugee camps in which vast populations actually live stand to these dreamworlds as one mirror reflecting another, rather than in dialectical opposition.[57]

But topologically speaking, an island is never just an island. Consider, for example, another a set of diagrams, in this case of Utopia itself as described by Thomas More in 1516. They are taken from one of Jameson's key sources, *Utopiques*, the well-known study of More's text by the semiologist Louis Marin, first published in 1973 as an explicit response to the events of May 1968.[58] They diagram the geography of More's Utopia, a circular island with a circular harbor or gulf inscribed into one of its edges, resulting in a crescentlike shape. In More's account, the island is actually produced by an act of civil engineering—a cut, which prefigures so many more modernist cuts and caesuras to come—in the form of a trench dug to separate the preexisting promontory from the mainland. Its harbor is therefore Utopia's sole point of contact with the outside (or "real") world. Ships come and go through its treacherous straits, which the resident Utopians control with strategic cunning. The three versions of the diagram represent three possible interpretations of More's text—three oscillating "figures" in the text—in which the size of the circular harbor and therefore the relative location of Amourotum, Utopia's centrally positioned capital city, varies with respect to the water's edge and therefore with respect to the "outside" world as such. As Marin puts it, "Utopia is a circular island, but it is both closed and open."[59] This description applies internally as well as externally since, according to Marin, the "spatial play" in More's Utopia involves, among other things, an irresolvable, internal tension between Utopian equality (and thus internal openness), as figured in the even, gridlike distribution of its fifty-four city states across the roughly circular island, and Utopian hierarchy (and thus power and inequity but also governmental authority), as figured in the added value attached to this central city, the *capital* city. On another scale, this reading of an irresolvable tension between bounded sites and networks reproduces the dialectical struggle that Manfredo Tafuri discerned during the modern period between two "utopias," thus confirming the general applicability of Marin's analysis. In Tafuri's allegory of modernization, the neoclassical monumentality of Washington, D.C., the nation's political capital, and the circulatory, gridded metropolis of New York compete for symbolic sovereignty over American capitalist development, to which postmodernism (or for Tafuri, "hypermodernism") supplies the inevitable, exhausted denouement.[60]

Toward the end of his book, Marin includes his celebrated reflections on Disneyland, which he describes as a "degenerate Utopia." Beginning with the islandlike enclosure of the original theme park, Marin demonstrates the persistence, in Disneyland, of what he calls "patterns of spatial organization that can be qualified as utopic." But with these and through these, he also demonstrates how, in Disneyland, the properly utopian dimension of its island topology—that is, the "spatial play" that allows it to remain simultaneously open and closed—degenerates into myth, where "American" values such as the "frontier spirit," historically "obtained by violence and exploitation," are re-coded and naturalized through the machinery of collective fantasy as the psychic infrastructures of "law and order" or, in another register, biopower.[61]

Disneyland has also been much discussed in architecture as a prototype of both the enchanted urban/suburban enclave and of postmodernist aesthetic populism, perhaps most notably and *avant la lettre* in an article published by Charles Moore in 1965 under the title "You Have Got to Pay for the Public Life."[62] Like Rossi's work on urban collective memory

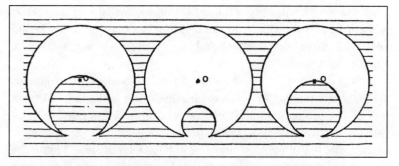

Diagrams showing three possible versions of the map of Thomas More's *Utopia* (1516), from Louis Marin, *Utopiques, jeux d'espaces* (Paris: Les Éditions de Minuit, 1973). Copyright 1973 by Louis Marin. Reprinted courtesy of Les Éditions de Minuit.

and Venturi and Scott Brown's work on Las Vegas, Moore's tour of the architecture and urbanism of California grasps at a communicative foundation for the postmetropolitan city. He finds its prototype in Disneyland where, in return for the price of admission, Moore argues that the visitor gains the closest thing to public space that southern California has to offer—a "whole public world," as he puts it. Though Moore goes on to concede that in fact this world-within-a-world falls short of manifesting an authentic "urban experience"—most notably because it fails what he calls his revolution test, whereby the success of urban space is measured by its hypothetical capacity to host a revolutionary uprising—he nevertheless winds up by offering Disneyland as a positive model for architectures and urbanisms to come.

We are familiar with how such a proposition would play out in Moore's own work, from his mountaintop fantasy drawings to the world-within-a-world of Piazza d'Italia in New Orleans. But it is more relevant here that he develops his celebration of Disneyland's pseudopublic nature by way of a critique of the rootlessness of suburbanization. Referring to the sprawl that was just beginning to overtake California, including what would later be called Silicon Valley, Moore complains that "[t]he new houses are separate and private . . . islands, alongside which are moored the automobiles that take the inhabitants off to other places. . . . The houses are not tied down to any place. . . . " He describes all of this as "a floating world in which a floating population can island-hop with impunity," equipped with drive-in everything, including Frank Lloyd Wright's drive-in Civic Center in Marin County.[63] So we are left to conclude that what distinguishes Disneyland from all these other islands is its scale: it is a private city, but it is big enough to contain an entire world and anchor its "floating population" and thereby to sustain the fantasy of a "public life."

This is exactly what Marin means when he describes Disneyland as a "degenerate utopia," in which the inside-outside oscillation of Utopia proper—its complex, ambivalent, and in a sense still negative relation with the real world—is frozen into a fixed representation: in a word, myth. In this case, it also means a mythical public realm organized around a mythical America: Disneyland as the capital city of a dream factory that does not merely represent or reflect American economic and political hegemony but rather helps to produce it and to organize it. Still, like Utopia itself, Disneyland has a hole in it. This hole is the channel by which the visitor gains access, having "paid for the public life" not merely by buying a ticket but by exchanging dollars for Disney money. This translation, this substitution of one system of representation for another, works to cover over the hole, the place where the outside enters in and the inside leaks out. As Marin says, it leads from "reality to fantasy" along the axis of Main Street USA, which, we recall, Venturi described a year after Moore's article as "almost all right." Whereas according to Marin, the reification of the imagination in the form of Fantasyland (Disneyland's privileged subsection) that awaits the visitor at the other end of the line accounts for the degeneration of Utopia into so many "banal, routine images from Disney's films . . . bankrupt signs of an imagination homogenized by the mass media."[64]

Still, like the gate in the gated community, the hole in the middle of Disneyland is real, whether or not it is covered up by Main Street USA and the fantasy of "public life" that it stages. Through it pass the networks (and the Main Streets, and the Wall Streets) of multinational capital. To describe it as a hole, however, is not quite correct. Instead, its topology is better described as a twist or a knot that enfolds the doubled-up island figure; architecturally, it is more like a revolving door than a passage. On one side of this door lies Utopia and on the other the camps, in an antinomy of the modern that has since been forcibly resolved by collapsing the two into a single, double-sided norm: on the one side the global, gated community and on the other the "planet of slums."[65] These two sides of the new, urban coin-of-the-realm now effectively require one another, in what may seem like an infinite regress of negative-positive reproduction.

In this way, the postmodern master narrative that claims that all utopias lead to the camps—a preoccupation that is traceable in architecture to Sigfried Giedion's *Mechanization Takes Command*—seems verified but as a self-fulfilling prophesy of biopower rather than as a historical truth. In such a narrative, what Jameson names the "desire called Utopia" is admonished and apparently satisfied, at once.[66] And yet, like the two sides of a Möbius strip at any point along its length, what seem like inverted mirror images remain distinguishable as limit cases on either side of the strip's historically sedimented thickness. Utopia and camp become visible as poles of an antinomy rather than as seamlessly connected norms only when one passes *through* rather than along the Möbius strip of history. Seen along its length or followed as a line, the doubled-up logic of inclusive, biopolitical exclusion can be summarized as follows: you can neither leave nor enter. Cut through at any point and seen crosswise, however, Utopia and camp begin to peel apart.

The effect of this separation is somewhat different from what Foucault famously called, also in 1966—the same year that Venturi and Rossi published their treatises—"thought of [or from] the outside."[67] With this expression, Foucault offered what would be one of many formulations of the exteriority of language, and of its authorless, subjectless textuality. But his own thought, including the underdeveloped heterotopology that he addressed to architects (in 1967), holds many clues that the open sites of textual iteration remain implicitly dependent upon humanism's stable interiors, if only as a kind of foil.[68] Reconceived as an inhuman island that perpetually threatens to revert to the equal and opposite inhumanity of the camp, Utopia breaks off, but not as an abstract ideal or limitless "frontier."[69] Instead, cutting through the twisted space that keeps Utopia both in and out at once, we discover a wholly thinkable set of options that have nothing to do with realizing the unrealizable, only with derealizing the real.

The utopian function of the island—and of the modernist cut more generally—is not compromised, therefore, by a plurality of interests that fragments its supposed organic unity (to be reconciled by Venturi's populism or by Rossi's myth) but by a topological sleight-of-hand. As biopolitics begins its work of normalization, modernity's two poles are forced together; Utopia and camp align, and the no-man's-land that separates them is displaced. In other words, the barbed-wire fence is internalized or, as the former East Germans say, the wall is now "in the head." The gate is no longer needed; the fence is now everywhere. But its strange topology can be cut through at a very practical level by recognizing that it represses a political-economic choice everywhere along its length. Here is an all too modest example. A possible translation of Moore's title into the context of Pruitt-Igoe and the discourse of defensible space would be "You Have Got to Pay for Public Housing." Such a formula tendentiously converts housing from a political right to a form of private property, demonstrating again that biopolitics and late capitalism go hand in glove. Whereas, to refuse this formula is to think an authentically (if distantly) utopian thought that conjures a *counterdiagram* to that of the camp and of the gated enclave, undoing its unity and its ubiquity from a crosswise distance. Put more concretely: The choice is whether or not to demand unambiguously *public* housing with all of its risks, responsibilities, and double binds and thereby to "risk" the dimly perceptible thought called Utopia again.

Not "affordable" housing, or "sustainable" housing, or housing provided by "public/private partnerships," but *public* housing. Power flows through architecture and lives are governed, whether by states, corporations, banks, or real estate investment trusts. And in cities from New York to Mumbai, as a matter of state housing policy, governance has increasingly devolved onto the markets. But the simple, unequivocal choice "not to be governed like that" metonymically denaturalizes postmodern narratives that have been built around the foreclosure of the public realm as a kind of socioeconomic hazard.[70] And the actual, material existence of such a choice, if not its "real" plausibility and its inherent risks, establishes the conditions for a far more ambitious political project that can be called utopian in the positive sense. It also marks postmodern architecture's moment of truth, the moment when it comes face-to-face with matters of life and death. That such choices are dissipated, on the one hand, into the statistical and probabilistic language of risk management and, on the other, into the equally defensive and securitized language of architecture-as-such is an eventuality to which we will presently return.

2 HISTORY

The Last War

REFERRING TO THE "CHECKMATE" performed by advanced capitalism on the Shklovskian "knight's moves" attempted by the modernist avant-gardes, the architectural historian Manfredo Tafuri announced, in 1976: "The war is over."[1] Tafuri was evaluating attempts by the neo-avant-gardes of the 1970s to replay such moves, mainly in the United States. And in a sense he was right. His text, titled "The Ashes of Jefferson," charted the exhaustion of the avant-garde project by way of its built-in contra-dictions, as exemplified by the melancholic contest over the stylistic leg-acy of architectural modernism known as the Gray/White debate, which overtook the American academy in the early 1970s. Tafuri's own melan-choly stems from his conclusion that, among other things, this "debate" was in fact stage-managed to conceal an actual crisis confronting the dis-cipline, namely, the collective failure of architects to substantially alter patterns of capitalist development at the urban scale.

The other, victorious side of this same checkmate is given in general terms by the American neoconservative philosopher Francis Fukuyama in his transposition, immediately following the fall of the Berlin Wall, of the neo-Hegelian "end of history" thesis elaborated in the 1930s by the émigré Russian philosopher Alexandre Kojève. For Fukuyama, a pessi-mistic view of modernity's overall historical arc is unwarranted. As with Tafuri, the arc itself is irreversible. But global capitalism, rather than being a driver, is portrayed as its inevitable consequence, driven in turn by the "economic self-interest" of a newly conscious class of consum-ers that replaces Lenin's "global proletariat," once the veil of dependency theory and other structural accounts of uneven development have been stripped away. In light of this "victory of the VCR," as Fukuyama calls it (a reference meant to identify the consumerism of "Made in Japan" with the postwar Asian economic "miracle"), class struggle is made to look nothing if not counterproductive.[2]

Fukuyama wagers his attempt at universal history on the unity of capitalist economic development with liberal democracy. Here too, the relationship is deemed "unquestionable." But by his own admission, he is unable to explain it in the economic terms on which he has relied. Enter, via Kojève, the figure of the "last man," the subject of history in a Hegelian struggle for recognition of man qua man. However, rather than adduce allegedly self-evident examples of historical inevitability for this figure, as is his pattern throughout (the fall of the Wall, etc.), Fukuyama appeals here to the full and recognizable actualization, in liberal democracy, of something like human nature, over and above what others might call the "postmodern" morass of cultural relativism.[3] To demystify this operation (and with it, the pseudohumanism on which the larger neoconservative edifice is built), it may be enough to point to Jacques Derrida's demonstration of the tautologies that organize Fukuyama's project, his "sleight-of-hand trick between history and nature."[4] Still, we must admit that we have here two versions of history's "end," bracketing the period from the early 1970s through the late 1980s.

What to make of this two-sidedness? Both are endings to the narrative arc of history. Checkmate: the war is over, the project has failed. Or checkmate: the wall has fallen, the war is over; there is no more outside, the project is complete. Is this merely a matter of left and right observing two "ends" of the same phenomenon and coming to opposite conclusions? Partly to avoid this too-easy conclusion, I want to claim a space for architecture in all of this that is slightly different from that occupied by the tragicomedy witnessed by Tafuri. Since, if there is anything at all that joins those disparate practices that have, in different combinations, been gathered together under the heading "modern architecture," it is a pretense to control the future. In *Architecture and Utopia* (1973), his first real settling of accounts with the avant-gardist legacy, Tafuri calls this the "project."[5] It is what slides into capitalist planification in his version of the narrative, most often through a rationalization of urban development that reproduces the exchangeability of empty signs by which Georg Simmel had already defined the money economy.[6] This projected (if eternally postponed) control of the future, just as visible in Dada as it is in Constructivism, constitutes both the modernity and the historicity of the avant-gardes. Whether manifestly nihilist or futurist in tone, the project does not secure entry into history so much as surrender to it and, in the process, attempt to guide it.

By contrast, whatever else architectural postmodernism is or is not, it has relinquished control over history. Content to recirculate existing languages that have been drained of their revolutionary content, so-called postmodern architecture in its myriad forms seems satisfied with its fate. That fate is by and large that of the *petit-bourgeoisie,* who have come to power with the "victory of the VCR." But Fukuyama's VCR metaphor is serendipitous in another way. The history that it inadvertently materializes is a history of reruns, of bootleg copies, of reproductions of reproductions, and of what Fredric Jameson, paraphrasing Raymond Williams, has called "total flow." And it does not take a trained eye to notice that the postmodern architectural rerun or reproduction, whether stylistically neomodern or neoclassical, is neither copy nor original. In which case, we can say that whatever else it does or does not do, "postmodern" architecture replaces the serial (call it cinematic) imagination of historical time frames with a not exactly circular (call it videographic) temporality that obeys commands like "rewind" and "fast forward." This, technically speaking, is also what we must mean when we speak of mass media and architecture's relation therewith since 1970: an uneven historicity, not of narratives big or small, interrupted or structured by breaks (montage but also passages of legible "meaning"); rather, an interleaved historicity of many-times-at-once.[7] In what Jameson is content to describe in still somewhat mechanical terms as a "ceaseless rotation of elements" in experimental video art, we can further specify as a temporality, and a sense of history or lack thereof, in which even the "untimely" or uncanny cannot be confidently determined by measuring it against a dependable sequence of one thing after another.[8] Hence, we are confronted with a temporality that is no longer quite that of mechanical reproducibility: the "victory of the VCR," indeed.

This is also how we should see (or really, watch) the Gray/White debate. In one corner (on the left side of your screen) the New York Five, led intellectually by Peter Eisenman and including architects like Richard Meier and Michael Graves, all of whose work at the time mined the abstract, protolinguistic "grammars" of prewar (or "white") modernism. In the other corner (on the right), the "Grays," led by Robert A. M. Stern and with Robert Venturi and Denise Scott Brown as fellow travelers, who were identified with more figural, "postmodern" mixes of classical and vernacular citation aimed at populist communication that accommodated a status quo. By 1976, the date of Tafuri's "Ashes of Jefferson" text, the debate had played itself out with both sides fully identified with postmodernism. And by that time, the Vietnam War was in fact "over."

But in announcing that "the war is over" Tafuri was not referring to Vietnam, nor to any other historical conflict in particular. He was referring instead to the revolutionary "languages of battle" characteristic of the avant-gardes that had given modern architecture its ethical charge. In this light, the actual war that formed the historical and televisual backdrop against which ideological battles on American campuses such as the Gray/White debate were fought during the late 1960s and early 1970s did not appear to have penetrated the disciplinary confines of architecture. Instead, according to Tafuri, under postmodernism (or hypermodernism, as he preferred to say) the anguished public battle conducted by the modern avant-gardes against capitalist planification had been driven into the private realm. There the aesthetic languages that led the charge were overcome with a Barthesian "pleasure of the text," and architecture was converted into "*a Marseillaise without Bastilles to take by storm.*"[9] Still, given the embeddedness of his American subjects in a historical milieu overdetermined, in effect, by the Vietnam conflict, Tafuri's choice of a vanguardist martial metaphor seems peculiarly anachronistic.

It is fair to say that even today Vietnam remains the "last war" in the American political imaginary, in the sense of the oft-used expression "fighting the last war." Despite the later Gulf War and the NATO-led action in Kosovo, to say nothing of the post-9/11 conflicts in Iraq and Afghanistan, Vietnam continues to haunt public discourse on war in the United States. This occurred on all sides of the debate over the 2003 American invasion and subsequent occupation of Iraq, whether in the form of suggestions that the United States became trapped in a Vietnam-style "quagmire" or in the form of the "Swift boat" attacks on Senator John Kerry's military record in Vietnam during the 2004 U.S. presidential campaign.[10] Likewise for the erosion of curbs on executive power put in place after the Watergate scandal, an erosion that was exacerbated, after 2001, by appeals to the exigencies of a new and terrifying "war on terror" and against the unproductive effects of Vietnam-style dissent on the prosecution of the Iraq occupation. To the extent that the cultural war over the legitimacy of actual war rightly or wrongly took Vietnam as its model, then, all sides can be said to have been fighting the last war.

If postmodernism also emerged in part out of the intertwining of culture and politics during the 1960s and early 1970s for which Vietnam was an organizing referent, architecture's internal endgames can offer interpretive guidance here. In arguing that certain works of architecture from the 1970s and 1980s helped draw the contours of postmodernism proper, Jameson in particular has found confirmation in the anguished dialectic charted by Tafuri, though in resolutely negative "anti-postmodernist" terms.[11] Seen retrospectively, and from an architectural perspective, this negativity seems justified. Today, the multicoded citationality generally understood to be characteristic of postmodern architecture, with its noncommittal mixed messages signaling an acceptance of the historical "inevitability" of capitalist development, has been eclipsed by an epic combination of neopragmatism and techno-triumphalism that leaves even less room for dissent. This acritical celebration of the imperatives of "practice" has been accompanied by an anti-intellectual *rappel à l'ordre* that is the true legacy of the Gray/White debate, filtered in the late 1990s through the euphoria of the "new economy."[12]

So the insights of Jameson, Andreas Huyssen, David Harvey, Jean-François Lyotard, and other theorists of postmodernism still apply: architecture still seems symptomatic of far-reaching cultural tendencies. The question is whether the modern/postmodern distinction captures the specificity of these tendencies. Though he rejects this distinction outright, it may still be necessary to let go of some of the theoretical underpinnings that inform a historiography like Tafuri's. Such underpinnings include, in "The Ashes of Jefferson" and elsewhere, the very notion of a dialectic of the avant-gardes tending toward ever more farcical, futile repetition of long-lost battles, culminating in postmodern ennui.

Tafuri's Jefferson reads as a cipher for the betrayal, by capitalist unreason, of the revolutionary dialectic of destruction and construction launched by modernism. Doomed from the start, the aesthetic and protopolitical acts of overthrow and (tragic, compromised) reconstitution that Tafuri charts in his polemical history of key avant-garde movements in *The Sphere and the Labyrinth* (1980, into which the earlier text was assimilated) have by the 1970s become mere parlor games. That history begins with Jefferson's near contemporary Piranesi, and it ends with the smoldering ashes of the only architect ever to occupy the U.S. presidency, whose designs at Monticello and elsewhere Tafuri sees as "aimed at placating the *Dialektik der Aufklärung* [Dialectic of Enlightenment]."[13] It is notable that Jefferson's own architecture attempted a synthesis of modern technology and postrevolutionary (neoclassical) aesthetics that prefigured liaisons between technology and aesthetics in so many later modernisms. Tafuri's emphasis, however, is on slippages between aesthetics and ideology. And though he had pursued these themes since the early 1960s, there is also a distinctly post-1968 sense of the exhaustion of revolutionary politics in his account, mirrored in the endgames of a revolutionary aesthetics cornered in a prison-house of linguistic play and reduced to incoherent babble.

But is it possible that Tafuri, too, may be fighting the last war, if only in the sense that he has little to offer in comprehending what we might call the epistemologies of Vietnam? To be sure, as a European writing on America, his perspective is potentially different, and in any case his despair at the effects of American hegemony is palpable. But in order to take full measure of the disconnect it would be inadequate merely to note, as a matter of context, the transformation of the war game called chess—and with it, the revolutionary "knight's move"—into one of many allegorical battlefields on which the cold war was waged. Nor would it be sufficient to recall that precisely this game had become a measure of machine intelligence in the military-industrial think tanks in which American computers were being taught to read Russian, and from which the "electronic battlefield" of Vietnam was being managed.[14] Yet each of these observations raises the possibility that Tafuri's war, the war of the modernist avant-gardes (a term with nineteenth-century military origins), was not over but rather obsolete.

In its place there did indeed arise something like a game with aesthetic languages. However, this formalist turn to language was accompanied, in architecture and elsewhere, by other, more technologically oriented games played with signs and symbols. Many of these were devoted to measuring environmental, geopolitical, and economic risk, and the corollary risk of ecological and/or social catastrophe (or, in the policy think tanks, nuclear war). Exemplary here are such exercises as Buckminster Fuller's World Game, begun in 1965. And it is only by considering these two dimensions of the postmodern epistemic modulation together—the technological and the aesthetic—that we get a sense of the difficulties faced by the frame of reference relied on by Tafuri and many others in charting the new cultural battlefields of what we now call postmodernism. Further to this, the encounter (or non-encounter) between Fuller and the (neo)avant-garde puts into play the biopolitical dimensions of the "language games" that would characterize these battlefields, in architecture and elsewhere.

Fuller, of whom Tafuri had nothing to say in *The Sphere and the Labyrinth* and scant little elsewhere, had been working for the U.S. military since the 1940s designing, among other things, lightweight deployable geodesic "radomes" that were used as enclosures for radar equipment along the Distant Early Warning (DEW) line near the Arctic Circle. These installations were part of the enormous, feedback-driven civil defense servomechanism called SAGE (Semi-Automated Ground Environment), the technical logic of which anticipated the remote-controlled warfare attempted by the U.S. military in Vietnam. During this period, Fuller exhaustively (if idiosyncratically) theorized the implications of a systems-based, feedback-driven cybernetic model of what he called "universe," or the global techno-economic network of networks in which architecture and engineering now operated. And by the late 1960s, having improbably become something of a hero for the counterculture, he was devoting much of his attention to turning swords into plowshares, or as he put it, converting the technological output of the military-industrial complex from "killingry" to "livingry."

As an instance of the latter, the World Game was originally designed to be played in the geodesic dome Fuller built for the United States Information Agency for Expo '67 in Montreal. Unrealized there, it took on a life of its own and was played in more ad hoc fashion in various institutional venues, often by students. The World Game is a game of "life," of the management of populations and resources in the interest of the survival of the human species qua species, rather than as a particular category of humans. Participants were invited to experiment with the environmental consequences of different scenarios for the distribution of resources on interactive world maps modeled after those used by the risk management strategists of the cold war. In its own way, then, the World Game is a language game—a game played with signs and symbols according to denotative and prescriptive protocols that turn technocratic positivism into a playful experiment, with a series of different narrative scenarios that unfold in a combination of linguistic and cartographic codes. But in the balances of trade and other quantities that are measured and rearranged in this game what is being contested is not this or that micronarrative in the heaving, directionless late-capitalist sea. Instead, like the futurists working at the RAND Corporation or at the Hudson Institute, the World Game posits a set of competing master narratives that tell the story of the global future as such.

Fuller's futurology reflects the general systems theory that lay behind it, which Lyotard would condemn at the end of the 1970s for its totalizing logics.[15] Yet at another level the World Game is more than just a game of possible futures that (as with futurology) inevitably resemble the system from which they are extrapolated. It is also an administrative game. Using maps, statistics, and other means of abstraction, the World Game attempts to reorient the world system from within by playing games with the very *idea* of a graspable, collectively charted direction for what Fuller called "Spaceship Earth." At stake here is architecture's presumed capacity to model the laws governing historical transformation, in a manner comparable to the discipline's classical vocation as construed by the Renaissance, of mapping the axiomatics of the cosmos onto the interior surfaces of a dome with a mixture of secular and religious subtexts. The difference is that in Fuller's case, as in many comparable practices operating on the shores of postmodernism, the stability of any such projection, stripped of its a priori metaphysical authority and condemned to inhabit secular, technical modern infrastructures like the geodesic dome, is very much in doubt from the start.

The World Game also indexes a postmodernist struggle with futurity in another, related sense. Its scenario-planning format was modeled on the war games played by cold warriors and thus offers some insight into the epistemologies of Vietnam. A notable difference however, was that the Manichean "drop dead," zero-sum premises of the latter (based on mathematician and computer scientist John von Neumann's game theory) were replaced here by a distinctly Fulleresque formulation: "Everybody must win."[16] This was utopian, to be sure, but with a certain tautological precision. Since if the objective of the game was to devise a redistribution of resources in which everybody wins, it was nevertheless impossible to win the World Game, not because this "ideal" scenario was permanently out of reach but because its availability was premised on an agonistics of knowledge (playing the game to win by devising the "correct" scenario) that, from the beginning, canceled the synergetic cooperation necessary for all players to win.

Thus the World Game was played on two contradictory levels at once—one intrinsic, another extrinsic. Intrinsically, it was a kind of postmodern language game, in which no one scenario had an a priori metaphysical or empirical claim over any other. Nor did it assume any power differential among the players (in other words, a politics of knowledge), in which sense it was "post-political."[17] Extrinsically, on the other hand, it remained thoroughly modernist, in the sense that it posited a space mapped and modeled by the geodesic dome itself in which something more than a temporary consensus could be reached, once the computer had, with the help of its human "players," played out all the possible scenarios. At this extrinsic or external level, the World Game remained a modernist game of optimization at the scale of the world system, rather than a postmodernist game of perpetual, competitive innovation.

Extrinsically then, the World Game was also not as postpolitical or postideological as Fuller often liked to claim. On the contrary, it entailed a displacement of politics to the level of cartography. It was a road map to a utopian future, but one in which the political question was, in part, who was in charge of the cognitive maps. For Fuller himself, this was a non-question comparable to asking who was flying the many airplanes in which he circled the globe. The ultimate arbiter in the World Game would be the mainframe computer rather than a political entity. As Fuller put it, "What I proposed was based on my observation that world people had become extraordinarily confident in the fundamental reliability of the computer and its electronically controlled processes," a state of affairs verified by "the equanimity with which world-around air jet travelers now commit their lives to the computer's reliability" as they come in for a night landing.[18]

This presupposed that the destination toward which Spaceship Earth ought to be headed was preprogrammed or, to put it another way, that the utopian future could be represented transparently and thereby optimized. But in contrast to the modernist utopias of Le Corbusier, for example, which were represented in panoramic aerial views and integrated master plans, Fuller's futures were represented discursively and probabilistically, in charts, graphs, and statistics describing world-historical "trending" (his term). It was assumed that these documents, archived at his "headquarters" at Southern Illinois University, were uncontestable and represented objective trends rather than an ideological project. At one level, this was nothing more than raw positivism. But at another level it was a wager, the stakes of which did not really lie in the question of whether the statistics were scientifically verifiable and therefore constituted a solid foundation on which an optimal future could be constructed, whether agonistically or consensually. Instead, the stakes lay most profoundly in the conversion of modernist utopias of form (Le Corbusier) into postmodernist utopias of risk (Fuller).

The risk/reward calculations underwriting both the World Game and the policy think tanks on which it was based depended on the translation of diverse environmental variables into a set of linguistic or protolinguistic units. This technical logic paralleled but did not exactly map onto those aspects of architecture's linguistic turn that later became identified with postmodernist discourse in general. For example, here is Jameson assembling the minimal "units" of an architectural grammar: ". . . these 'sentences'—if that is indeed what a building can be said to 'be'—are read by readers whose bodies fill in the various shifter-slots and subject-positions; while the larger text into which such units are inserted can be assigned to the text-grammar of the urban as such (or perhaps, in a world system, to even vaster geographies and their syntactic laws)."[19] What worries Jameson is the increasing difficulty of mapping such multiscaled "texts," which he describes with the help of Frank Gehry's house in Santa Monica as "the sixties gone toxic, a whole historical and countercultural 'bad trip' in which psychic fragmentation is raised to a qualitatively new power, the structural distraction of the decentered subject now promoted to the very motor and existential logic of late capitalism itself."[20]

Another name Jameson uses for this socio-spatial "bad trip" requiring a new set of cognitive maps is "corporate space."[21] But in his inclination to read "texts" like Gehry's house or John Portman's Bonaventure Hotel as allegories of this newly globalized space and the multiple dislocations it entails, he is compelled to overlook (or at least underestimate) some of the actual properties of more literal corporate spaces, like office buildings. These spaces were produced by new organizational regimes increasingly dedicated to technological and aesthetic principles like flexibility, which allowed for a responsive, interactive relationship with naturalized and increasingly mobile forms of capital. This meant that, as with the scaleless geodesic patterns that organized both Fuller's domes and the World Game maps, the inherently scaleless dynamics of such buildings, as well as their technical reproducibility, supported a decentered and apparently disorganized, postindustrial mode of production. But at another level, these same dynamics worked systematically to reorganize the human-environment assemblage into integrated, pattern-based networks. In aesthetic terms, aura was therefore both lost and regained as a result of technical reproducibility, in the form of recognizable patterns like the omnipresent (post)modernist grid. In that sense, many such office buildings are both originals and copies, at once.

The curtain walls that enclosed many office buildings during the 1950s and 1960s, in the United States in particular, are exemplary in this regard. In the hands of an architect like Ludwig Mies van der Rohe (in collaboration with Philip Johnson) at the Seagram Building in New York (1958), the modular, metal and glass curtain wall can appear as the epitome of modernist abstraction—a Greenbergian reduction, not so much to the flat painterly surface as to the plastic three-dimensional grid, an empty sign. The same wall can also appear as the very diagram of capitalist rationality, in the form of a gridded parcelization of qualitative, lived space into quantitative real estate. The resulting tension between autonomous artwork and reified commodity has caused a number of interpreters, Tafuri principal among them, to see in the Seagram Building a kind of limit case in which architecture, like a Liebnizian monad reimagined by Theodor Adorno, bears tragic witness to the ravages of capitalist expansion even as it stands in silent, heroic juxtaposition to them. Seagram's reflective/transparent curtain wall thus allegorizes a kind of last stand for the autonomous artwork as a mirror of environmental dissolution.[22]

But there is another logic at work between the lines of the curtain wall, particularly in office buildings for major corporations like Seagram. This is the logic of what I have called an "organizational complex," or the aesthetic and technological extension of the post–World War II military-industrial complex.[23] Particularly in its more commercial variants such architecture, which is often referred to as postwar modernism, has long been understood (again with Tafuri's help) to represent the full capitulation of interwar modernism's emancipative (if tragically flawed) social project to the imperatives of the culture industry, most vividly through the supposed reduction of modern architecture to corporate image. But this architecture and the discourse that surrounds it is also evidence of a historical shift in the organization of power and knowledge into increasingly horizontal, pattern-based networks of control characterized by a systems-based *organicism,* rather than by the denaturalization and disenchantment implied by the loss of aura through reduction to reproducible image.

If the World Game is a playful allegory of biopolitics, the organizational complex is an outright biopolitical machine. Within its modulated networks of spatiotemporal control, architecture organizes and is organized by an exchange of images in the form of regulatory patterns, in a scaleless cascade ranging from corporate organization charts, to office interiors, to exterior curtain walls, to urban planning diagrams. This patterned cascade, of which the maps, charts, and diagrams of Fuller's game also form a part, anticipates the image-based production of architectural postmodernism. But significantly, in its scalelessness and in the interchangeability of its patterns, the topologies of exchange (including relations of inside and outside, front and back) have also been flattened out. Thus, one of the key postmodernist figures—what Robert Venturi and Denise Scott Brown called, in their 1972 analysis of Las Vegas, a "decorated shed," or a utilitarian structure overlaid with imagery (a building, in other words, that declares on a loud billboard atop its roof: "I am a monument!")—becomes less convincing as an interpretive model.[24] Rather than signification simply overtaking or overshadowing utility (or ornament trumping structure), within the organizational complex media such as architecture, as well as the signs and images circulating through them, become in effect technologies of organization, image-machines in which structure and ornament, form and function, base and superstructure, time and space continually trade places in a hall of mirrors comparable to that which Jameson found inside Portman's Bonaventure Hotel in Los Angeles.[25]

As the technical and aesthetic matrix out of which this hall of mirrors is assembled, however, the organizational complex also deploys its new, systems-based organicism to integrate these levels into a single, self-regulating network of networks. Here, it may be helpful to recall that for Jameson, Portman's hotel stands homologously side by side with the hallucinatory dislocation and disorientation associated (in the United States) with the Vietnam War and represented in texts such as Michael Herr's *Dispatches,* which recounts Herr's experiences working as a journalist in Vietnam. From the point of view of a Tafurian dialectic of the avant-gardes this is to be expected, since Portman's spatial gymnastics had already brought vanguardist architectonic experimentation into the service of multinational capital (the hotel's plan might be said to synthesize the experimental spatial languages of Piranesi and Louis Kahn). But the mirrored-glass curtain wall in which the hotel is clad, when reconnected to the office buildings in which it originated, requires a slightly different interpretation.

In his important "Chicago Frame" essay of 1956 the critic Colin Rowe took pains to distinguish between office buildings designed by commercial architects and those designed by architects like Mies. Reiterating such a distinction in his 1972 introduction to *Five Architects* (a key document in the Gray/White debate), Rowe found it necessary to refer indirectly to the curtain wall, which by then had become a hallmark of corporate architecture. There, he cast the work of Peter Eisenman, Michael Graves, Charles Gwathmey, John Hejduk, and Richard Meier against the backdrop of a post-ideological American reception of European modernism, which had converted modern architecture's revolutionary rhetoric into what Rowe called "a suitable veneer for the corporate activities of 'enlightened' capitalism."[26] According to Rowe, the evident "gap" between the utopian promises of the 1920s and the commercialized postwar modernism delivered to American consumers in the form of such a veneer "establishes the base line for any responsible contemporary production." The five architects' (the "Whites") return to European sources, and in particular to Le Corbusier, was therefore a salvage operation.

But the very fact that an architect like Mies had already long employed techniques that could be catalogued alongside those employed by commercial firms also suggests the inseparability of his work from a *mass* phenomenon, despite claims to the contrary by critics like Rowe. Which means that the crisis in architecture here (if there is one) ultimately bears little resemblance to that experienced by Odysseus, tied to the mast and exposed to the Sirens' enchantments while his oarsmen steer the ship with ears plugged, thus dividing aesthetic experience from practical life and in the process securing rigid abstraction as the basis of both.[27] It is therefore not enough to locate the Miesian silence within a dialectical oscillation, at the other end of which hangs a guilty, sublimated indulgence, dimmed almost to the point of unrecognizability, in the pleasures of mass communication. Why? Because the apparent crisis does not issue from a confrontation between architecture *and* the modern mass media. It issues from that moment when architecture recognized itself, reflected in the curtain wall, *as one among many media.*

The Gray/White debate is symptomatic of this moment, marking a kind of architectural mirror stage in which neo-avant-garde and rear guard joined together in an attempt to restore the internal, disciplinary coherence of architecture as such. This is why Rowe is in near violation of the debate's unwritten codes when he measures the work of the New York Five against the "base line" constituted by the "gap" opened up by American corporate modernism with respect to its European antecedents. No contextualizations of this sort were attempted by any of the respondents to *Five Architects* who were gathered together in another key document in the debate, the "Five on Five" critique published in *Architectural*

Forum in 1973. Those other ("Gray") five, bound as they were to the terms of a discourse that they construed as internal to architecture, were both unwilling and unable to inquire directly into their own roles in articulating an indistinction between artwork and mass medium. And so Robert A. M. Stern, Jaquelin Robertson, Charles Moore, Allan Greenberg, and Romaldo Giurgola looked into the mirror at their doubles. What they saw, and what they wrote about, were eleven houses designed by five architects—no "base lines" and no "gaps" organizing the field, just works of architecture that could be assessed as such.[28]

Above all, they did not see any curtain walls. Certainly, the domestic scale of the work largely precluded the use of this device. But the mirror itself, in which five were reflected as five and architecture as such could still be discussed—by architects—was invisible for different reasons. It was invisible because it was everywhere, in sublimated form. It was there in the form of the "cardboard architecture" associated with the five Whites (and with Eisenman in particular), in the sheer whiteness of their walls, in the hollowness of their "structures," and in the empty surfaces through which *architecture as such* asserted its precarious autonomy. It was also there (as an agent of dematerialization) in the overdetermined tendency of their five respondents to confront this blankness with "materials," or rather, images of materials—messages bearing the name of *architecture as such:* shingles, sticks, and siding.

Rowe's counterpart as apologist for the other (Gray) five, Vincent Scully, demonstrated as much when he summarized the attributes of certain nineteenth-century American houses in the preface to the 1970 revised edition of *The Shingle Style and the Stick Style,* an important source for postmodernist citation:

> Regarded purely as architecture, those houses were surely even better than I thought they were when I wrote about them, and they have proved to be even more important in an historical sense as the inspiration for new architecture themselves. . . . In their own way they were also the gentlest forms: the most relaxed and spiritually open. . . .
>
> Generous and gentle: they are not words which we can easily apply to ourselves in these years of blood and madness. There was evil in the nineteenth century too. All the more reason to value these houses and their architects, long dead, whose purposes were humane.[29]

And so we return to Vietnam. Enjoining his readers to look into the mirror with him, Scully saw wars, but he did not see the architecture in which their "blood and madness" was made visible. He saw only an image of humanity, "generous and gentle," embodied in a system of architectural signs (the "shingle style") projected as an archive for postmodern practice against the backdrop of wartime atrocities flickering across a screen.

But the war in Vietnam was not simply a context for the architecture in question (though it was this), nor did it merely supply this architecture with some kind of latent subject matter (though it occasionally did this). Just as art-historical efforts such as Scully's countered the televisual emptiness of the curtain wall with images of plenitude drawn from "history," historians to date have generally distinguished the singularity of Seagram (understood as an authentic artwork) from the mass of copies that it spawned. But like the many deformed historical repetitions executed by Scully's admirers, these copies—the curtain wall as a mass phenomenon—exhibit a singularity of their own, which is not the singularity of the artwork but of the medium. As a mass and as a medium, they constitute a field in which Mies's building appears, to borrow an expression from J. G. Ballard, as a "mere modulus."

As Ballard puts it in *The Atrocity Exhibition* (1969):

> In the perspectives of the plaza, the junctions of the underpass and embankment, Talbot at last recognized a modulus that could be multiplied into the landscape of his consciousness. The descending triangle of the plaza was repeated in the facial geometry of the young woman. The diagram of her bones formed a key to his own postures and musculature. . . .[30]

Units of image are exchanged throughout this book (for Jameson, a signal instance of literary postmodernism), wherein the atrocities of the title, figured in the car crashes, assassinations, and war crimes that appear in disarticulated, televisual segments, are shown ultimately to lie in the exchanges themselves, which lay to ruin all spatial contiguity and communicative coherence. Again the curtain wall bears witness: "The glass curtain-walling formed an element in a vertical sky, a mirror of this deteriorating landscape."[31]

But if Ballard's book charts the new regime of commodified, regulated flux also exemplified by television, the curtain wall's role as mirror conceals another, more instrumental function. In a vein similar to Jameson's notion of "total flow," Jonathan Crary has suggested that Ballard's heterotopic juxtaposition of media fragments—the Zapruder film, Jacqueline Kennedy, the Vietnam War, wrecked automobiles—"coincides with a dissolution of legibility generated by the very efficacy and supremacy of the spectacle."[32] The undecipherability of these collisions is secured by the equivalence of their content and with the cybernetic commodification of information as data flow. In place of objects there are only switches, channels, and—we can add—recording and playback devices like the VCR. This type of abstraction correlates with the abstraction of the curtain wall. In Mies, but also in Skidmore, Owings & Merrill, Emery Roth & Sons and many others, the curtain wall acts as both a recording device bearing witness to the violence effected on the city fabric by its own reduplication and, through the modulations of its grids, as a switching device that channels the very same flows of both labor and capital that it records. The resulting landscape, diagrammed in and by the organizational complex, is no longer an assemblage of autonomous or semi-autonomous aesthetic processes. It is a landscape in which all such processes tend toward integration through mediatic linkages like those catalogued in Ballard's book.

In *The Atrocity Exhibition,* body parts, sexual positions, buildings, highway interchanges, and images of mechanized death become mirrors of one another in a continuous, undecipherable modulation cascading through inner and outer landscapes, up and down in scale. Each unit in the exchange is a "mere modulus," marking the utter neutralization of the very limits of subjective experience—sex and death—in what Ballard calls a "conceptual game." As his Dr. Nathan puts it, brutally:

> Any great human tragedy—Vietnam, let us say—can be considered experimentally as a larger model of a mental crisis mimetized in faulty stair angles or skin junctions, breakdowns in the perception of environment and consciousness. In terms of television and news magazines the war in Vietnam has a latent significance very different from its manifest content. Far from repelling us, it *appeals* to us by virtue of its complex of polyperverse acts. We must bear in mind, however sadly, that psychopathology is no longer the exclusive preserve of the degenerate and perverse. The Congo, Vietnam, Biafra—these are games anyone can play.[33]

So in the "conceptual games" of the New York Five, as in the semiotic games of their Gray adversaries, the war was anything but over. Withdrawing in horror from its own dissolution into the switching device of the curtain wall, architecture could not shed its complicity with the violence of the mass media. Instead, it internalized this violence, in the form of a "mental crisis mimetized in faulty stair angles or skin junctions, breakdowns in the perception of environment and consciousness"—the dislocations and "polyperverse acts" that became characteristic of post-modernism. Thus the war in Vietnam and the wars in the cities were written into the very grids and shingles of the supposedly architectural objects around which the Gray/White debate turned. Each element of each house, including its architect, was a modulus in a chain of equiva-lences. The possibility of the autonomous artwork was lost in this mir-rored cascade, even as one pole of a dialectical sweep. In its place were only media, reproducing one another and interfacing with one another, ad infinitum.

In that sense, *contra* Tafuri, the pleasures of architecture's postmodern texts were entirely public. They were the very same pleasures that Bal-lard associates with television, the pleasures of witnessing an atrocity at a safe enough distance to react in moral outrage even while experiencing perverse satisfaction through the mimetic reduplication of such acts in aestheticized form. The curtain wall with its A-B-A rhythms was, like the maps organizing Fuller's World Game, among the many chessboards on which these moves were made. This is also to say that the linguistic games played on the surfaces of postmodern architecture were, precisely, *war games*. And I do not mean this metaphorically. These games were played by combatants going through the motions of avant-gardist militancy, the pleasures of which derived not from private withdrawal but from the publicity of war itself—an abstracted yet very real war that, like Vietnam as seen on American television sets, must be called a *media* war.[34]

Here we approach the category of *risk*, which is indispensable to any analysis of the epistemologies of Vietnam. The efforts of thinkers like Jameson to map the cultural, social, and economic dimensions of a world-historical shift with the occasional help of architecture have been paralleled and sometimes challenged by variants on modernization dis-course that take risk as a central epistemological figure. This discourse sees transformations such as the articulation of environmental risk at the level of abstract signs and symbols (and away from direct experience) as continuous with modernity, rather than marking a passage into a prop-erly *post*modern regime. Illustrative here is the work of the sociologists Anthony Giddens (with whom we find Jameson occasionally sparring) and Ulrich Beck. In different ways, both Giddens and Beck have argued that the balancing of environmental and ontological risk is a hallmark of a new, self-correcting "reflexive" modernity.[35] Jameson is, I think, rightly suspicious of the homeostatic, centrist political project with which this thesis is often aligned, particularly in the case of Giddens. Risk/reward calculations are, after all, equally applicable to nuclear war, environmental threats, and financial investments. To the degree that Giddens and Beck offer a risk-based paradigm and its feedback loops as models of reflexivity, they appear not so much to have stepped *outside* the technical logic of late capitalism as to have internalized it.

Still the cybernetic feedback loop, which underwrote the systems-based organicism of the curtain-walled office building, the game theory (and war games) played out in cold war think tanks, as well as Fuller's playful World Game, offers a different interpretative model, and a different model of causality, than the historical dialectic on which both Tafuri and in a different sense, Jameson, rely. From this perspective, the problem may not be just that postmodernism brings with it the ultimate form of disenchantment but, rather, that its disorienting hall of mirrors also conceals new naturalizations that track the movement of the "system" as such into ever more dreamlike stages. These naturalizations are familiar in neoliberal economic discourse where the "self-organizing" magic of markets, analogized to biological systems, frequently takes over from the invisible hand as a prime mover. But they are all too often overlooked as markers of a different but related kind of epistemological modulation characteristic of postmodernism.

Such naturalizations, and their accompanying restorations of aura, are at odds with postmodernism's delirious, fragmented, and schizophrenic character as emphasized by Jameson and others. In historical terms, any given period is necessarily shot through with its own counterexamples. And yet as Jameson has suggested, reflecting on the historiographical and philosophical fragility of all periodizing gestures, we nevertheless "cannot not periodize" if we are to combat the mythologies of an eternal present.[36] But these apparent anomalies, such as Fuller's mixing of modern and postmodern techniques, are more than merely idiosyncratic or transitional. Instead, they index a dynamics of periodization itself which, rather than drawing lines between historical epochs, yields clusters of oscillations of the sort named by the more technical term *periodicity*. Periodicity operates like a recurrent pulse or a modulation. It moves in self-reflexive cycles that trace more than just the eternal return of the same. These cycles or loops reach backward even as they move forward, in effect fighting two wars at once.

I therefore want to suggest that the closure implied by the various "ends" of postmodernism, and preeminently by the "end of history," is the (semi-open, pulsating, modulated, and videographic) closure of the feedback loop rather the coming-to-an-end of the narrative arc. In an essay that identifies a largely Hegelian posthistory (differentiated from the French *posthistoire*) with postmodernism, Jameson has suggested, by way of a comparison with Frederick Jackson Turner's "The Frontier in American History" (1893), that in any case the "end" in question with Fukuyama is more spatial than temporal in character. For Jameson writing in 1998, the anxieties captured in Fukuyama's thesis "bespeak the closing of another and more fundamental frontier in the new world market of globalization and of the transnational corporations."[37] Another version of the claustrophobia provoked by the lobby of the Bonaventure Hotel, this near-total ambience is beset by a failure of the imagination defined on the one hand by a sense of impending ecological catastrophe that constrains industrial expansion (think here of Fuller's World Game) and on the other by the intensification of postindustrial linkages within the cybernetic order of things that make "delinking" nearly impossible to conceive (think here of the curtain wall as mass medium). But whether in space or in time, or better, in the transition from modern temporality (evolution, progress) to postmodern spatiality (claustrophobia, schizophrenia), we still seem to be dealing with a passage from one historical stage to another.

So what to make of the "last war" replayed endlessly (as if on television? Another version of postmodern closure, history's ultimate cybernetic joke, a feedback loop of infernal proportions? Or, more counterintuitively, an opening onto new spatiotemporal (that is, *historical*) terrain, with past, present, and future, inside and outside slightly offset from one another, rather than joined by narrative or estranged by montage? Architectural analysis might help here to reconstruct a sense of postmodernism's surprising, asynchronic periodicity, one that challenges the naturalized forward motion of the feedback loop by watching it replay on top of itself or feed back into itself, without completely closing itself off.[38] Such analysis can also help make sense of the anachronism generally called "postmodern." In Benjaminian terms, this might look something like dialectics at a standstill. But mapped onto the economies and ecologies of risk that organize corporate globalization, it might also chart circular paths through postmodern interiors that otherwise seem only to house disengaged parlor games and paranoid think tanks.[39] Such paths might even lead to a post-postmodern exterior that, Jameson notwithstanding, cannot be captured in its entirety in the atrium of a 1970s hotel. At minimum, they offer a map of a different battlefield.

It is only necessary to look to Vietnam itself. An imperial war at the very frontier of imperialism, with no real territory at stake, the Vietnam War was, from the American perspective that much postmodernist theory occupies, a schizo-symbolic war, though a deadly one. From the Vietnamese perspective (both North and South) it was surely different. Here is a glimpse, from a RAND Corporation interview with a North Vietnamese soldier who had defected: "If I knew when the war would be over, I would have tried to remain in the [National Liberation] Front to fight until the end."[40] Perpetual war, with no end in sight, organized around a series of experimental laboratory tests of risk-managed "weapons systems," including, among other things, cluster bombs, antipersonnel heat sensors, and the chemical defoliants responsible for the destruction of over 1.5 million acres of rural land in 1967 alone.[41] All of which helped to clear the ground, so to speak, for another incremental move in the polyperverse doubling back of late capitalism from, as Fuller would have it, "killingry" to "livingry."

Fast forward to 1994. The asynchronic periodicity that echoes through the phrase "fighting the last war" can be measured in untimely events such as this: That year, Skidmore, Owings & Merrill (SOM), the architects of so many canonical office buildings who would also control the design for Ground Zero in New York, won an urban planning competition to design "Saigon South," in Ho Chi Minh City. In addition to offering housing, offices, and cultural facilities, the plan incorporated "amenities" like universities, sports facilities, botanical gardens, a zoo, a water park, fair grounds, a race track, and golf courses, "all linked by a landscaped parkway."[42] Among its keywords was "sustainability," which describes an integrated "environmental framework" designed to manage risks to the city's hydrology, water quality, flooding, shorelines, and air quality posed by urban growth. Without irony, this "framework" was applied to a landscape previously subject to the risks posed by napalm, among other postmodern environmental technologies.

In that sense, the plan emblematically replaces (but also replays) earlier U.S. environmental initiatives in Vietnam such as Operation Igloo White (1967–72), whose line of sensors, disguised as twigs and rocks and strewn across the Ho Chi Minh Trail, fed back information on Vietcong troop movements to a central U.S. command post in Thailand. That same operation also included a proposed (but unexecuted) plan to use chemical defoliants to clear an uncrossable ten-mile-wide strip of jungle all the way across Vietnam at the demilitarized zone.[43]

The war in Vietnam was a war of modernization, fought with the social sciences as much as with technoscience. It was a war in which, for example, Fukuyama's former teacher, the political scientist Samuel P. Huntington, suggested in a classified report to USAID written in 1969 that the United States accelerate existing programs of "inducing substantial migration of people from the countryside to the cities" as well as build "marketing and transportation links" throughout South Vietnam.[44] This, in hopes of demoralizing or co-opting NLF (National Liberation Front) resistance in the impoverished countryside, by offering the incentive of economic development. Though such recommendations are recognizable as belonging to a "hearts and minds" approach to counterinsurgency, the actual techniques they entail tell a more elaborate story. In the case of Huntington's report, it was evidently assumed that accelerated urban migration would continue to be "induced" through "relentless bombing, the creation of free-fire zones, and crop destruction."[45] In other words, a biopolitics, or a politics enacted not at the level of political ideology or of jurisprudence and the law but through the technospatial management of a population and its territory. This is a politics for which it ultimately did not matter whether the South Vietnamese peasants actually switched loyalties, only that they were appeased by the promise of a better life under capitalist modernization.

It is one of the uncounted ironies (read: feedback loops) of history that Huntington had to wait until the cold war was over (only to be replaced by a fictive "clash of civilizations") for his recommendations to be carried out. By 1994, the global real estate market had replaced applied social science and technowar as an organizing instrument in a reunited Vietnam. Instead of sensors and napalm, SOM's plan offered "a range of competitive economic and development incentives." This was an improvement, perhaps, but not without a certain compulsive repetition. It was as if Tafuri's announcement were perversely emblazoned on every contextually appropriate facade and well-manicured lawn proposed for Saigon South: "The war is over."

Which war? By the 1970s, the mechanized shock tactics of modernist "languages of battle" had not exactly run aground in the absence of overall societal transformation, as Tafuri would have it. They had instead been assimilated, during the misnamed "postwar" period, into organicist architectural systems developed by firms like SOM and built into corporate curtain walls and other technologies of organization. Simultaneously, the ontological dislocations amplified by the technologies of war (cold or hot) were being managed in cybernetic games of environmental and geopolitical risk like Fuller's World Game. These two projects eventually came together in the architectural postmodernism exemplified by SOM's proposal for Saigon South. They did so in the form of a homecoming, in which the aesthetic dislocations associated with mixtures of linguistic codes (Charles Jencks called this "radical eclecticism") found, in their very repetition within a globalized monoculture, a perverse capacity to appear—in Ho Chi Minh City and practically anywhere else—as rooted, "local," by virtue of their compensatory appeals to cultural continuity. While at the same time, the very specter of intensified geopolitical and environmental risk confronted head-on (with modernist swagger) by Fuller was increasingly domesticated through the production of lifestyle amenities assembled under the sign of "sustainability," a word that performs its own risk-managed naturalizations by referring at once to the ecosphere and to the global markets.

Though they were there at the outset, these reflexive regroundings were overshadowed by the sense of world-historical synchronicity that often accompanies battles in the "last war." And so a theorist like Jameson could see "postmodernism" as primarily a process of disembedding, rather than as the asynchronic reterritorialization that it has also turned out to be. In that sense, architecture comes both early and late to postmodernism. Early, in that it was able to offer raw material with which to chart the initial deterritorializations. And late, in the sense that it now offers signal evidence of how the very specters that were let loose in the echo chambers of corporate space have returned not so much to haunt us—and therefore to threaten our stabilities at some other level—but to soothe us. By the mid-1990s, postmodernist disorientation had thus come full circle, having been cognitively remapped, regrounded, and domesticated in Vietnam itself. This is how feedback loops work. Likewise, hallucinatory collaborations between technology and aesthetics originating in the 1960s have been recycled and resold, in the form of a mass-mediated, thoroughly postmodern "sense of place" in any number of plans that, like SOM's, now serve as the biopolitical instruments of a neoliberal economic order. And between the lines of these "adaptable frameworks" offered in support of phantasms like a "dynamic Ho Chi Minh City market" is written, perhaps, another phrase even more ominous than that which marked Tafuri's melancholy. The war, it seems, has only just begun.

3 LANGUAGE

Environment, c. 1973

ONE CONDITION FOR THE EMERGENCE of architectural postmodernism was the transformation of "environment" as an epistemological category during the late 1960s and 1970s. Architecture was thought during this period either to belong to "environment," understood as a mixture of natural and cultural effects, or to be ontologically excluded from it, and therefore from the instrumentalities of environmentalist theory and practice. In and of itself, this was not new. But these two positions shared a largely implicit understanding that the scope and nature of "environment" had become so vast, so encompassing, and so *abstract*, and had gathered such independent momentum, as to escape (or threaten) architecture's capacity to model it, whether through metonymy or as an *imago mundi*.

Environment as a type of postmodern sublime, then, was either defended against in the name of autonomous aesthetic practice or subjected to the domesticating imperatives that guided much ecological research and activism. The basis for both options, however, was what Michel Foucault had tentatively and somewhat awkwardly identified, in notes to himself written in the late 1970s, as an expansive "environmentality"—a set of technical procedures and protocols that the philosopher-historian saw appearing on the horizon of his own historical experience.[1] In architecture, this somewhat unexpectedly included a whole range of comparisons to language, of which we will only deal here with those that most explicitly sought an architectural grammar and syntax thought capable of defining an autonomous realm of practice.

To recognize the consequent implications, we must examine the challenges posed by a new, risk-based notion of environment as they were addressed in architectural discourse as well as in public policy. We must also be prepared to discard any absolute distinction between what lies "inside" a discipline and what lies "outside" it, without discarding the notion of disciplinarity as such. As with the problems of space and territory we have already encountered, I propose instead that we regard the question of disciplinary autonomy as fundamentally topological in character. In this light, what formalist analysis in architecture, painting, or literature might take to be a move inward, toward the grammars and syntax of the aesthetic object qua object or text, also constitutes a movement outward, toward "environment" and all that it implies: autonomy as a condition for immanence then, rather than an alternative to it.

We begin outside. On 1 January 1970, U.S. president Richard M. Nixon signed the National Environmental Policy Act (NEPA), declaring that "the nineteen-seventies absolutely must be the years when America pays its debt to the past by reclaiming the purity of its air, its waters and our living environment. It is literally now or never."[2] On 10 February of the same year Nixon outlined a thirty-seven-point antipollution program, noting further that "as we deepen our understanding of complex ecological processes . . . much more will be possible."[3] On signing NEPA and in announcing the antipollution measures, Nixon implicitly called forth a series of constructions that were simultaneously being tended to by architects and theorists of architecture, among others. Primary among such constructions was an implied human subject, the inhabitant of "environment." For Nixon, as for much of environmental and ecological discourse, this subject was an instrument of integration into a sociopolitical totality, albeit to different ends. But what I hope to clarify here is the degree to which architectural discourse has also called forth this same subject in an attempt to isolate architecture-as-such from the sociotechnical and sociopolitical forces at work in the discourse on "environment." I emphasize this, because architecture's immanence with respect to these forces turns out to be most active and most visible at precisely the moment that it seems to withdraw into a protectionist, disciplinary autonomy.

For Nixon, the signing of NEPA, with its "now or never" injunction followed up by his thirty-seven points, pointed toward what he called "an urgent common goal of all Americans: the rescue of our natural habitat as a place both habitable and hospitable to man."[4] In invoking environment as an object of governmental regulation, Nixon thereby repeatedly invoked a people—"our" environment, "our" natural habitat. But his words also acted to force this people together as a unified subject, while collapsing two territories to which this subject and its environment implicitly corresponded, the national and the supranational, when he identified the "common goal" of environmental "purification" both with "all Americans" and with "man" as such. With this collapse also comes the peremptory collapse of the habitability and hospitality Nixon presumably sought in "environment," because during the era of the Vietnam War and napalm it was hardly self-evident that the goals of all Americans, including their environmental goals, coincided. Nor was it clear that these coincided with the interests of so-called man. This conflict is obscured in Nixon's language, which merely borrows from that of mainstream environmentalism during the period in calling forth a universal human as the inhabitant of environment. In the details of the legislation that environment is converted into an object of technoscientific knowledge associated with the logico-mathematical regime of risk. Thus Nixon's language, the language of ecology, also reconstitutes the human (one can also read: "nation") as a subject *at* and *of* risk, an only apparently stable subject, who in practice occupies the position of a *variable* or a parameter in a complex ecological *and* economic calculation.

At this point we find environment disengaged from its nineteenth-century origins in the form of the more proximate sociobiological "milieu," because as a rule environmental risk does not present itself to direct observation or experience but rather, as Ulrich Beck observes, is "localized in the sphere of *physical and chemical formulas.*"[5] At work here is what Foucault had already described in 1966 as "the principle of a primary decipherment" that promised to overturn "man" as both a pre-constituted object and implicit addressee of scientific knowledge. It is a principle given in its historical specificity by what Foucault calls the "counter-science" of linguistics, through the apparatus of a logical, rationalized "structure" also found in mathematical description—in which, as Foucault puts it, "things attain to existence only in so far as they are able to form the elements of a signifying system."[6] So too for environment, because it is also through a signifying system, or a system of signs—an ecosystem as described by physical and chemical formulas—that what Beck calls "risk society" perceives connections between environmental modulations and their geographically and/or zoologically remote effects. On the basis of such a system both environmental risk *and* ecological solidarity (or what Beck calls "the solidarity of living things") are articulated.[7] But these same signs can also be refunctioned economically (as, for example, in the case of both oil consumption and exploration) by translating probabilistic environmental projections into probabilistic financial projections through such techniques as cost-benefit analyses and risk-reward calculations.

Among the provisions in the act signed by Nixon (which resulted in the formation of the Environmental Protection Agency later that year) was one that authorized and directed all federal agencies to "utilize a systematic, interdisciplinary approach which will insure the integrated use of the natural and social sciences and the environmental design arts in planning and in decisionmaking which may have an impact on man's environment."[8] On this matter, the "environmental design arts" were well prepared. For example, in 1972 there appeared the seventh volume in the Vision + Value series edited by the artist and visual theorist (and MIT professor) Gyorgy Kepes, called *Arts of the Environment*. This book, like the other volumes that preceded it in the series, took the interdisciplinary requirement quite literally, not by responding to it directly (Kepes was no Nixonite) but rather in employing what the legislation called a "systematic, interdisciplinary approach" integrating the "natural and social sciences" with the "environmental design arts," a framework that had for some time been typical of ecological discourse. Indeed, Kepes saw both art and humanity poised on the cusp of a second order of evolutionary adaptation, a "self-conscious evolution" regulated by social communication, in which the art-into-life aspirations of the early-twentieth-century avant-gardes (where Kepes had his roots) had mutated into a man-and-environment symbiosis regulated by a complex of interdisciplinary knowledge.[9]

Nixon's environmental initiative left its own traces on this discourse when, for example, the historian Leo Marx, author of *The Machine in the Garden* (1964), mentioned it in his contribution to the Kepes volume in the context of a suspicion that the focus on environmental policy might have also represented an attempt to distract attention from the war in Vietnam and to neutralize the increasingly frustrated civil rights and antiwar movements with the palliative of environmental activism converted into government policy.[10] Marx also wondered aloud whether the initiative was in fact designed "to provide the cohesive force necessary for national unity behind the Republican administration." But in pointing out the failure of crusading politicians and ecologists alike to acknowledge the origins of imminent ecological crisis in expansionist consumer capitalism (in other words, to recognize the links between *ecologies* and *economies*), Marx still posited what he called "national unity" as the basis for effective action, designating the pastoral tradition in American literature as a guide for thinking "an organic conception of man's relation to his environment." For a sensibility informed by this aesthetic tradition, according to Marx, "Nature as a transmitter of signals and a dictator of choices is now present to us in the quite literal sense that an imbalance of an ecosystem, when scientifically understood, defines certain precise limits to human behavior."[11] What he is alluding to here is what ties the ecosystem to systems theory: the notion of a natural environment, which he calls a "transmitter of signals," as a communicative organism or (eco) system with which human beings interact. Marx borrows this idea from ecological discourse in his attempt to unify the technological with the social at the level of the nation, guided by a national literature.[12] The result, in Marx's discourse, is that the human subject of "environment," split by the incommensurable interests of a divided nation willing to destroy remotely while conserving locally, is welded back together by the signals, or what we can call the "language," emitted by an environment construed as a signifying system.

Nixon's environmental initiative also made a brief appearance at the time in Tomás Maldonado's *Design, Nature, and Revolution: Toward a Critical Ecology,* which was the English translation and revision, published in 1972, of his *La speranza progettuale* of 1970.[13] Maldonado, who directed the Technische Hochschule für Gestaltung at Ulm from 1954 to 1967 with an emphasis on a rationalized design science, noted the origins of the term *ecology* in the Greek *oikos,* meaning "household" or "home," which also forms the root of *economy,* with the two terms translating etymologically as the "study" and the "management" of the household, respectively. Though Maldonado noted the etymological sense of *ecology,* he did not note the connection to *economy,* preferring instead to take up the systems approach of Ludwig von Bertalanffy via an analytics of the "social system" constructed around an opposition between open and closed systems, derived from the post-Weberian school of American sociology formed in the 1950s around Talcott Parsons. This framework compels Maldonado to read the failed rebellions of the late 1960s through the notion of a system's tendency toward "dynamic equilibrium" that absorbs and neutralizes conflict. And so we find him referring sarcastically to Nixon's environmental campaign as evidence of a neutralizing, authoritarian closure imposed on the social system, reflected in its appropriation of ecological protocols, or what Maldonado calls the "fashion of ecology."[14] As he puts it in one of the book's many extended footnotes: "In fact, from one day to the next, as though they were responding to a *Diktat*, the most important organs of the American press—*Time, Newsweek, Life, Fortune, Business Week,* and even *Playboy*—all became very concerned with the subject." Hence for Maldonado the travesty was simple: "The scandal of society is now culminating in the scandal of nature."[15] But the real scandal, to which Maldonado remains insensitive despite his critical insight, lies in the naturalization of "environment" as a signifying system.

This scandal becomes evident in Maldonado's indictment of what he calls the "semiological abuse" perpetrated by Tom Wolfe and by Robert Venturi and Denise Scott Brown in their presentations of Las Vegas as a model for environmental richness. He sees the closure of these "exercises in conformist gymnastics" (as he calls them) exemplified by Venturi and Scott Brown's work in particular, when they present Las Vegas as a communicative environment, or what Maldonado calls a "system of signs."[16] For Maldonado, what is objectionable is not communication but its absence in Las Vegas, as it is drowned out by the "noise" of urban signage. He calls this "fictitious communication, a simulacrum of communication," which is another way of lamenting that city's unreality or unnaturalness.

Measured against such abuses, for Maldonado "the only truly well-articulated semiotic set of ideas is the one by Charles W. Morris," the important American semiotician who had been attempting to read works of art as systems of signs since the late 1930s.[17] Maldonado dismisses the well-known association of Morris's thought, and of semiotics in general, with behaviorism, preferring instead to emphasize Morris's roots in the philosophy of C. S. Peirce and his ties to the Vienna Circle of logical positivism, as well as to American pragmatism, both of which were consolidated during his tenure at the University of Chicago. While in Chicago Morris had also befriended Kepes and taught courses at the New Bauhaus/Institute of Design led by Kepes's friend and colleague László Moholy-Nagy in the late 1930s and mid-1940s. Morris's semiotics were also an important source for Kepes's *Language of Vision* of 1944, an attempt to reconcile questions of formal and spatial organization in modern art and modern architecture with the dissemination of visual meaning in modern advertising.[18] Indeed, in his critique of Venturi and Scott Brown, Maldonado discerns notable parallels between their account of Las Vegas and the visual, urban geographies mapped by Kepes's MIT colleague Kevin Lynch in *The Image of the City* (1960), a book that relied heavily on notions of visual orientation and Gestalt recognition that Kepes had formulated earlier through his reading of Gestalt psychology.[19] Lynch's substantial debt to Kepes, who had collaborated closely with him on background research for the book, is clear in his opening chapter, "The Image of the Environment," as well as in the title of the book itself, which announces its author's intention to remap the city as a visual field.[20] As early as 1946 Kepes had extended the perceptual framework guiding *Language of Vision* into the urban scale in his contribution to a major conference at Princeton University, "Planning Man's Physical Environment." Kepes's presentation referred to a "second nature," a "man-shaped environment" distorted by the marketplace, and sought a humanistic restoration of visual order and thence meaning through modernist visual techniques.[21] Among the techniques enumerated in *Language of Vision* was what Kepes referred to in general terms as "transparency," or the effect of interpenetration generated in modern painting through the superposition of planes. And so when, in their seminal essay of 1955–56 (published in 1963), Colin Rowe and Robert Slutzky take up this notion, quoting Kepes at length to distinguish between "literal" and "phenomenal" transparency or between what they called "an inherent quality of substance" and "an inherent quality of organization," they complete the inversion: from Kepes's projection of a visual language as an organizational system onto the external, urban environment (later taken up by Lynch) to the contraction of this visual field into that occupied only by the object itself, which they reformulated as a relativized perceptual system.[22]

Rowe and Slutzky acknowledge as much in part II of the same article, published in *Perspecta* 13–14 in 1971, when in comparing Vignola's Villa Farnese at Caprarola with I. M. Pei's Mile-High Tower in Denver they declare themselves unconcerned with every aspect of the two buildings' historical, social, and technical context except "the manifestations which reveal themselves to the eye."[23] This contraction ultimately corresponds to a further abstraction of "environment" in the Kepes/Lynch sense, an abstraction that Rowe and Slutzky indirectly acknowledge in quoting another source they share with Kepes, Rudolph Arnheim, who asserts with respect to the Gestalt-psychological premises of figure-ground oscillation on which phenomenal transparency is based that "the processes of organization active in perception somehow do justice to the organization outside in the physical world."[24] For Rowe and Slutzky, "gestalt supposes that mental activity and organic behavior are subject to the same laws," which they take to be laws of visual perception. This connection, this semiabstract internalization of environment, thus authorizes their dehistoricizing and decontextualizing readings as more than merely arbitrary, because it presupposes a commonality at the level of subjective experience, the experience of the ahistorical, acontextual subject of Gestalt psychology.[25]

In a series of articles published between 1970 and 1973, Peter Eisenman developed a theory of environment tightly woven into this discourse. He did not do this in so many words. Nor did he do this by simple, implicit contrast with other, more explicit reformulations of architectural or urban theory around environmentalism or around environmental technologies, like that attempted by Reyner Banham in *The Architecture of the Well-Tempered Environment* (1969) or *Los Angeles: The Architecture of Four Ecologies* (1971) or by Ian McHarg in *Design with Nature* (also of 1969). Nor again did he directly address the cybernetic notion of environmental "fit" formulated in Christopher Alexander's Cambridge dissertation, which was published as *Notes on the Synthesis of Form* in 1964, and against which Eisenman later acknowledged his own Cambridge thesis was written.[26] Instead, Eisenman's theory of environment is discernible only within a discursive network for which, in Foucault's terms, "things attain to existence only in so far as they are able to form the elements of a signifying system."

Eisenman's first notable words on the subject are as follows: "Modern architecture demanded of the individual a new attitude toward understanding and perceiving his physical environment."[27] This is the opening sentence of "From Object to Relationship: The Casa del Fascio by Terragni," published in *Casabella* in January 1970. At first glance Eisenman's use of the term *environment* seems casual or generic, and he does not qualify it further in the rest of the article or in subsequent writings. But already symptoms of a broader discourse are showing through when he offers Le Corbusier's Maison Dom-ino as evidence of a technological medium in which was embedded a shift "from the conception of space as a result of pragmatic limitation to the product of semantic intention."[28] This example is followed by Giuseppe Terragni's Casa del Fascio—a choice obviously provocative in its political connotations—as evidence of a subsequent turn "from the semantic domain to the syntactic domain" in which form ultimately detaches itself from technological structure, with corresponding semantic connotations likewise bracketed out. For Eisenman this detachment demands a new mode of apprehension because "such an architecture, in addition to being experienced perceptually as an aesthetic object, must also be understood at the conceptual level of formal relationships."[29]

At this point Eisenman transposes the linguistic hypotheses of Noam Chomsky into the architectural realm by correlating Chomsky's distinction between contingent "surface structure" and a universal "deep structure" in language to two attributes of architectural form. The first level is that of the object itself, including its elements—floors, walls, columns—capable of accruing meaning as nonliteral though potentially archetypal "signs," while the second is that of the internal relation between these elements that "furnishes the matrix to render the object intelligible."[30] Significantly, Eisenman further correlates this distinction with that made by Rowe and Slutzky between literal and phenomenal transparency, with "surface structure" corresponding to the literally perceptible spatial qualities of a building and "deep structure" to their underlying formal logics. And so, with this transposition of terms that Eisenman finds in Chomsky onto Rowe and Slutzky's categories (which relied in turn on Kepes), we return to the linguistic hypothesis formulated by Kepes in *Language of Vision* with the help of Morris.

For Kepes the "language of vision," or "optical communication," is a potentially universal medium for the dissemination of a new, modern semantic. But this language is first given the task of engaging the viewer's participation in what Kepes describes as "a process of organization . . . a discipline of utmost importance in the chaos of our formless world."[31] Kepes calls this process of subjective reorientation "thinking in terms of structure," a process summarized in its linguistic dimensions in a preface to *Language of Vision* by S. I. Hayakawa, professor of English at the Illinois Institute of Technology, author of *Language in Action* (published one year later), and leader in the General Semantics movement. In Hayakawa's terms, "[Kepes] gives us the 'grammar' and the 'syntax' of vision . . . a reorganization of our visual habits so that we perceive not isolated 'things' in 'space,' but structure, order and relatedness of events in space-time," a distinction that Hayakawa refers to elsewhere in his comments as the difference between an "object-minded" and a "relation-minded" visual orientation.[32]

However the point of contact with Eisenman, the author of "From Object to Relationship," is not General Semantics but, rather, Morris's semiotics. In a footnote to the second, expanded version of "Notes on a Conceptual Architecture: Toward a Definition," published in *Casabella* in 1971, Eisenman refers to Morris's distinction between the pragmatic, semantic, and syntactic dimensions of language.[33] But where Morris assembles these three branches in order to describe more clearly and synthetically what he calls "the unitary process . . . of semiosis as a whole," Eisenman, via Chomsky, refers to them in order to isolate syntax as a privileged object of study.[34] Likewise, where Kepes sought a unitary synthesis between the organizational (or syntactical) dimension of visual signs—what Morris calls the relations between signs—and the iconographic (or semantic) dimension—what Morris calls the relations of signs to the objects to which they refer—Eisenman follows Rowe and Slutzky in isolating what he takes to be the syntactic, relational level of perception.

Here Eisenman introduces a further distinction, between the perceptual aspects of an architectural syntax as treated by Rowe and Slutzky and what he calls "conceptual structure" or "that aspect of the visible form, whether it is *[sic]* an idea, in a drawing, or in a building, which is intentionally put in the form to provide access to the inner form or universal formal relationships."[35] Because for Eisenman architecture, unlike painting, will always imply both use and semantic meaning in the form of walls, doors, bathrooms, and so on, which must therefore also be bracketed off from a "conceptual matrix" that he calls "structure." The argument thus proceeds as follows:

> Most environments, whether they be linguistic, biological, social or physical have a structure. That is, they have a series of elements which have both definable properties and definable relationships between these elements. These structures can usually be described in terms of their differences or similarities to other structures. While many attempts have been made comparing architecture and language, mainly using linguistic analogies, the semiological classification of pragmatics, semantics and syntactics [Morris], can serve as a useful beginning, if only to describe the different aspects of architecture.[36]

With respect to subjective experience, Eisenman goes on to make a further distinction, between the individual's sense impressions, which he compares to Chomsky's notion of surface structure, and the apprehension of conceptual syntax, Chomsky's "deep structure" or (for Chomsky) "the underlying abstract structure that determines [a sentence's] semantic interpretation."[37]

Although Eisenman carries out the remainder of his exposition primarily with respect to painting and sculpture, his ultimate aim is to establish the parameters under which a truly "conceptual" architecture can be generated. Indeed, the entire operation is conducted under the sign of an implicit critique, in the form of a comment made in passing in the text's opening sentence, of what he calls architecture's "present commitment to a social and technological polemic."[38] Among the key aspects of such a commitment, far-ranging as it was during the late-1960s, was that summarized by Maldonado in his reflections on the notion of environment as a receptacle for architecture's technological and social project. But where Maldonado saw the effacement of social relations in the sublimation of environment under a technocratic consensus in Nixon's rhetoric and found in the "semiological abuse" of Venturi and Scott Brown an intolerable, populist conformism against which he felt compelled to mobilize the totalizing force of an integrated ecological consciousness, Eisenman moves in the opposite direction. In a word, Eisenman pursues the *abstraction* of environment discernible in Rowe and Slutzky's borrowings from Kepes to its logical conclusion.

In "From Object to Relationship II: Giuseppe Terragni Casa Giuliani Frigerio," published in 1971 in the same double issue of *Perspecta* (13–14) as the second Rowe/Slutzky "transparency" article, Eisenman returns to the notion of a virtualized, conceptual "structure" lurking within buildings analogized, in part, to painting. He repeats: "The structure of a linguistic environment, or more explicitly a language, can be said to exhibit similar characteristics to a physical environment—and in this case to an architecture."[39] And so, Eisenman's theory of architecture-as-language turns out—again—to be a theory of environment, with linguistic environment substituted for physical environment. Again there is syntax and again there is an invisible, mentalistic "deep structure," which he notes is "concerned with providing an abstract or conceptual framework for the formal regularities common to all languages."[40] In other words, deep structure is deep in that it is common, universal, and thus indicative of that which is proper to architecture-as-such, independent of semantic or pragmatic variation.[41]

Two years earlier, in 1969, Eisenman had published a celebratory review of *Perpecta* 12, the volume immediately preceding that in which his own article was published. For him, *Perspecta* 12 was to be distinguished from its immediate predecessors by virtue of an implicitly polemical focus that imparted to architecture something like an internal, disciplinary rigor through theoretically informed historical analysis.[42] And yet, a closer look at *Perspecta* 11, which appeared in 1967 and was among those *Perspecta* volumes that Eisenman specifically identified as unfocused, suggests that the situation might be rather more complex, because as with Kepes's Vision + Value series of the same period, *Perspecta* 11 sought out what its editors called "a new concern with the whole synthetic and natural environment" through a *mixture* of disciplines.[43] Thus we are given an interview with the liberal economist Robert Theobald, a conversation on urbanism with Shadrach Woods, a text by Buckminster Fuller, questions posed to John Cage, a text on "World Dwelling" by John McHale, and Marshall McLuhan's "The Invisible Environment: The Future of an Erosion," among other contributions. Frequently invoking a systems model, what this material had in common was the challenge it posed to the notion of architecture-as-such—what would later come to be called architecture's autonomy, or for Eisenman, its "interiority"—an internal, linguistic universality or commonality that Eisenman sought, during these years, in Chomsky's "deep structure."

McLuhan's text is telling in this regard. He, too, sees a virtualization of the physical environment through the application of a linguistic hypothesis, though one significantly different from the one Eisenman finds in Chomsky. For McLuhan, the theorist of media, language is a medium of communication embedded in the material substrate (that is, the communication systems) through which it circulates. Using a combination of cybernetics, systems theory, and communications theory, he postulates the human subject as an opaque black box communicating with and constructed by a multimedia environment through constant feedback. In *Perspecta* McLuhan observes the necessity of what he calls "pattern recognition" as a new form of environmental awareness. Among its instruments would be language, held together by *invisible* relational patterns (what McLuhan calls in his title the "invisible environment") that we can recognize as akin to Eisenman's syntax but made available to human beings only through interaction with machines. For McLuhan, "The future of language, as a complex structure which can be learned without learning the words at all, is a possibility that the computer presents increasingly."[44] So whether you are a machine or a human, your access to language is conditioned by your ability to recognize hidden patterns.

McLuhan, writing here in an architecture journal, underscores the pedagogical implications for environmental design, which would be required "to program the environment in such a way that we can learn a second language as we learned the mother tongue."[45] In other words, for McLuhan pattern recognition is a process comparable to that of acquiring a new mother tongue, a linguistic home that gives shelter to the human subject awash in a delirious, multimedia environment, by training him or her to "see" the hidden, regulating patterns—the grammar, but also the software, if you like—that was running the new machines that were running the new environments, in a recurrent feedback loop.

In such a light Eisenman's attempt to retrieve a ground for architecture in linguistic "deep structure" becomes recognizable as a defensive measure undertaken to defer absorption into the media-ecological spectacle described by McLuhan, by pointing architecture inward rather than outward. Nevertheless, it too functioned as training in pattern recognition, or the recognition of an architectural "mother tongue," that ultimately worked to *integrate* architecture and its subject—the subject of language and the subject of environment—into that very same media ecology.

Thus the materiality of the architectural medium became Eisenman's next target, in what must be seen as an effort (whether conscious or unconscious) to remain one step ahead of the communications juggernaut led by figures such as McLuhan. In 1973 Eisenman published "Cardboard Architecture" in *Casabella,* with critical commentary (on "Linguistics in Architecture") by Mario Gandelsonas. Eisenman defines *cardboard architecture* as "a term which questions the nature of the reality of the physical environment," marking a shift toward a notational understanding of architectural form thereby submitted to direct study.[46] Here we are offered four projects, two of which (Houses II and IV) are presented with the article, that set off what Eisenman calls a "feedback process" between theory and practice, in which physical form might be "used as a marking to produce, as it were, a new mental image of an environment different from that which we are actually seeing," thereby effecting a final conversion of the physical, perceptible environment, for architecture, into a (pre-)signifying syntactical system.[47]

In 1976 Manfredo Tafuri thus finds Eisenman, in the houses presented as cardboard architecture, as having arrived at a "perfect 'virtuality' of the object itself."[48] Indeed, he quotes Eisenman on the alienation of the subject, specifically with respect to the environment of the house, as follows:

While the architectural system may be complete, the environment "house" is almost a void. And quite unintentionally . . . the owner has been alienated from his environment. In this sense, when the owner first enters "his house" he is an intruder; he must begin to regain possession—to occupy a foreign container.[49]

In other words, the subject of the linguistic environments projected by Eisenman is potentially alienated only to the degree that he or she engages them at the now voided pragmatic or semantic level, but he or she is perfectly capable of "regaining possession" through the reconstitution of subjective interiority at the syntactic level of pattern recognition made available by what Eisenman refers to as the completion of the "architectural system." Again recalling that the term *ecology* refers etymologically to the logic of the household, or *oikos,* we can say that to reoccupy a house as though it were a "foreign container" is to submit the foreign, alien space of the linguistic environment to a specifically domestic economic policy grounded in the law of an absolute and pure environmental grammar, or what Eisenman calls, after Chomsky, a set of "transformational rules."[50] The same holds for Nixon's call to integrate the natural and social sciences with the environmental design arts in the interest of purifying "our living environment," but from the opposite direction. These rules, these policies that project the domestic onto the foreign, call forth both a unified *oikos* and a unified subject no longer tied to the physicality of either nation or house but *to the grammars in which these are constituted as signs.*

So while Tafuri accomplishes a certain demystification that reveals the closure of the neo-avant-gardist critique as taken up by Eisenman and the other members of the New York Five, he bypasses the critical question of what is *conserved*—rather than what is alienated—in Eisenman's encounter with Chomsky. Pursuing noncommunicative linguistic closure to its logical conclusion with the Five, Tafuri outlines "the limits of this cell where they are only able to leave *graffiti* on the underside of the walls."[51] But Eisenman's graffiti, both written and built, must also be measured against the otherwise incommensurable standards represented by Chomsky, who sought a "universal grammar" calibrated to the competence of what he calls elsewhere an "ideal speaker-hearer," and by Nixon, who commanded the restoration of environments "habitable and hospitable to man," even as "man" became an abstract variable in the calculation of environmental risk.[52]

Given Chomsky's long record of courageous political activism, such a conjunction might seem unfair or bizarre. And yet it remains necessary, if only to underline the shift in register required here by discourse analysis. Although Chomsky takes care to distinguish between the universal grammar he outlines and the particularities of speaking subjects, he continues to insist on the origins of "deep structure" in what he calls "human nature," precisely to account for the "generative" creativity made possible by the unwavering rules of language. This insistence is amplified somewhat in the pseudo-oppositional format of a "debate" with Foucault that was broadcast on Dutch television in 1971, just as Eisenman was quoting Chomsky. Although Chomsky has long been reluctant to draw definitive parallels between his linguistics and his politics, it becomes clear in the debate that what ultimately connects these two aspects of his thought is a certain humanism centered on this notion of linguistic creativity based in human nature, which gradually becomes "freedom" in his conversation with Foucault.[53] For Foucault, Chomsky's "human nature," and thus the "human" to which his universal grammar was addressed, is a specifically historical concept that cannot be translated into a universal ground for political justice (however self-evident the justification might seem), because it remains indifferent to the question of power. Respectfully characterizing what he calls Chomsky's war on the police, Foucault observes rather dryly, "One makes war to win, not because it is just."[54]

Thus, by grounding the discourse on environment in the universal needs of an idealized human subject, Nixon is able to appropriate a just cause as an instrument of war. This exertion of power took the form of a unifying national and ecological project at precisely that moment when the unity of the environment *and* the nation, a nation at war, was in crisis. So again, when Tafuri announces, in his subsequent requiem for the avant-gardes that spirals around the language games conducted by the New York Five, that the "war is over," he could not be more wrong.[55] What had occurred instead was a confusion of the battle lines at the level of the subject of language and the subject of environment. In architecture this confusion was to be found most vividly in the supposed inhospitality and uninhabitability of Eisenman's writings and his houses, both of which effectively abstracted the overdetermined ecologies of the city and of the visual field posited by others into an architecture of pure syntax. Following Chomsky (and despite Tafuri), this was precisely the deepest, most secure home any human could have. In that sense, in borrowing Chomsky's notion of "deep structure," Eisenman also borrowed his humanism. Likewise, Eisenman's withdrawal into the house of language had the presumably unintended consequence of carrying with it the *oikos* of both ecology and economy, effectively retooling architecture as both an instrument and an object of pattern recognition that *secured* rather than resisted its integration into the new media-ecological economies organized as systems of signs. This withdrawal, this supposed abstraction, was therefore only apparently alienating and, if anything, neither abstract nor alienating enough, because it also worked covertly to preserve the universality of an architecture reconstructed as "linguistic environment."

On 15 August 1971, Nixon performed another speech act, which he reported in a televised address on economic policy: "I have directed Secretary [of the Treasury John B.] Connally to suspend temporarily the convertibility of the dollar into gold or other reserves."[56] This measure, a protectionist attempt to stem rising inflation, became permanent by 1973. That year also saw a massive increase in the influx of speculative petrodollars as a result of the fourfold increase in energy prices during the OPEC oil embargo, which effectively undermined the efforts of the state to protect its currency. Until Nixon's executive action, the value of the dollar had been fixed to that of gold as a result of the Bretton Woods Accord of 1944, which sought a stable U.S. currency as the basis for what became known as "world trade." But in the subsequent decades, through successive inflationary cycles, the supply of dollars on the international market had come to far exceed that of gold held in trust by the U.S. Treasury. In other words, in the language of semiotics, the sign had become detached from its referent, or the signifier from the signified.

In their challenge to the postulates of a Chomskian linguistics circa 1980, Gilles Deleuze and Félix Guattari found a similar process at work in another governmental speech act from an earlier era: on 20 November 1923, the German reichsmark was replaced by the rentenmark, which was declared by fiat to be backed up by the state's physical assets, including land, when in fact it was not. Refusing to bracket off pragmatics as external to semantics or syntactics, Deleuze and Guattari describe this act as a "semiotic transformation" that, although indexed to the land and to material assets, acted incorporeally yet pragmatically to refunction a very real economic regime at the level of signification.[57] In other words, at an economic level changing the rules of signification has very pragmatic consequences, even in 1923. Like Foucault, and arguing specifically *against* the autonomy of Chomsky's hierarchically branching grammatical trees rooted in deep structure, Deleuze and Guattari elucidate what they call a "politics of language" that presupposes the material existence of a collective apparatus, like a state or a socialized subject, through which circulate what they call "order-words" that "compel obedience" at the level of language itself. Thus, "a rule of grammar is a power marker before it is a syntactical marker." And so with Deleuze and Guattari we see that "Chomsky's trees establish constant relations between power variables. Forming grammatically correct sentences is for the normal individual the prerequisite for any submission to social laws. . . . The unity of language is fundamentally political. There is no mother tongue, only a power takeover by a dominant language."[58]

So while Eisenman was enacting his own protectionist policies in the form of a semiotic transformation of the architectural object, Nixon was performing a semiotic transformation on the status of the dollar, officially converting it into a floating signifier exchangeable on its own terms, delinking it from a stabilizing referent in the form of property (gold), and—quite pragmatically—identifying it as an object of financial speculation that ultimately undermined his protectionist intentions. Though the gold standard itself had merely grounded currencies in yet another signifier (gold), the year 1973, when the delinking became permanent, has thus been seen by some as marking the emergence of a new phase in a global economy dominated by the speculative exchange of statistical *risk*, fully abstracted from the value of any underlying goods or services, in the form of new financial instruments such as derivatives.[59]

It was in such a context that Nixon also declared, upon signing the United Nations Environment Program Act of 1973, that "we hold the Earth—its environment and its resources in trust for future generations," an enunciation that again acted specifically to obscure the pragmatic function of his environmentalism, at a moment when ever-increasing layers of logico-mathematical abstraction separated the virtualized, risk-based speculations of a global economy from the materialities—whether in the form of labor, land, oil, or buildings—from which value had initially been extracted.[60] Nixon's environmentalism thus assisted in perpetrating a blind economic and ecological violence that was enabled by the very distance of its instruments from what was supposedly held in trust as "environment," through its instantaneous and pragmatic effect of designating "environment" as always already subject to the extraction of risk, whether couched in the language of ecology or of economics.

With his borrowings from Chomsky, Eisenman, well versed in the formation of "grammatically correct sentences" imbued with the rigors of a properly architectural history, performed a comparable series of speech acts called "theory." "Order-words" like "deep structure" acted pragmatically to preserve the syntactic "unity of language" in which architecture-as-such could finds its proper home supposedly sealed off, like Chomsky's trees, from external pragmatic and semiotic factors, or what Maldonado called the "scandal of society." And if, as Deleuze and Guattari remind us, all such linguistic operations presuppose a social apparatus immanent to language, Eisenman found himself provided with such an apparatus in the form of a teaching-machine (The Institute for Architecture and Urban Studies, 1967) and a discourse-machine (*Oppositions*, 1973). Thus, also in 1973, elements of this apparatus interacted with those of another apparatus speaking its own dialect in the Gray/White debate, an in-house power struggle of five against five, for which architecture-as-language was a foregone conclusion. It made no difference that one side spoke of semantics while the other spoke of syntactics, because these two levels ultimately converged—again, quite pragmatically—in architecture's new home within an ecology and an economy of signs.

Whereas, if the delinking of the dollar sign under the Nixon administration can be seen as a last-ditch effort on the part of the nation-state preemptively to control its economic sovereignty at a moment of politico-economic, cultural, and technological deterritorialization that is now called globalization, Eisenman's progressive delinking of the architectural sign from both the physical environment and from meaning can itself be seen as a preemptive effort, on the part of what the legislation called the "environmental design arts," to retain sovereignty over an environment that attains to existence only as a signifying system. To be sure, by attempting to reground architecture in an abstract "deep structure," Eisenman was countering the semantic play advocated by his postmodernist "gray" adversaries (Robert A. M. Stern, Charles Moore, Allan Greenberg, Romaldo Giurgola, and Jacquelin Robertson), which had already begun to prove its worth in the corporate marketplace. But Eisenman's inward turn interfaces with global capital on another level. As Michael Hardt and Antonio Negri have pointed out, at precisely that moment when the assessed risk of impending ecological crisis points to an outer limit to the exploitation of the physical environment, the self-perpetuating "ecology of capital" also turns inward, toward the reflexive circulation and exchange of signs themselves.[61]

In the late nineteenth century, the historian Frederick Jackson Turner had charted the beginnings of this process in his famous commentary on the closing of the American frontier; much later, Fredric Jameson updated this to describe postmodernism.[62] In short, when there is nothing left to consume, capital consumes itself. There is no contradiction, then, between Nixon's environmentalism and his economic policies. The former identifies an outer limit to the exploitation of the external physical environment, while the latter compensate on the inside, at the semiotic level of capital-as-such. So, too, do we find with Eisenman, on the *interior* of the linguistic environment constructed by architecture, a new grammaticality that exists not in the mind of an alienated subject condemned to inhabit a virtual house of language but, rather, in a very real global economy naturalized as a global media-ecology. Indeed, the further inside we go, the further outside we get, as we approach that pure exteriority in which all signs (including architectural signs in circulation since 1973 in which some have read the words *world trade*) remain subject to deadly speech acts that elicit further executive action from those who—in theory at least—make the rules.[63]

4 IMAGE

Have We Ever Been Postmodern?

IN HIS FOREWORD to the 1984 English translation of Jean-François Lyotard's *The Postmodern Condition*, Fredric Jameson goes so far as to say, with respect to Jürgen Habermas's denunciation of postmodernism's "explicit repudiation of the [revolutionary or critical] modernist tradition" as expressing a "new cultural conservatism," that "[Habermas's] diagnosis is confirmed by that area in which the question of postmodernism has been most acutely posed, namely in architecture."[1] However, while regretting postmodern architecture's abandonment of both political and aesthetic utopias, Jameson defends its playfulness, its self-conscious superficiality, as well as its populist willingness to "learn from Las Vegas," against Habermas's recalcitrant modernism. He also defends postmodern architecture against what he sees as a master narrative lurking within Lyotard's attack on master narratives: a neomodernist promise of the "new," now in the form of *scientific* rather than aesthetic innovation, sneaking in through the back door of postmodernist allusion and historical quotation.

But if Jameson can describe this moment in Lyotard's argument as a productive contradiction, his own references to architecture tend to overlook narratives that architecture draws from science, including the peculiar afterlife of a systems model that we have already encountered. Considered together with the architecture of science itself, which was also to "learn from Las Vegas," these lesser-known narratives approach a kind of science fiction, a literary genre about which Jameson has had much to say.[2] This becomes most evident when the architecture of the scientific laboratory extrapolates a systems model into the image-sphere. In doing so, a nominally postmodern architecture modifies the stakes of the "science wars" as they appear, for example, in the political ecology developed at around the same time by Bruno Latour. All of which pivots around the many problems that arise when architectural discourse tries to distinguish between what is true and what is false, as well as between what is real and what is not, in a manner that inverts what we can call modern architecture's "jargon of authenticity."

In 1964, Theodor W. Adorno used this phrase, the "jargon of authenticity," to frame dialectically his critique of Heideggerian existentialism, on the argument that a certain set of philosophical colloquialisms circulating in academic and popular discourse (including "the elevated diction of the representatives of business and administration") mystified the historical processes by which an ultimately fascist absolutism and essentialism, masked in theology that had been masked in philosophy, had finally taken refuge in language.[3] *Authenticity* is among these terms, which Adorno associates, again dialectically, with Walter Benjamin's celebrated reflections on the decline of the "aura": "As words that are sacred without sacred content, as frozen emanations, the terms of the jargon of authenticity are products of the disintegration of the aura."[4] For Adorno, this is evidence not so much of language converted into ideology but rather of "ideology as language," a certain standardized "tone of voice" that inveighs against soulless standardization even as it reproduces its formats.[5] Something similar can be said about the postwar critique of modern architecture that sought a poetics of authentic experience or of situatedness that eventually found its own jargon in Heidegger. But its tone was set, during the same years that Adorno was writing, in a cryptotheological quest for occulted meaning that is discernible, for example, in such works as Sigfried Giedion's *The Eternal Present.*[6]

What is commonly called postmodernism in architecture is usually thought to have rejected these earlier metaphysical efforts in favor of the playful, more or less arbitrary exchange of signifying elements. But this exchange spoke a jargon of its own. Its most salient terms were formulated in 1972 by Robert Venturi and Denise Scott Brown in *Learning from Las Vegas*. There, Venturi and Scott Brown assert the dramatic possibility of classifying the whole of architecture into two categories: the "duck" and the "decorated shed." The "duck" is named, drolly, after "The Long Island Duckling"—a duck-shaped store that sells ducks. As a category, it refers to a building in which architectural particulars such as space, structure, and function are synthesized into an "overall symbolic form" or image from which they are inseparable, as in many modernist monuments. In contrast, a "decorated shed" is, like the casinos that lined the Las Vegas strip in the late 1960s, a building to which symbolism, in the form of signage and ornamental imagery, is distinctly applied like a marquee.[7]

Translated into the rudiments of an aesthetic theory, in a "duck," form and content are inseparable; while in a "decorated shed" their relation is contingent, and thus a (sometimes literal) gap opens up between them. Or again, in the language of semiotics, in a "duck" the building *is* the sign, to the degree that signifier and signified are inseparable, while we might risk calling the sign stranded in the parking lot of a "decorated shed" a "floating" signifier. But most significantly for the polemics that Venturi and Scott Brown inherited from modern architecture, in a "duck," structure and ornament are indistinguishable, whereas in a "decorated shed," ornamental imagery and signage are disengaged from the structure supporting the building itself and are at liberty to proliferate across its surfaces, appearing to suffocate the epistemological lucidity of structure-as-such that was so dear to modern architecture.

To illustrate this, Venturi and Scott Brown provide a number of examples, including one that contrasts two mid-rise buildings designed for elderly occupants: Paul Rudolph's Crawford Manor in New Haven, which they describe as a "heroic and original" late-modernist duck, and Venturi's own Guild House in Philadelphia, which they describe as an "ugly and ordinary" decorated shed. But this is not simply a matter of one building (Crawford Manor) expressing its spatial structure visibly on its surfaces, and thus partaking of modernist narratives of foundational truths and attendant technoscientific myths of historical progress, which the other (Guild House) sacrifices to the ironic play of exchangeable signs. In fact, it is nearly the opposite, since Venturi and Scott Brown effectively accuse Rudolph's building, with its monolithic, rough-hewn concrete exterior, of occluding its internal truths (including its rather conventional structural frame, invisible on the surface), in favor of a mythic spatial plasticity. In contrast, they describe the articulation of Guild House, where windows are "frankly windows" rather than abstract spatial elements, in prosaic terms that reproduce the building's artful claim to a sort of truthfulness by virtue of its avowedly Pop use of culturally communicative—not to say stereotypical—elements in a kind of architectural common sense.[8]

Such a characterization might seem like a reversal, since the reader of *Learning from Las Vegas* understands throughout that, on the whole, Venturi and Scott Brown clearly prefer decorated sheds over ducks. And yet they seem to defend Guild House as if it were a duck—a building in which "[t]he windows look familiar; they *look like*, as well as *are*,

Venturi and Rauch, Guild House, Philadelphia, 1963. Photograph by William Watkins. Courtesy of Venturi, Scott Brown and Associates, Inc.

windows. . . ."[9] But this is not merely a case of visually oriented architects writing ambiguous prose. It is indicative of a foundational displacement. Characterizing their own building as a "decorated shed" in contrast to Rudolph's "duck," Venturi and Scott Brown effectively transpose modern architecture's search for irreducible truths into the realm of ornament and signage. In other words, according to its architect(s), what is authentic rather than contrived at Guild House is its decoration, which includes straightforwardly communicative graphics, appropriate materials used to signify specific meanings, overscaled yet familiar windows, and a heraldic (fake) golden television antenna mounted on the roof like a billboard, intended as a an "imitation" abstract sculpture as well as a "symbol for the elderly."[10]

As Venturi and Scott Brown describe them, these are stable, transparent signs rooted in popular culture and applied to an otherwise unremarkable, functional shell. And so if Guild House is indeed a decorated shed it is only because the cognitive, spatial transparency, celebrated by historians like Giedion in *Space, Time and Architecture* three decades earlier and still sought by architects like Rudolph in a visceral plasticity bursting with the rhetoric of functionality, had been transferred to the two-dimensional surface by architects like Venturi and Scott Brown. Rather than building *spaces* that verified the functionalist zeitgeist at the symbolic as well as at the practical level and could thus be construed as authentic, Venturi and Scott Brown essentially claimed to be building authentic *images*. It is but a short step from here to full-blown metaphysics of the image that turns Benjamin's notion of the decline of the aura on its head. Seen in retrospect, not only has the proliferation of images failed to deprive architecture of what Benjamin called "cult value"; it has elevated the depthless image to the status of an icon, a quasi-theological authority fully capable of emitting an aura of its own.

But did this image-based metaphysics make Venturi and Scott Brown *post*modern? At least one influential observer at the time did not think so, though for slightly different reasons. According to Charles Jencks, Venturi and Scott Brown's communicative, aesthetic populism merely inverted orthodox modernism's noncommunicative, aesthetic elitism, while remaining committed to an "argument by taste . . . modernist at its core," rather than to a theory that took advantage of recent developments in semiotics readily available in other fields.[11] Thus Jencks set out to correct this oversight by describing architecture systematically as a "language." But this, too, had its roots in modernism.

As we have already seen, the work of the American semiotician Charles Morris was an important source for the notions of visual communication articulated by the artist and visual theorist Gyorgy Kepes in his widely read *Language of Vision* of 1944.[12] Morris's work helped bring the visual in line with the linguistic in a way that was readily transmitted to architects and urbanists while also recalling iconographical approaches in art history. At MIT, Kepes worked closely with Kevin Lynch on strategies of visual organization and "imageability" at the scale of the city that would form the basis of Lynch's book *Image of the City*, published in 1960. There, using Kepes's Gestalt-psychological notions of visual communication to represent the city as a system of legible signs, Lynch elaborated the techniques of what Jameson would later describe, with reference to Lynch, as "cognitive mapping."

So we are led back to Jameson, who called for an "aesthetic of cognitive mapping" by which a bewildered subject might regain orientation in the delirium of postmodern space while taking into account its irreversible decenterings.[13] *Learning from Las Vegas* serves as an emblem for what Jameson identifies as a postmodernist "effacement . . . of the older (essentially high-modernist) frontier between high culture and so-called mass or commercial culture," with architecture seen as one among many aesthetic practices that no longer merely "quoted" mass culture (à la Joyce or Mahler) but rather, thoroughly incorporated "this whole degraded landscape of 'schlock' and kitsch" into their fabric. This "rise of aesthetic populism" was but one feature of the correlation of culture with late capitalism, the scope of which was so vast and encompassing (today: "global") that it defied older modes of cognition and therefore required new tools of orientation and analysis, while another and perhaps more poignant feature of this correlation was a type of spatial (and cognitive) disorientation supremely exemplified by the intricate, disorienting "public" interior spaces of the Westin Bonaventure Hotel in downtown Los Angeles, an assembly of mirrored cylinders designed by the architect John Portman and completed in 1977.[14]

According to Jameson, what makes the hotel's architecture postmodern is precisely that it is neither mere style nor mere symptom (a mere surface expression of economic forces). Rather, it is a world unto itself, an enormous perpetual motion machine that effectively *models* the vast decenterings of global capital. In this "new machine," cause and effect, base and superstructure, time and space continually trade places in a manner that can be compared with the decenterings of postmodern warfare, exemplified by Jameson in a hallucinatory quotation from the journalist Michael Herr's account of his experiences in Vietnam:

> In the months after I got back the hundreds of helicopters I'd flown in began to draw together until they'd formed a collective meta-chopper, and in my mind it was the sexiest thing going; saver-destroyer, provider-waster, right hand-left hand, nimble, fluent, canny and human; hot steel, grease, jungle-saturated canvas webbing, sweat cooling and warming up again, cassette rock and roll in one ear and door-gun fire in the other, fuel, heat, vitality and death, death itself, hardly an intruder.[15]

For Jameson, Herr's linguistic efforts here represent an attempt to devise a mode of description adequate to a new kind of war, characterized by the "breakdown of all previous narrative paradigms, along with the breakdown of any shared language."[16] Elsewhere, Jameson describes this in psychoanalytic terms as a Lacanian "breakdown of the signifying chain."[17] In both cases, the result is a heterogeneous field of nonreferential signifiers unmoored from their orientation in narrative time and set

John Portman & Associates, Westin Bonaventure Hotel, Los Angeles, 1977. Interior. Photograph by Nakashima Tschoegel and Associates.

adrift in a temporal disequilibrium that, in turn, corresponds to a "crisis in historicity." This crisis would eventually be written as the end of history and its replacement by an eternal present of simultaneous, interchangeable signs. All of which is, again, given its most tangible manifestation in what Jameson calls the "postmodern space" exemplified by Portman's hotel, since:

> . . . something else does tend to emerge in the most energetic postmodernist texts, and this is the sense that beyond all thematics or content the work seems somehow to tap the networks of reproductive process and thereby to

afford us some glimpse into a postmodern or technological sublime, whose power is documented by the success of such works in evoking a whole new postmodern space in emergence around us. Architecture therefore remains in this sense the privileged aesthetic language; and the distorting and fragmenting reflections of one enormous glass surface to the other can be taken as paradigmatic of the central role of process and reproduction in postmodernist culture.[18]

Taken at face value, this assertion would suggest that we might find further evidence of postmodernism's counterintuitive authenticity—its powerfully euphoric, schizoid affect—within architectural discourse itself. Yet in *The Language of Post-Modern Architecture* we find Jencks condemning Portman's hotel as an overblown, mirrored "jewel," the lavishness of which reflects the increasing privatization of large-scale public works, in the form of large hotels and other commercial buildings, monuments to "private wealth and public squalor."[19] Elsewhere, Jencks illustrates more favorably an explicitly "schizo" mixed-use building in Rome—so designated by critics for its superimposition of three architectural styles, one atop the other—as stark evidence of a postmodern stylistic "impurity."[20] But he assimilates both Portman's commercialism (a more literal reading of the late-capitalist hotel than Jameson's metaphorically spatial one) and "schizophrenic" stylistic juxtaposition into an overall narrative of historical development that also domesticates the impurities identified by Venturi and Scott Brown in the promiscuous slippages of Las Vegas's signs.

Jencks does this by reproducing the systems model that had already entered architecture, through the discourse of Kepes and others, by way of innovations in theoretical biology and communications theory that had coalesced into the multidisciplinary science of cybernetics. As we have also seen, by the early 1970s this assemblage had been articulated as a science of "environment"—visual, technological, and biological—by figures as diverse as Lynch, Marshall McLuhan, Buckminster Fuller, and others.[21] In the second, revised edition of *The Language of Post-Modern Architecture* (1978), Jencks internalizes this external environment in an "evolutionary tree" of architectural styles illustrating the emergence of distinct strains of postmodernism gradually converging in a Babel of architectural languages that he calls "radical eclecticism." Modeled after a linguistic tree, his roots-and-branches version of architectural history posits a pluralistic future that corresponds with the choice-driven

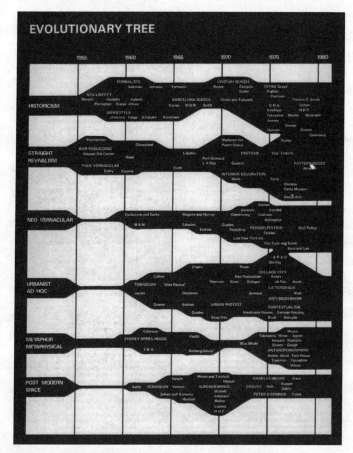

Charles Jencks, "Evolutionary Tree," from *The Language of Post-Modern Architecture,* 2d rev. ed. (New Haven: Yale University Press, 1978). Courtesy of Yale University Press.

pluralities of global consumerism. As Jencks puts it, "eclecticism is the natural evolution of a culture with choice."[22] And further, in distinction to the piously univocal modernist past out of which it evolved, such a future finds its architectural expression in the diverse, image-based codes he tracks throughout the book, some of which draw from historical styles (including modernism) and others from various vernaculars.

In that sense, the "evolution" toward a postmodern future as described by Jencks was, oddly enough, natural. With its systems and its trees, it, too, belonged to a reorganization of the epistemic field hinted at in Michel

Foucault's notion of environmentality, though in a way that is quite different from that elaborated by the environmental sciences. Consistent with Jameson's characterization of postmodernism's late-capitalist exuberance, one consequence of this was the naturalization of consumerist variety in architectural form. Describing the rapid dissemination of diverse visual codes around the world, Jencks observes that "any middle class urbanite from Teheran to Tokyo is bound to have a well-stocked, indeed overstocked, 'image-bank' that is continually restuffed by travel and magazines."[23] Jencks attributes to this state of affairs, as the natural outcome of evolutionary processes traceable linguistically within the images themselves, a certain inevitability whereby any effort to transform the situation structurally is absorbed preemptively as just one more utterance spoken into the void of radical eclecticism.

Earlier in the book, Jencks offers another, related chart describing what he calls "three systems of architectural production" intended to account for the "crisis in architecture" out of which postmodernism emerged.[24] The result, in this instance, is a quasi-structuralist—indeed, even crypto-Marxist—account of forces of production ("systems") conspiring to disarm an ultimately superstructural modern architecture of its transformative potential. Seen as deep background, Jencks's "three systems" represented by three kinds of clients—private individuals, public institutions, and developers—constitute a kind of external economic environment in which the internal stylistic evolution announced by the second evolutionary chart occurs, while linking the two charts brings to the surface another linkage that extends far beyond the quasi-populist theories expounded by Jencks himself and accounts, in architectural terms, for the rhetorical capacity of postmodernism to assert late capitalism as its sine qua non. As with the grammatical experiments conducted on houses by architects like Peter Eisenman, written into the economies represented by Jencks's three systems is the *oikos,* or home, that confers upon the word *economy* the sense of something like the law, or *nomos,* of the home. As expressions of this *oikos,* the home lying within all economies, Jencks's three systems can be described as an *eco*system, both in the sense of that term's traditional association with *ecologies* and in the sense of that term's association with *economies.* Another name for this ecosystem is consumer capitalism, built on cycles of stylistic innovation that upset systemic equilibrium in order that it may be restored at a higher level. It is the given, the taken for granted, the new or second nature that is not only uncontested but actually *sought* by Jencks's book.

. . .

Jencks was by far not the only writer to assimilate the proliferation of images into an ecological model during the 1970s. For example, on two occasions in his *Postmodernism*, Jameson cites Susan Sontag's 1977 classic, *On Photography*, to describe the suffocating totality or closure of the postmodern system of images. In one case, Jameson cites Sontag's recommendation, in her book's closing lines, of what she calls a "conservationist remedy" or, as she puts it, "an ecology not only of real things but of images as well."[25] For Jameson, this is a "classically liberal" solution to the challenges of postmodernism—"nothing in excess!"—that is overdetermined by more radical alternatives figured negatively for Sontag by the suppression of images in Maoist China. The ecological model, then, while therapeutic, tends to foreclose any utopian alternative by virtue of its emphasis on homeostatic balance, despite the frequent association of the two terms *ecology* and *utopia*.

Similarly, in his evolutionary chart of languages proliferating in the polyphony of "radical eclecticism" Jencks deploys a homeostatic, ecological model precisely to avert any radical, unforeseen break in a global economy of architectural styles circulating within a global economy of architectural production and consumption. In other words, there is nothing radical about "radical eclecticism." Instead, the phrase encodes an unspoken anxiety that corresponds quite closely to what Jameson has called the "anxiety of Utopia," but it is a fear in this case not so much of a revolutionary event (à la 1968) but of a revolutionary image that negates the system itself and that the system therefore cannot simply absorb, an authentic innovation within the image ecology that Lyotard might well have called "postmodern."

This anxiety is played out vividly in Jencks's earlier and most overtly prospective book, *Architecture 2000: Predictions and Methods*, published in 1971. There, in an opening chapter on the methodological pitfalls of futurology, Jencks links his efforts to predict the future of architecture to what he calls "critical evolution," which is based on recombining the dissected elements of a "system" rather than accepting its totality as inevitable.[26] At one level, what he means here by "system" is close to what structural linguistics had called *langue*—the organizing structures of language, as distinct from their specific manifestations in *parole*, or everyday speech. Thus, *Architecture 2000* already contains the architecture-as-language premise of Jencks's later book on postmodernism. Moreover, in describing linguistic change as evolutionary, it much more explicitly attributes to the deep structures of architectural language all the characteristics of a biological system.

Jencks acknowledges as much by comparing, in a footnote, the structuralist *langue* with the closed system of systems theory (which originated in theoretical biology).[27] Taken to a logical conclusion, according to Jencks, this amounts to a fatalistic view of history held by apologists for a technocratic future, such as Daniel Bell. In his own effort to steer away from such fatalism, Jencks prefers to follow systems theory in describing history as an "open system." Thus the term *critical* in his notion of "critical evolution," which indirectly modifies the arguments of the biologist and patron of modern architecture Julian Huxley in *Evolution in Action* (1953), whom Jencks also cites. In this popular work, Huxley develops his thesis on the emergence of a second-order evolution, in which humanity is able to shape its destiny through intervention in biological evolution with the instruments of culture, including both science and art. For Huxley earlier in his career (in the 1920s) this meant eugenics, while for Jencks in 1971 it meant genetic engineering, the future impact of which on architecture is the subject of his concluding chapter.

There, Jencks proposes something like a recombinant genetics operating on multiple subsystems within the bounds of the "general system" called architecture, since, as he puts it, borrowing the language of the biologist Ludwig von Bertalanffy, "In general systems theory the machine, nature and culture are all just different levels of organized system working in opposition to the trend towards entropy or disorganization."[28] In that sense, Jencks continues, "We can combine semi-autonomous systems to direct our evolution in a variety of ways: through piecemeal shopping, through *ad hoc* legislative reform, through political action and even through transplant surgery and genetic engineering."[29] According to Jencks, the latter would yield various counter-entropic genetic hybrids, mutants, and chimeras, underlying all of which would be the homeostatic "general system" itself—for Jameson, late capitalism—that, through internal feedback–driven processes of natural selection, would reterritorialize or domesticate any mutation. For architecture, this would mean that there would be nothing authentically "new" under the sun, only slightly modified repetitions of existing archetypes comparable, according to Jencks, to Le Corbusier's *objets-types,* acting like what he calls "evolutionary universals." Language becomes the primary evidence for this hypothesis, when Jencks asks, rhetorically: "What [i]f the linguistic universals that Noam Chomsky postulates underlie all natural languages, some of which would have to be built into any information-processing automata; or the structural universals which Lévi-Strauss contends can be found in every society?"[30]

Lying between this concluding chapter of *Architecture 2000* and the book's opening reflections on futurology is the architecture itself. Again utilizing a kind of mild, nondialectical structuralism, Jencks diagrams six different architectural traditions—logical, idealist, self-conscious, intuitive, activist, unselfconscious—along intersecting X-Y-Z axes. This, in turn, gives both the content and the form of another evolutionary tree extending to the year 2000. This tree is more like a swamp, a primal soup or ecosystem in which a plurality of styles float, compete, and mix, each hewing loosely to one or more of the six basic traditions. And in contrast to its successor in the later book this evolutionary tree reaches far forward in time, acting as what Jencks claims is a "framework for speculation" regarding the future of architecture. Here we find what Jameson has called a "colonization of the future" comparable to those frameworks for speculation that organize the equally naturalized growth of finance capital—diagrams, charts, and projections of future performance, with all conceivable variables factored in.[31]

Though the actual categories developed by Jencks in both evolutionary trees are dubious or interchangeable at best, they share a status as images, a common denominator that allows the crossbreeding. Indeed the point of all the diagramming and all the classifying is, as Jencks puts it, "to obtain a complete picture of events that can subsequently be *distorted* as surprising things start to happen."[32] That is, the point is to supply architects with images, the raw material—the genetic material, if you like—that allows them to produce new mutations in compliance with mutations in the general system. Like Le Corbusier's *objets-types,* six different types of images are said to exist ahistorically and universally and therefore to preclude the appearance of anything totally unexpected. This is also Jencks's answer to futurologist Herman Kahn's "surprise-free" projections for the year 2000, which were extensions of paranoid fantasies circulating in the Hudson Institute in the late 1960s. In Jencks's futurology as in Kahn's, surprises are factored into the evolutionary equation but now under the guise of an open-ended pluralism where, as Adorno and Max Horkheimer once said about capitalist growth in general: "chance itself is planned."[33] This, finally, is the deep structure of architectural history that organizes Jencks's later characterization of postmodernism just as it does his futurology: six great lineages persisting over time, cross-breeding along structural axes and yielding uninterrupted stylistic innovation while in effect still maintaining a status quo: evolution, rather than revolution.

It is worth noting here that minus the structuralism, this (albeit popularized) systems model, with its emphasis on internal heterogeneity, also bears some comparison to the far more rigorous emphasis on dissensus and paradox in Niklas Luhmann's notion of art as an autopoetic "social system." For Luhmann, all such systems maintain "organized complexity" in continual, dynamic evolution through recursive self-referentiality. Distinguished by the primacy of "second-order observations" made by an observer observing her/himself or others observing the artwork, a distinctly "modern" (i.e., post-Enlightenment) art in this instance multiplies its terms of reference internally, while maintaining its systemic coherence or autonomy externally. Second-order observations work to increase differentiation through a paradox of observability: one can only observe oneself observing if one forgoes rooted "first-order observation" in favor of contingent "second-order observation." But in distinction to Lyotard and, in a different sense, Jameson, and in accordance with the second-order or autopoetic cybernetics on which Luhmann relies, the unity of the system is maintained through its relentless drive to expand (for Luhmann: to "evolve," for Jameson: like capital), through constrained innovation rather than through consensus.[34] In the place of homeostatic balance is an apparently open-ended self-differencing, through which (again somewhat paradoxically) the "system" nevertheless consolidates itself, an effect read by Lyotard and other critics of Luhmann as a self-regulating postmodern twist on modernist administrative rationality.[35]

Taken on their own, however, it would be difficult to say whether the traces of a systems model, which carry through into Jencks's postmodernism book as the architectural gene pool is described in more explicitly linguistic terms, makes Jencks himself more modern or more postmodern. Jameson, for his part, is content to treat him as a spokesman for the postmodern in architecture who is nevertheless attuned to the persistence of the modern in its various guises. He further commends Jencks for emphasizing the manifest populism of postmodern architecture, which Jameson regards more as evidence of a crisscrossing of high and low, classical and vernacular, rather than a switchover from one to the other. However, as is also typical in architectural discussions of postmodernism, Jameson makes no mention of the proto- or pseudoscientific pretensions underlying Jencks's "evolutionary trees." Given that the substance of Jencks's often contradictory and loose argument is not necessarily central to Jameson's overall thesis regarding architecture's postmodern credentials, this may not be an issue. Still, if we are to believe that what is called postmodernism in architecture, as represented discursively by works such as *Learning from Las Vegas* and *The Language of Post-Modern Architecture*, bears any relation to the "postmodern space" of distinctly nondiscursive buildings such as Portman's hotel, we must pursue the question further.

In his 1991 *Postmodernism*, Jameson also writes architecture into the late-capitalist equation through different channels, analyzing the early work of Frank Gehry as modeling, somewhat involuntarily and in the form of a spatial puzzle, the nearly ungraspable totality of the "power networks of so-called multinational capitalism itself."[36] But if Jameson's vocation as a literary critic as well as his focus on postmodernism as a "cultural logic" may incline him to note the contemporaneous tendency of architectural theory toward proto-literary narrative analysis, the foregoing discussion suggests that perhaps we should insist on equal representation for architecture's encounters with science.

Much of what has passed as postmodernism in science has, from the point of view of its detractors at least, come precariously close to deserving the appellation "science fiction." When applied to scientific knowledge itself, this would either be an oxymoron, in the sense that science can by definition *never* be fiction, or the opposite, where *all* science is, in a sense, fiction—that is: narrative, text, social construction. One figure who has traditionally been associated with the constructionist position but who has also attempted to declare a sort of truce in the science wars by revising the terms of the debate is Bruno Latour. Unwilling simply to transfer the source of scientific authority from a universalized "nature" to a relativized "culture," Latour has systematically explored the multifarious alliances between the two as constitutive of—rather than as deviations from—the truth claims (and the truths) of science. So it may not be entirely fortuitous that Jameson reproduces Latour's 1984 list of sardonic synonyms for "the modern world," all of which exhibit an aversion to the impure, networked hybrids that Latour argues constitute the true firmament of scientific knowledge.[37]

All the while eschewing the label postmodern, in *We Have Never Been*

Modern (1991) Latour designates as "nature-cultures" the hybrid impurities on which a nonreductionist, nonessentialist, "non-modern" science works. Their pragmatic, irreducible complexity joins these "quasi-objects" (Michel Serres) into networks of alliance and/or antagonism. These networks seem to reverse the breakdown of the signifying chain discerned by Jameson, by making sense of otherwise senseless, schizoid juxtapositions found within such postmodern conditions as controversies over AIDS research as reported in newspapers, where "heads of state, chemists, biologists, desperate patients and industrialists find themselves caught up in a single uncertain story mixing biology and politics."[38] In collecting hybrid networks together into what he has elsewhere called "assemblies of assemblies," Latour attempts to put them to work in the service of a constructive renovation of the institutions, or the "constitution," of parliamentary democracy. Hence his proposal for an encompassing "parliament of things," which overcomes the great nature/culture divide by bringing to the surface the political and scientific networks of humans and nonhumans—Donna Haraway's "cyborgs"—that proliferate just beneath modernism's dogmatic absolutes.

Latour intends this model to take the place of a representational one, whereby politics is a function of representatives making representations in a contractually limited space that pre-sorts or divides materials into rigid classes of objects. Among these are nature, society, and discourse, which he contends (in 1991), the postmodern condition has

> recently sought to juxtapose . . . without even trying to connect them. If they are kept distinct, and if all three are separate from the work of hybridization, the image of the modern world they give is indeed terrifying: a nature and technology that are absolutely sleek; a society made up solely of false consciousness, simulacra, and illusions; a discourse consisting only in meaning effects detached from everything; and this whole world of appearances keeps afloat other disconnected elements of networks that can be combined haphazardly by collage from all places and all times. Enough, indeed, to make one contemplate jumping off a cliff.[39]

Under Latour's alternative model, questions of authenticity become questions of authentication in which truth is a function of testimony, record keeping, demonstration and counterdemonstration, and so on. And though Latour makes no mention of architecture, like Jameson he does rely on concrete spatial exemplars to make his case. Principal among these is the scientific laboratory, where, since the seventeenth century, apparently well-organized, objective experiments are seen to be highly mediated through—in one historical example—the complex interplay of vacuum pumps, leaky gaskets, chicken feathers, annotation techniques, and the testimony of expert witnesses, among other things. Only through such mediation does something emerge that can be called a scientific fact.[40] By virtue of their practical function within expansive philosophical and political debates, scientific facts, the veracity of which is authenticated pragmatically through their participation in nature-culture assemblages, in turn bear witness to the fact that "we live in communities whose social bond comes from objects fabricated in laboratories."[41] Although the emphasis on contingency would seem at least to make Latour a relativist if not a postmodernist, he is quick to object that the semiotic turn that underwrote most postmodernisms (including, we must insist, the architectural ones) ascribed to language an undue degree of autonomy and thus overlooked its actual, mediating role in a field made up concretely of "quasi-objects" and "quasi-subjects," or again, networks connecting politics, philosophy, vacuum pumps, leaky gaskets, chicken feathers, annotation techniques, and the testimony of expert witnesses. In other words, for Latour as for so many others, the problem of postmodernist semiotics is that its signs (and, we must assume, its decorated sheds) are insufficiently concrete, in the sense of their capacity to mediate human social relations in practical terms.

And yet architects like Venturi and Scott Brown had already discovered the contrary in designing real scientific laboratories. By Latour's own admission, the output of the late-twentieth-century laboratory consisted mainly of linguistic elements, in the form of tables, charts, notes, data sets, reports, grant applications, refereed articles, and the like. In an early work devoted to this argument, he and his colleague Steve Woolgar documented the ethnographic research that they had undertaken at one such laboratory, which also happened to be a major work of late-modernist architecture designed by Robert Venturi's mentor, Louis Kahn: the Salk Institute for Biological Science in La Jolla, California.[42] The Salk Institute was representative of Kahn's quest for an architecture of unmediated metaphysical content—what Venturi and Scott Brown would call a "duck." It was among those modern institutions, including other scientific laboratories and a house of parliament, rendered by Kahn throughout his career as monuments that dug deep into architecture's transhistorical reservoir of symbolic affect, manifest in the building's ponderous concrete walls and poetically empty courtyard. More generally, Kahn's architecture was frequently invoked in neo-Heideggerian attempts to recover an authentic "ground" for architectural discourse.

Kahn himself described the Salk Institute's internal, spatial hierarchies as separating the realm of the "measurable" (the laboratory rendered as a utilitarian shell) from the "unmeasurable" (the offices and social spaces, rendered as a symbolic screen).[43] Such myths, both written and built, formed an important target of the postmodernist revolt personified by Venturi and Scott Brown and codified by Jencks, while also representing one of its most enduring models, as exemplified by the ongoing sponsorship that Kahn received from Venturi's supporter, the historian Vincent Scully, whereas in their account of what they called "laboratory life" at Salk, Latour and Woolgar simply ignored architectural attempts to communicate. In their place was the architecture of taking notes, labeling samples, compiling data, inputting that data into computers (which only output more data), and so on.[44]

"We shall emphasize image," wrote Venturi and Scott Brown in *Learning from Las Vegas*.[45] And so they did. In many ways this process reached its apotheosis in a series of scientific laboratories designed by their firm in the 1980s and 1990s, which must be seen in relation to those designed earlier by Kahn, including both the Salk Institute and the Richards Medical Center at the University of Pennsylvania. In Venturi, Rauch and Scott Brown's "postmodern" laboratories, images applied to the surfaces of sheds were inseparable from the life of the laboratory itself, inside and out. This corresponded with the thesis of *Signs of Life: Symbols in the American City*, an exhibition installed by Venturi and Scott Brown at the Smithsonian Institution in Washington in 1976. There, the lessons of Las Vegas regarding the iconography of a building's exterior on "The Strip" and on "Main Street" were complemented with the interior iconography of "The Home," in which everyday domestic objects and environments were decoded for their latent semantics. Venturi and Scott Brown brought this applied domesticity to their laboratory projects, most visibly at the Lewis Thomas Laboratory for Molecular Biology at Princeton University, completed in 1986.

The Princeton laboratory was designed in a collaboration with Payette Associates, a firm recognized for its technical expertise in the design of hospitals in the 1960s and 1970s, with VRSB in charge of the outside of the building (its image) and Payette supervising the planning of the technically complex interior, in a division of labor that, like the building, seemed to follow the logic of the decorated shed. The result was a variation on Kahn's separation of the "measurable" space of the laboratory from the "unmeasurable" symbolism dedicated to the external, social

Venturi, Rauch, and Scott Brown, Lewis Thomas Laboratory, Princeton, New Jersey, 1986. Exterior with protruding lounges. Photograph by Matt Wargo for Venturi, Scott Brown and Associates, Inc. Courtesy Venturi, Scott Brown and Associates, Inc.

collective. Venturi described the laboratory in prosaic terms as a "generic loft building" designed for maximum flexibility, with a patterned facade adjusted to the visual rhythms of the adjacent campus buildings.[46]

But at either end of the building's rectangular volume, Venturi and his colleagues had requested an anomaly in the spatial rhythms. Payette Associates complied by supplying small, informal lounges, intended to encourage social interaction among researchers so that they might better share their knowledge in a field that only exists by virtue of its interdisciplinary linkages. These, along with many of the other details of the building's interior, were executed by VRSB in keeping with the user-friendly iconographic accessibility for which the firm had become known. Like the windows that are "frankly windows" at Guild House, those portions of the building's interior devoted to socializing—also acknowledged by Latour and Woolgar (as well as by Venturi's clients) as instrumental to the linguistic output of "laboratory life"—carried a rhetorical straightforwardness that Venturi described as "accommodating a permanent ambience where one anticipates the comfort of the familiar." This was in contrast to the relative neutrality of the laboratory spaces themselves, which were flexible sheds designed to anticipate change in a "clutter of creative action, analytical, intuitive, physical" no different from the clamor of inscription that Latour had found at Salk.[47]

Thus at Princeton specialists in higher eukaryotes could socialize in a soft, comfortable VRSB-designed window nook with specialists in lower eukaryotes, and virologists could share their insights over coffee with botanists. And so, the "signs of life" that Venturi and Scott Brown had read into suburban domesticity now helped organize the life of the scientific laboratory. To what end? Not only to domesticate science within the postmodern *oikos*, or home, offered by an ecology of codified images first mapped out with scientistic earnestness by Jencks, but also to feed such imagery back into science itself, as a functional necessity for the postmodern scientific innovation on which Lyotard wagered. Aesthetics and technoscientific knowledge are inseparable here; the lounges and other trimmings, and the "laboratory life" they represent, are more than mere ideology. They are real, in the sense that the building deploys the communicative functionality of images side by side with the mechanized functionality of space. Whether modern or postmodern, Venturi and Scott Brown's laboratory architecture thus also conforms with Jencks's homeostatic project by translating a reassuring domesticity into the realm of the scientific imaginary: a familiar, fragile image of a home, supporting a schizoid, postmodern science presided over by nature-culture hybrids with interchangeable names like Genentech and Genzyme—in other words, science fiction.

The imaging of science would be carried forward in other laboratory commissions that fell to the Venturi, Rauch, and Scott Brown firm in the 1980s and 1990s. And if the instrumental feedback of positivist theories of social communication into the laboratory environment would also seem to confirm Latour's early account of the laboratory as a social field that is constantly writing and rewriting itself, the difference is that by now architecture had entered the picture, making its own contribution to all the socializing, all the writing, all the "communication." But it had not entered the picture merely as a flexible loft space that accommodates these practices. Architecture had entered the agonistic field of postmodern science *as an image*—an image of domesticity, a sign of life, of couches, coffee, and community, the raw materials of the *oikos* of both economics and ecology.

An ecological model is also at the center of Latour's expanded "parliament of things" (or of nature-culture hybrids). But unlike Jencks's, Latour's ecology is not a naturalizing one. As he elaborates it elsewhere, it is a political ecology that refuses the reduction of nature to the terms of either of the two "eco" sciences—the "'warm, green' nature of the ecologists" or the "red in tooth and claw" law of the jungle of a fundamentalist economics.[48] In Latour's model, the naturalized *oikos,* or home, of both ecology and economy is split into two houses of parliament, in a "new bicameralism" that displaces the modernist partition of facts versus values onto two levels of political activity. The first house is charged with "taking into account" and with asking "how many are we?" by staging the manifold perplexities of hybridized nature-cultures as practical, always politicized questions of enumeration and verification, in which the pragmatic authentication of data replaces the metaphysics of authenticity. Meanwhile the second house is charged with asking the question "can we live together?" and with arranging in rank order the priorities associated with each fact and each constituency.

Latour's proposition revolves around a new division of labor for professionals, a redistribution of "skills for the collective" in which each is expected to make an equal if distinct contribution. There are roles for scientists, (to "make the world speak"), politicians (to mediate and compromise), economists (to model), and moralists (to force the collective to see itself from the point of view of those who have been excluded).[49] But given that Latour follows this list with instructions for what he calls "the organization of the construction site" in preparation for erecting the new parliamentary edifice, it may surprise that there is no designated role for architects. Or rather, architects (including, perhaps, Latour himself) seem to perform a kind of metapolitics here by constructing the space in which it all happens—again, a doubled-up house of parliament modeled on a scientific laboratory. According to its metaphorical architect, this new double house actually contains "flowing basins, as multiple as rivers, as dispersed as tributaries, as wild as the brooks on a map of France." Before such multiplicities, camouflaged as houses, "no entity is asked to declare, before its propositions are taken seriously, whether it is natural or artificial, attached or detached, objective or subjective, rational or irrational" or, we can add, authentic or inauthentic.[50] Thus to postmodernist multiculturalism is added what Latour calls "multinaturalism," and the science wars, far from being concluded, are extended into a "war of the worlds" that seeks to replace the transcendentalism of modernist science and the relativism of postmodernist multiculturalism with—again an architectural metaphor—the "common world to be built," the *oikos* of both economy and ecology.[51]

But here is Latour's subterfuge, his rhetorical sleight of hand. He claims, "I have no utopia to propose, no critical denunciation to proffer, no revolution to hope for. . . . Far from designing a world to come, I have only made up for lost time by putting words to alliances, congregations, synergies that already exist everywhere and that only the ancient prejudices kept us from seeing."[52] And so he takes architecture for granted. That is, in contrast to Jameson, who perhaps overplays architecture's antimetaphysical postmodernity, Latour treats it as a near-metaphysical constant, by failing to take architecture's own discourse and production "into account" as an element of the dynamic, nonmodern assemblages he enumerates—not only in the sense of the a priori spatial organization of politics into two houses but also in the sense of the proliferation of images that architecture had historically and concretely become, including the architecture of the scientific laboratory. And yet, as a political ecologist supplying what he calls "the designation of the edifice to be built," Latour assumes the duties of an architect, a custodian of the future who nevertheless refuses to name himself as such, who declares that it all exists already—in other words, an architect truly deserving of the name "postmodern."

But if Latour's parliament is modeled on a scientific laboratory, his concluding propositions might be different if the architecture in question here is seen less metaphorically and more literally. After all, since at least the 1970s what was called ecology amounted in political terms not to a set of imperatives drawn from direct experience of the ecosphere but from calculated assessments of *risk* generated in the laboratory, including the risk of ecological and/or economic catastrophe. Thus the linguistic units coming out of laboratories constitute, among other things, the actual, raw materials of a "risk society" and as such are comparable to the risk/reward calculations organizing Jameson's "colonization of the future."[53] In this light, the function of Jencks's evolutionary trees and of Venturi and Scott Brown's domesticated laboratories was to manage both the ontological and the practical risks, and both the crises of authenticity and of authentication, brought about by the recognition that signs, symbols, and images were real and not merely ideological decoration applied to utilitarian sheds. This, then, was and remains architecture's image problem: the problem of taking into account architecture-as-image. Not as some grand illusion or mere surface effect but as a concrete instrument that writes what we might call a science fiction, in this case about science itself.

Jameson, for his part, would find a different postmodernity in certain authors of science fiction. As with his appreciation of Herr's linguistic innovations in narrating the war in Vietnam in nonlinear anti-narratives, Jameson sees in the writings of J. G. Ballard, for example, a way of narrating postmodern space-time. He associates Ballard's science fiction with what he calls a "spatialization of the temporal" imbued with a disaggregating tendency toward entropy, which is precisely the opposite of the anti-entropic, homeostatic naturalism of Jencks's evolutionary trees and of Venturi and Scott Brown's docile laboratories.[54] And if, as Jameson is at pains to show, his privileging of architectural examples to describe this spatialization is not intended to restrict postmodern space-time to a leisure-entertainment experience, whether in Los Angeles or Las Vegas, Portman's hotel becomes a kind of science-fiction architecture, a defamiliarized world unto itself in which the human subject is metaphorically (if not literally) lost in space.

It is also worth noting that in the mid-1970s, as architects like Venturi and Scott Brown were actively rejecting modernist utopias with their slogan "Main Street is almost all right," while Jencks was drawing up the family trees of "radical eclecticism" and Latour was stalking scientists at the Salk Institute, Jameson was working through the utopian science fiction of Ursula Le Guin, among others. He concluded that Le Guin's ambivalent or even dark projections of utopian socio-ecological experiments, such as the rough-and-ready anarchism of the planet Annares in *The Dispossessed* (1974), are evidence not of "utopia as such, but rather our own incapacity to conceive it in the first place."[55]

To Le Guin's novels we can add the science-fiction architecture of Venturi and Scott Brown and many others climbing Jencks's evolutionary trees, but in reverse. For what we have here, in the ecology of styles of which these laboratories and the discourse surrounding them form a part, is a willing concession, a sigh of resignation, that it is almost all right not to be able to imagine any alternative. For his part Latour, the political ecologist, has attempted from the side of science to denaturalize a related system of signs without giving up entirely on their content. Such a perspective would identify the trees on which Jencks's architectural "languages" hang, as well as the paradoxical teleology they uphold, as still belonging to the species "modern" for their uncontested naturalism. The same applies to Venturi and Scott Brown's attempts to advance a theory of authentic architectural language attuned to messages coming from below. By contrast, if the scientific laboratory is among the sites in which modernity's legitimation crises are played out and where a real, material struggle over signs and their meaning occurs, its architecture, too, must be among the variables in the post-postmodern equation.

After all, is it not possible to imagine that the *politics* of political ecology might lie in some small part in the struggle over specifically and irreducibly *architectural* images—images of laboratories as images, perhaps—that actively reimagine and reorganize, rather than domesticate, the relation between nature and culture? Far from constituting one more set of consumables for Jencks's "radical eclecticism," and unlike those images that make up the *oikos*, the well-kept if more inclusive house of both ecology and economics on which Latour ultimately stakes his claim, such images could be called authentic. But their authenticity would lie neither in their immediate legibility nor in their free play. Instead, it would lie in their very real capacity to stir the imagination toward something different, something like what modernists used to call Utopia, which to our tired, postmodern eyes might yet again be new.

5 MATERIALITY

Mirrors

TWO DARK, CRYSTALLINE SOLIDS are poised corner to corner on a diagonal and separated by a tense, narrow gap. For twenty-eight stories, each of these consists of an extruded trapezoid, in the form of a rectangle with one of its corners cut off. From floors twenty-nine through thirty-six, each volume has another corner cut off in section at a forty-five-degree angle but in opposite directions. Seen frontally (and at some distance), the resulting figure resembles an elongated, archaic house form with a slit down the middle. Seen from other angles (and closer in), the figure breaks up and the two solids vie for dominance, as right angles and diagonals bounce off one another in what their tinted, reflective surfaces capture as an overlay of lines and planes. At the base, these reflections become literal on the exterior and virtual on the interior, as two mirrored-glass planes stretch up from the sidewalk on opposites sides of the site, and into the ten-foot-wide crevice that separates the two volumes. Inside, this atrium roof is supported by a latticework of triangulated trusses that match up with the gridded curtain walls in which the two volumes are wrapped.

The object (if, indeed, a composition of two elements can still be called an "object") has many corners. There are inside corners and outside corners; there are corners that turn at right angles, at acute angles, and at obtuse angles, in both plan and section. At each turn of each corner, something happens. The figure either asserts itself by aligning certain corners while setting others in counterpoint, or it disintegrates, its contours falling away as corners compete in three dimensions, one turning this way, the other that—an effect that is particularly evident as one looks up from the base at the vertiginous play of one chamfer against the other at the top. These competing effects pose a series of difficult

Philip Johnson and John Burgee, Pennzoil Place, Houston,
1976. Photograph by Richard Payne, FAIA.

questions with remarkable efficiency: Is this a symbol, or is it simply a
form? Is it representational or abstract? Or is it both? Neither? Regardless
of how such questions are answered, their very posing secures one indis-
putable fact about the object: It is a work of architecture.

Or is it? In 1992, the novelist and cultural critic Amitav Ghosh asked
why the transnational oil economy, unlike the spice trade in earlier days,
had yet to produce great literature.[1] The same might be asked about its
architecture, though the oil industry has produced, directly or indirectly,

a great number of buildings. Among these are several designed and built by the firm of Philip Johnson/John Burgee in Houston, Texas, including the object described above, Pennzoil Place (1976). These are not necessarily works executed on behalf of oil companies but rather works executed in and by a milieu fueled by the petrodollars that flowed freely into the U.S. economy during the 1970s. Philip Johnson belonged to this milieu and profited from it. But both Johnson's activities and the commissions his firm received were only indirectly linked to the oil industry. For example, his long friendship with members of the de Menil family, whose wealth derived from the Schlumberger Oil equipment company, translated mainly into art institutions such as the Amon Carter Museum in Fort Worth (1961).[2] All of which poses significant methodological problems for any analysis concerned with the interrelation of architecture, materiality, and capital.

If we can imagine such a thing as "oil money," what role does architecture play in its circulation, if any? Conversely, what role does the circulation of oil as capital play in the production of architecture, if any? To avoid reductive equations between architecture and money or, more to the point, between the ephemerality of postmodern architectural imagery and the perceived immateriality of finance capital, Fredric Jameson suggests that we "elaborate a series of mediations between the economic and the aesthetic," beginning with the mediations effected by "new technologies." Thus intermediated, aesthetics and economics operate as two among many semi-autonomous yet mutually interpenetrating "levels."[3] Still, there remains the question of value, in respect to which Jameson usefully compares Manfredo Tafuri and Rem Koolhaas shadowboxing over questions of "beauty" or "spirituality" in their respective interpretations of Rockefeller Center. Having already hinted that the actualities on which Rockefeller Center is built are primarily symbolic rather than immediately productive (oil and land speculation, etc.), Jameson assigns to each of his boxers an antithetical resolution of the ambiguity inherent in the artwork understood as a "symbolic act." Such an evaluation breaks down along its axis of symmetry, indicating either a merely *symbolic* act (Tafuri) or, conversely, a productively symbolic *act* (Koolhaas).[4] Jameson provisionally resolves the ambiguity by appealing to David Harvey's extrapolations from Marx on the long-term virtualization of "ground rent" as "fictitious capital." This refers to the extraction of value from land not based on labor but on what Harvey calls "a flow of money capital not backed by any commodity transaction," based solely on the expectation of future value, "a claim upon future revenues."[5] Risking (or courting) what we might call an aestheticization of economics, Jameson imputes to this essentially symbolic economy an analogy with what many critics have taken to be the "symbolic" (i.e., aesthetic) value of Rockefeller Center. Which in turn allows him to name, with the help of vivid imagery from Charles Jencks, an isotropic "modernism to the second power" of which, we can assume, Rockefeller Center is an avatar.[6]

The displacement of use value by what is in effect an exchanging of exchange values, enabled in the economic sphere by the technosocial mediation of global financial networks, leads Jameson to that "aspect of late-capitalist abstraction, the way in which it dematerializes without signifying in any traditional way spirituality: 'breaking down the apparent mass, density, weight of a fifty storey building,' as Jencks puts it. The evolution of the curtain wall 'decreases the mass and weight while enhancing the volume and the contour—the difference between a brick and a balloon.'"[7] Though we might disagree that this process is not spiritual in "any traditional way," it is only a short distance from here to other aesthetic forms, such as "Barthesian connotation . . . or reflection about reflection."[8] That Jameson, with Derrida, sees a ghost in this hall of mirrors gives some indication that the commodification of the future (Tafuri's "planification") brings with it dead bodies but also the possibility of returns, disappearances, and reappearances.

Jameson is well aware of the possibility, whether in Rockefeller Center or in its spectral postmodern futures, that the question of value can simply be excluded on principle, in the eventuality that "we have to do with a bad, or at best a mediocre, set of buildings."[9] Still, however commercial it may seem, even so-called developer architecture is never entirely reducible to the economic interests behind it. It remains, in some sense, architecture. As such, its liminality might even serve to illuminate otherwise obscure properties of more canonical works. In that sense, Johnson's long-standing commitment to architecture as an art form—we can call it architecture with a capital A, or Architecture—was both tested and affirmed in his collaborations with developers and petrodollars in Houston and elsewhere. The context for this was the increasingly global marketplace also invoked by Jameson that, during the 1970s, generated new combinations of finance capital, cultural capital, and real estate speculation. But despite his increasing celebrity, Philip Johnson did not exactly become a "brand" during this period. Nor was he reduced to a mere commodity (or "whore," to use his own terminology). Instead, he and his work were, in a technical sense, media. That is to say: Johnson was not only a media figure, he was also, with his architecture, a medium and a mediator, both in Jameson's sense and in the sense of a figure who channels ostensibly spiritual or—more to the point—otherworldly forces. And in Houston, he and his architecture specifically channeled the force called "oil."

Circulating as it does in the mass media but also in various semischolarly contexts, "oil" is, strictly speaking, a fetish.[10] A fetish is something that both reveals and conceals at once. That is why Americans could be told in 2006 that they were addicted to oil by George W. Bush, the man who started an oil company with the comical name Arbusto Energy in 1977.[11] Simply put, "oil" is a thing that is named, desired, and sometimes gone to war over whose aura actually works to conceal the complex and often violent social and historical processes that make it possible in the first place. In that sense, buildings like Johnson/Burgee's Pennzoil Place, designed and built for the developer Gerald Hines between 1973 and 1976, do not really represent "oil"; rather, they *produce* it, in the form of a fetish—an object with special powers.

In other words, these buildings do not merely symbolize the power of oil companies. This is partly because what we call "oil" is really a hybrid plurality of actual objects, including the chemical called petroleum in its various states of refinement, as well as the various mechanisms via which it is extracted, and those via which it is processed, and those via which it is transported, and those via which it is sold and burned, and the gases thereby emitted, and the human bodies thereby propelled in machines, and those (perhaps in Nigeria) whose land is expropriated that these machines may receive more fuel, and the various organizations that do the expropriating, refining, selling, burning, and so on. All of these actualities are, in a sense, forced together into the phantasm called "oil," which in turn only exists by virtue of its capacity to keep the inherent contradictions and competing interests that it harbors at bay, to say nothing of its periodic, outright savagery. In helping to channel these objects and the forces flowing from and through them—amplifying some, screening out others—architecture helps quite literally to build this phantasm, the existence and effects of which are inescapably real.

But, pace Jameson, all of this occurs indirectly, through varying degrees of mediation. In fact, despite its name Pennzoil Place was not even built directly for an oil company. It was built for a real estate developer who had been approached by an oil company to build an office building in downtown Houston. As it turned out, the building involved two oil companies. In 1954 Pennzoil's chairman and Hines's client Hugh Liedtke had formed a partnership with the elder George Bush in an entity called Zapata Petroleum (named after the film *Viva! Zapata*). In 1959, Bush sold his interests in Zapata Petroleum to Liedtke's Pennzoil conglomerate, while spinning off the Zapata Offshore Oil Company for himself.[12] During the planning phase of Johnson's building, Hines and Liedtke brought in Zapata Petroleum as an additional major tenant and with it, the criterion that both companies be recognized in the building's architecture.[13] The result was a kind of twinned Seagram Building skewed along the diagonal that runs from one corner of the site to the other. Each tower has a distinct, but counterposed, diagonal roof. At the base, the atrium joins the two together as it presents another, lower diagonal volume to the street. · Other major tenants of the complex included the Pennzoil-owned United Gas Pipeline Company and the Houston office of Arthur Anderson, which later became involved in the collapse of Enron.

But Johnson's architecture also channeled *itself*, as Architecture, in a kind of feedback loop of mediation. Stylistically, Pennzoil Place was among Johnson's last recognizably "modern" buildings. In 1954 he had already theorized the diverse forms of fetishism characteristic of modern architecture, calling them "crutches," even as he admitted to relying on them himself on occasion. But according to Johnson, architects who rely too heavily on these crutches obscure the aesthetic essence of architecture—its true, unfettered status as an art object.[14] Crutch-free architecture is autonomous architecture, architecture standing on its own, a position with which Johnson's name has long been associated. And so we can test out his theory by applying it to his building.

First crutch: The crutch of history. Though in 1954 Johnson could declare this crutch relatively inoperative, by 1973 it was certainly an issue and included, in this case, the history of modernism itself. That history is captured here in the form of a mannered quotation of Seagram's 4'-7 ½" module, squashed into 2'-6"-wide units and spread in what Johnson called an "all over pattern" that stretches over Pennzoil's canted "roofs."[15]

Second crutch: The crutch of pretty drawing, or the "pretty plan." Johnson once compared the plan of Pennzoil to the then-new NBC logo, inverted with a gap in the middle. Still, it is true that presentation drawings were not very important at Pennzoil. In their place was a twelve-foot-square model of Houston, a five-foot-tall model of the building, two interior models of the atrium, and a fifteen-screen slide show starring Johnson himself, in which he explained to potential tenants the oceanic swell of emotion they would experience upon entering the building each morning.[16]

Third crutch: The crutch of utility. Here is Johnson in 1954: "They say a building is good architecture if it works. Of course, this is poppycock. All buildings work."[17] Pennzoil certainly works, and by most accounts works well. What does it do? Among other things, it helps to produce the phantasm called "oil."

Fourth crutch: The crutch of comfort, in which "environmental control starts to replace architecture." In an echo of Johnson/Burgee's earlier, environmentally controlled atrium space in the aptly named Investors Diversified Services (IDS) Center that defended against cold winters in Minneapolis, the air-conditioned atrium at Pennzoil is among its most distinct architectural features. Given the cost pressures of a speculative office building, it would probably not exist but for its capacity to defend oil industry workers against the extreme heat of a Houston summer.

Fifth crutch: The crutch of cheapness, or what Johnson called the "economic motive." As speculative office buildings go, Pennzoil was relatively expensive. Still, its economics were never far from the surface, and as Gerald Hines suggested at the time, its high level of design—its proximity to Architecture (and we must assume, to the name of Philip Johnson)—made it attractive to tenants willing to pay a dollar or so more per square foot.[18]

Sixth crutch: The crutch of serving the client. As Johnson put it, "[S]erving the client is one thing and the art of architecture another."[19] True. But at Pennzoil, among the services offered by Johnson's firm to their client Hines was to produce a work of Architecture, an artwork. Why? Because it would fetch higher rents.[20]

Finally there is the seventh crutch: The crutch of structure, of which Johnson happily admitted, "I use it all the time myself."[21] And indeed it is there at Pennzoil, in the regular column grid and in the trusses carrying the atrium roof, one precedent for which is the atrium-like roof covering the multilevel space of the sculpture galley at Johnson's New Canaan estate, completed in 1970. But in a perfect reversal, the actual structure at Pennzoil was built by "oil" itself: in this case, by Zapata Petroleum's affiliate, Zapata Warrior Constructors.[22]

Does this mean that architecture, having become dependent on, or addicted to, these seven crutches, is unable to stand on its own at Pennzoil? Yes and no, because Architecture also helps to prop up all the crutches. To demonstrate, I would like to add an eighth crutch—or really, a counter-crutch—to Johnson's list. Call it the "crutch of the corner," since it is often said that the real test of any Architect (capital A) is how she turns the corner (consider, for example, Ludwig Mies van der Rohe at the Illinois Institute of Technology). Johnson himself was fond of this criterion, as when he suggested that Mies had achieved at the Seagram Building a corner of sufficient nuance to merit comparison with the pilastered turn executed by Karl Friedrich Schinkel at the Altes Museum in Berlin. According to Johnson, such a comparison offered a salutary demonstration of the degree to which "architecture can be judged by corner treatment."[23]

As I have already suggested Pennzoil is, in a sense, all corners, inside and out. It is therefore potentially all Architecture, inside and out, at least to the degree that the turning of its corners is aesthetically pleasing, if not at times sublime. But the building's evident reliance on crutches one through seven seems to contradict this possibility, or at least to reduce it to an honorable compromise between the architect and a developer-patron who knew good architecture when he saw it. Since Pennzoil's corners also sublimely serve the client with some of the most dramatic corner offices around, to say nothing of the relative ease with which they accommodated Hines's budget, or the relative comfort of the multicornered atrium, or the elegance of the plan, or the structural resonance of the module, or the economy with which program is accommodated or, subliminally, history is invoked.

Johnson's former mentor-collaborator Mies rather notoriously used to say that God (read here: Architecture) is in the details. Bearing in mind that the theories of commodity fetishism to which I have been alluding with respect to "oil" begin with a definition of the fetish as a religious object most often found in so-called pagan religions, and given the possibility that for the quasi-Miesian Johnson Architecture was one such religion, it is only logical that we seek out its gods in Pennzoil's details. Among these, one stands out. This is the turning of the corner at the peak of each tower, as the curtain wall folds diagonally across the building's volume to produce the double-canted profile that gives the building its distinctive identity. Johnson called the resulting effect "pure shape" and celebrated the economy of means by which it was achieved. Apparently, this architectural bonus added only eighty cents per square foot to the building's bottom line.[24] In return, Hines got what some (including Johnson) saw as the ghost of Minimal art or, again in Johnson's words, "basic prismatic shape."[25]

The detail by which this was achieved is not particularly elegant. In fact, one member of the Houston firm that actually worked it out, S. I. Morris Associates, called it "a real dude."[26] Still, the corner detail did what it had to do. It even contributed a little crypto-classicism to Johnson's still-evolving aesthetic grab bag, in the form of the barely perceptible split pediment at the scale of the entire building that Frank Gehry later (and rather perceptively) identified as a possible predecessor to the Chippendale roof atop Johnson/Burgee's AT&T building of 1984.[27] So, as Pennzoil's temple form comes into view and with it the god called Architecture, it seems difficult to say that it also worships the god called "oil." But again, this is not necessarily a question of representation per se; nor is it merely a question of a so-called iconic building paying symbolic homage to the powers that be. It is a question of what you do not see as much as what you do see, when you watch Architecture appear and disappear on the skyline of history.

Juan Pablo Pérez Alfonzo, the former Venezuelan oil minister and founder of OPEC, once called oil "the devil's excrement."[28] Its corrupting promise of instantaneous wealth, in the form of a "black gold" worthy of El Dorado, operates on a mythic level. It works in a way that is comparable to the holy grail that currency traders call arbitrage, which is in effect a nearly risk-free exploitation of a momentary imbalance in the financial markets. Perhaps no place in the world exemplifies this better than Nigeria, where the brutalities of what Michael Watts has called "petro-violence" have included a civil war, a succession of military coups, and other internecine conflicts that are in large part wars over the control of oil sold to major transnational corporations. Watts has shown how this economy finds its phantasmagoric expression in Lagos, where periodic mob violence erupts over rumors of the organized theft of male genitalia, the spoils of which are thought (like oil) magically to produce instant wealth.[29] That Nigeria is sometimes called the Texas of Africa should give pause in this respect. Since, though there may not yet have been any cases of genital theft reported in Houston, that city too harbors a dreamlike, specular economy in which fetishes like "oil" circulate with their promises of magical powers.

Referring to the financial interests that it served, one critic favorably described Pennzoil Place as a "monument to liquidity."[30] It was designed for the purpose of making money and was 60 percent leased by the time of groundbreaking and 97 percent leased—at about 5 percent higher than market rates—by the time of occupancy. The risk-reduction strategy of "pre-leasing," common today, unleashed what the same critic called a "river of revenue" that in turn made possible a $60 million mortgage based on 75 percent of the building's presumed value, backed up by the leases that were in turn made possible, as Hines himself claimed, by the building's distinguished architecture.[31]

In Houston in the mid-1970s, the liquid called "oil" was at the base of all of this liquidity. Rather uncannily, the basement level of Pennzoil Place feeds a series of air-conditioned subterranean tunnels that crisscross the city. Distant relatives of the nineteenth-century Parisian arcades in which Walter Benjamin discerned a dreamworld of wish images, these cool, dark interiors connect Pennzoil's street-level lobby (which was first occupied by a bank) and its below-grade shopping arcade with its Houston neighbors. Among the latter is Number One Shell Plaza, the office building designed for Hines by Bruce Graham of Skidmore, Owings & Merrill and leased to Shell Oil (a principal actor in Nigeria) that set a precedent for Hines's hiring of well-known architects like Johnson. In the years that followed, Johnson/Burgee would add a number of nodes to this network. It is a network that is both virtual (in the sense of a space through which the fetish called "oil" circulates) and real, in the sense of the financial, technological, political, and cultural infrastructures linking oil companies, banks, and governments in Houston and across the world. These infrastructures are visible, we can say, in the circuitry of the tunnels but also in the buildings above.

Among other nodes in this network are Johnson/Burgee's stand-alone Transco Tower of 1983, located ten miles to the west, and, just next door to Pennzoil (and linked to that building by a tunnel), their RepublicBank Center of 1984. When seen in series with Pennzoil, these buildings tell a story about liquidity and about circulation. It is a story about the air-conditioned air that fills these buildings and the oil money that flows through them. But most important for any reconsideration of architecture's transition from the modern to the postmodern, this story is about the irresistible fetish called Architecture that both reveals and conceals such flows and the violence they frequently entail, as it helps literally to produce that magical, dangerous thing called "oil."

. . .

In 1990, borrowing a quote from the 1988 U.S. presidential campaign, David Harvey described the underpinnings of postmodernity as "economics with mirrors." In the campaign, this characterization referred to what had become known as Reaganomics. For Harvey, it captured the speculative nature of finance capital more generally. Together with the economic policies that supported it, what George H. W. Bush had also called "voodoo economics" summarized what Harvey and many others took to be a postmodernist dematerialization of cultural production into a specular play of images. Following Neil Smith and others, Harvey took this apparent dematerialization to signal a "crisis of historical materialism." That the empirical evidence suggested something less than a full-scale replacement of "Fordist modernity" with "Flexible postmodernity," and more like a coexistence or juxtaposition of the two regimes, he took as confirmation that these two were in fact poles in the historical dialectic of capitalist development itself, in both a synchronic and a diachronic sense. Within this dialectic, as Harvey put it, "wherever capitalism goes its illusory apparatus, its fetishisms, and its system of mirrors comes not far behind."[32]

In appending to this analysis Marx's famous dictum that "we erect our structure in imagination before we erect it in reality," Harvey seemed to assign to culture a premonitory function, one of signaling in aesthetic terms the economic juggernaut that underlay it, while covering up its real effects.[33] He thereby also assigned to postmodernist cultural production an ideological function that Marxism has traditionally assigned to the fetish: that of concealing economic violence, which in this case was aided and abetted by a cultural turn in which "ethics is . . . submerged by aesthetics."[34]

Mirrors, which have been used as construction materials at least since the seventeenth century, have often been thought to possess unique characteristics. At times they seem to reveal hidden secrets, while at others they appear to deceive or distort.[35] So the fact that many of the buildings constructed in cities like Houston and in their outlying suburbs in the 1970s and 1980s were clad in mirrored, reflective, or tinted glass could potentially confirm Harvey's hypothesis. What, after all, could be more illusory than an edifice erected for an energy company that dissimulated its function in a thin, uniform surface that repelled optically (but also metaphorically) all efforts to disclose its contents?

But these buildings were also real things, clad with real glass that had been coated or infused with real metals. There is nothing particularly illusory about such postmodern monuments, unless the modernist equation between optical and cognitive transparency is carried along, together with a counterintuitive distinction between authentic and inauthentic materiality. In that sense, reversing the perspective in which we discerned a phantasmagorical material—"oil"—in the architectonic materiality of Pennzoil Place, we should be able to look at these mirrors—and not at their images—and thereby glimpse a different sort of relation between culture and capitalism, or art and politics.

Look at a mirror. Not in it, at it. This is our task with respect to postmodern architecture's preoccupation with mirrored or (as at Pennzoil) tinted glass. Though it can hardly be said that the material was everywhere during the 1970s and 1980s, it is plausible to suggest that that was its function—to be "everywhere" and thereby to stage a kind of ubiquity, a kind of placelessness that, in effect, took the place formerly occupied by modernist universality (in architectural terms: transparency) in the capitalist imaginary. Thus certain tricks with mirrors were favored. Among these was the technique of rereflection. Based on the turning of corners, rereflection can be defined as a mise en abyme produced by placing mirrors at specific angles to one another. Johnson/Burgee utilized this technique at the IDS Center in Minneapolis, completed in 1974. The fifty-one-story office tower is an elongated octagon in plan, the four diagonal sides of which are serrated with seven right-angled notches, extruded to the top. The entire volume is clad in reflective glass, on a half-size (i.e., 2'-6") planning module. As a result, four of the building's eight sides are broken down into rows of seven inside-out corners that reflect themselves even as they reflect strips of the surrounding city and sky. The effect is compounded at the base, where a cubic, glazed latticework atrium known as the Crystal Court is attached to two of the sides. Inside this atrium, the gridded repetition of the roof structure is broken down and repeated in the cladding of the mirrored serrations on the building skin to which it is attached but which it also seems to pass through.

At IDS, the interior junction of gridded atrium roof and gridded, reflective curtain wall reminds us that the content of the reflections is not the point. What counts is their modular structure, the repetition of reflection upon reflection. But the Crystal Court, like the tower that rises above it, is not a house of cards, or even a hall of mirrors in the Baroque sense.[36] Rather than produce an illusion of spatial extension that disguises what

Philip Johnson and John Burgee, Investors Diversified Services
Center, Minneapolis, 1974. Photograph by Richard Payne, FAIA.

lies behind it—the regime of flexible accumulation superimposed on
an outsourced Fordism, perhaps—it reveals its basic principles. In this
respect, the building might even be called axiomatic, since at an architectural level it plays out the principle of the reflective, inside-out corner
with relentless consistency. Look at these mirrored corners and you are
looking at the materiality of flexible accumulation. Yes, it is an "immaterial materiality," to borrow (and to invert) a neologism from another
architect (El Lissitzky) from another, more utopian time. Its function is

not to hide but to reveal, to make visible the actual abstraction of finance capital, its spectral capacity to be here and here and here at the same time.

This kind of ubiquity is different from what Harvey calls "time-space compression."[37] For Harvey the expression, extended out of modernism, means accelerated rates of production, consumption, and information flow. In contrast, I use "ubiquity" here to refer to a quasi-stasis, a running in place, a circularity capable of taking everything into its feedback loops. That is what a mirror is; it is a feedback loop. We see this when we look at Johnson/Burgee's mirrors: input output input output input output. Or, referring to the two sides of an inside-out corner: right left right left right left. Or again, to the unsyncopated modularity of the atrium roof, which echoes the curtain wall's corners as it steps down in section: horizontal vertical horizontal vertical horizontal vertical. These mirror images are less oppositional or complementary than they are redundant, a doubling back of the surface onto itself, in which the screening function of the glazed architectural enclosure—the building as a giant "iron cage" or system of windows—is exchanged for sheer iteration. There is nothing behind the curtain. Not even more curtain. This is it.

But what is it? What, in the end, is a mirror? Despite the traditional equation between mirrors and mimesis, an architecture of mirrors does not merely reflect, whether directly or through a sort of disciplinary transliteration, the protocols of new socioeconomic arrangements. It helps to produce those arrangements, in space and in time. Architecture therefore does not (or does not only) represent or "mirror" late capitalism as its cultural equivalent. It *belongs* to late capitalism. Asserting this might seem like attributing or conceding to architecture a near absolute immanence. But seen from another direction, it also extends the dialectical model that both Harvey and Jameson deploy, perhaps to a point of no return, a point at which what is culture and what is capital cannot be distinguished in any useful way. One name for this point could very well be "Philip Johnson," who, together with his architecture and despite his high bourgeois credentials, stands as an instance of something like absolute immanence. But this does not mean that, even with Johnson, architecture devolves into pure service, a standard bearer for capitalist development. It means that with postmodernism, architecture's immanence is secured by its status as an artwork: as Architecture, that is.

Jameson intimated as much when he compared the mirrored cylinders of the Bonaventure Hotel in Los Angeles with the alienating power

John Portman & Associates, Westin Bonaventure Hotel, Los Angeles, 1977. Photograph courtesy of Westin Bonaventure Hotel.

play of hiding behind mirrored sunglasses.[38] Indeed, in a different but compatible reading, he goes so far as to suggest that for postmodernism, "[a]rchitecture therefore remains the privileged aesthetic language; and the distorting and fragmenting reflections of one enormous glass surface to the other can be taken as paradigmatic of the central role of process and reproduction in postmodernist culture."[39] For him, the privileging of the reproduction over the putative original, of Warhol's diamond-dust shoes over van Gogh's peasant boots, corresponds to a "waning of affect" that, dialectically, verges on something like a postmodern sublime which, like the monolithic surfaces of Skidmore, Owings & Merrill's prismatic

Wells Fargo Court (also in Los Angeles), "renders our older systems of perception of the city somehow archaic and aimless, without offering another in their place."[40] Again, and in support, Jameson cites Jacques Lacan's account of a paradigmatically schizophrenic moment of derealization that turns on the "breakdown of the signifying chain" and the isolation of the signifier as a vividly material presence, "bearing a mysterious charge of affect, here described in the negative terms of anxiety and loss of reality, but which one could just as well imagine in the positive terms of euphoria, a high, an intoxicating or hallucinogenic intensity."[41]

This, however, suggests that self-isolating mirrored surfaces like those wrapping Portman's cylinders reflect something other than the "other" of the city. And yet, with Lacanian overtones, Jameson seems content with the thought that they register the urban "other," which for him is not exactly the hotel but rather "the distorted images of everything that surrounds it."[42] But he is not really looking at the mirror itself. Rather, he seems to be looking into it, at its contents, which have been reduplicated and distorted by the curved surfaces to the point of unrecognizability.

As the topological obverse of the cylinder, Johnson/Burgee's *inside-out* mirrored corners at IDS encourage a different reading. In them, the mirror itself is what appears in the mirror; its contents are secondary, or at least held in suspension—delinked, as Jameson suggests, from the signifying chain. So too with the doubled-up towers of Pennzoil Place, which, by virtue of the gap between them and the offset, mirrored N-shaped site plan, generate an enormous, acute-angled inside corner that is itself mirrored on two sides of the site. As with the offset towers of Minoru Yamasaki's World Trade Center (1964–73), the doubling is not exactly that of the classically modern doppelgänger, an instance of mechanical reproducibility that for Freud and his followers captured the uncanniness of the self/other dyad, which Friedrich Kittler has already watched disintegrate into the matter-of-fact, frame-by-frame trickery of film, circa 1900.[43] It is more like a series with no beginning and no end, of the type explored by Minimal artists like Donald Judd and Sol Lewitt but also by Warhol. It is a seriality on the cusp of the transition from an industrialized imaginary organized around mechanical reproducibility to one—post- but also neo-industrial—organized around feedback. That is, like Portman's building, it is a circular and tautological seriality, a seriality turned in on itself. In that sense, each of the Bonaventure's cylinders can be understood as a single, gradual turn of a single, continuous corner that engulfs the entire volume while expelling its contents. While in revealing contrast, the volumetrics of Pennzoil Place make each of its two "fronts" into a single, sharp turn of a single (inside) corner that makes no reference to the exterior in the first place. Like a diagram of a recursive feedback loop, Pennzoil reflects itself and only itself in its doubled-up volumes, producing a time-space that is neither interior nor exterior, neither here nor there, neither this nor that, neither now nor then.

This is the ubiquity that I am arguing offers a more accurate diagram of postmodern spatio-temporality than Harvey's all-too-modern "time-space compression." Further, in place of Harvey's implication that aesthetic experience mirrors the techno-economic accelerations of post-Fordism, I suggest again that what we have been witnessing is more like running in place, wherein aesthetics and economics are not linked vertically, as image to substance, but horizontally, as node to node. This suggestion finds substantial backup in Jameson's version of the crisis of historical materialism, which he associates with "end of history" narratives in literature and in political discourse. But the fact is—and this is the point of even naming "postmodernity" in epochal terms—that this sense of inescapable ubiquity and recursivity is itself historically materialized. Still, Jameson is very specific about what he believes is behind the mirror, simultaneously concealed and revealed in its dissimulating, disorienting glare: "a network of power and control even more difficult for our minds to grasp [than digitalization]: the whole new decentered global network of the third stage of capital itself."[44]

Which raises the question: When we look at the mirror play on Houston's skyline, what are we looking at? The "global network of the third stage of capital" or just mirrors—or both? Ten miles from Pennzoil Place and marking another, more suburban node in the network of power, knowledge, and desire that takes physical form in the tunnels linking the city's downtown to itself is the aforementioned Transco Tower, completed by Johnson/Burgee in 1983. At Transco, another Hines development project for another energy company, the stepped-back tower of Bertrand Goodhue's Nebraska state capitol is blasted forward from the 1920s and stretched to about double the height (thirty-four stories, nine hundred feet) of the "original," without a corresponding increase in width or breadth. The sense of vertical extrusion is heightened by the all-glass skin, most of which is mirrored. At intervals, however, triangular crenellations of gray tinted glass are cut into the monolith, introducing a rhythm of dark vertical bands into the reflective sheen. According to the architects, the point was to achieve in glass the solidity normally associated

Philip Johnson and John Burgee, Transco Headquarters,
Houston, 1983. Photograph by Richard Payne, FAIA.

with stone, by way of the contrast between the two types of glass, which
reproduced the contrast of light stone cladding and dark strips of vertical
glazing on many towers designed in the 1920s by architects from Goodhue to Raymond Hood. At Transco, the effect was further enhanced by
reducing the mirrored glass module to a scale normally associated with
stone, while allowing the vertical gray crenellations to revert to a module
subliminally recognizable as normal for glass.

The building's stepped profile is complemented by a stepped plan
where, again, outside corners are turned into inside corners, causing the
mirrored glass to reflect itself, though this time more locally than globally.
The gray-glazed crenellations perform a similar inversion: protruding yet

reading optically as cuts. The elementary, almost parodic inside-outside game going on here with glass has little to do with that material's purported transparency as celebrated by a previous generation of architects, including Johnson himself in an earlier incarnation. But neither is it merely evidence of the dematerialized "precession of simulacra," as Jean Baudrillard might have said. It is a material thing that manages in crude and unsophisticated ways to seem spectral, both there and not there at once. To the extent that in looking at it we are also looking at Jameson's "global network," the same can be said about what supposedly lies behind the mirror. What we are looking at—or more properly, what we are watching—is not the network hiding behind a mirror, but a network of mirrors, unfolding.

This is the "space" of techno-economic globalization. Anything but flat, its folded surfaces perform topological transformations of the highest order: from in to out to back in again. There are many other objects designed by many other architects in which we could follow such folds in our pursuit of the mirror's materiality. There is I. M. Pei's faceted Fountain Place development in Dallas (1982–86), or the two massive, mirrored ciphers that Roche Dinkeloo designed for Hines in Denver in 1981, which went unrealized due to a declining local real estate market. Back in Houston, there is the Allied Bank Plaza designed by Richard Keating of Skidmore, Owings & Merrill and completed in 1983. But perhaps the most revealing clues are to be found in Pittsburgh, at the base (or, depending on orientation, the top) of that city's Golden Triangle commercial development, which lies at the point where the Allegheny and Monongahela Rivers meet to form the Ohio River. There, in 1984, Johnson/Burgee erected what is surely among postmodernism's most complete mirror worlds, known as PPG Industries Plaza and Tower, or PPG Place.

Unlike Houston, a city whose postindustrial pedigree is uncontested, the buildings of downtown Pittsburgh bear names such as U.S. Steel, Alcoa, and PPG. These are buildings designed both symbolically and pragmatically to house the entities that produced the materials of which the age of mechanical reproducibility was made: steel, aluminum, and glass. And at first glance, Johnson/Burgee's PPG complex is no different. Like the aluminum Alcoa Building by Wallace K. Harrison and Max Abramovitz and the steel U.S. Steel Building (by Abramovitz and Charles Abbe), it consists of a series of all-glass buildings designed for a glass manufacturer. Signifier and signified seem happily, almost comically united here. Though a deadpan, almost Warholian irony is discernible in the sheer

Philip Johnson and John Burgee, PPG Place, Pittsburgh, 1984. Photograph by Richard Payne, FAIA.

quantity of glass used at PPG Place (as if to render the association as obvious and as meaningless as possible, in Warhol's hometown, no less), the most important fact is that the glass is, again, mirrored.

Again there is reference to stone, this time in the pared-down Gothic Revival forms from which the buildings are assembled. Johnson reports that Charles Barry's Victoria Tower at the Houses of Parliament in London (1835–67) supplied the source material for the PPG Tower, while others have seen the afterimage of the University of Pittsburgh's Gothic Revival Cathedral of Learning, though again it hardly matters whether these arbitrary references are legible in Johnson's overscaled mirrored-glass version. Another copy without original, the PPG Tower stands to one side of PPG Place, which is the official name given by Pittsburgh's practitioners of "urban revitalization" to the rectangular plaza centered on an obelisk that is at the core of the complex. PPG Place is an urban enclave configured as a mirrored interior. It is as if the Bonaventure Hotel, whose Piranesian interiors so troubled (and excited) Jameson, has been turned inside out, its smoothly reflective exterior skin now folded into pseudo-Gothic encrustations, the absolute stillness of which approaches that of the crystalline, petrified forest that gives J. G. Ballard's 1966 novel *The Crystal World* its title.

Petrifaction, turning to stone; this is the postmodernist endgame. Not acceleration but deceleration. But again we risk drifting toward the realm of metaphor, of looking into the mirror at its images rather than at it, to comprehend its materiality. Almost one million square feet of vacuum-coated PPG Solarban 500 clear reflective glass cover the building's surfaces. Solarban is a low-emissivity ("low-e") glass that significantly reduces heat gain through solar radiation. According to the architects,

Philip Johnson and John Burgee, PPG Place, Pittsburgh. Curtain wall detail. From Darl Rastorfer, "Reflections on a Curtain Wall: PPG Place," *Architectural Record* 172, no. 12 (October 1984): 196.

increased energy prices recommended this choice.[45] However, the urban context in which the complex was situated contained little in the way of buildings thought suitable by the architects to be reflected in PPG's mirrors. Their response was to devise a hermetic self-referentiality. As Johnson/Burgee's monograph puts it, "[I]n an area awaiting the effect of PPG as a catalyst, the mirror could be expected to have little beyond itself to display. The complex makes the most of this situation by exploring the possibilities inherent in the material, through the use of a jagged façade that offers limitless reflections and rereflections."[46]

Thus the mirror returns us to the domain of commodity fetishism. Not because it seems to conceal the inner workings of the late-capitalist machine but because it renders the outer world—the city—invisible at its moment of crisis. That is how what Jameson calls the "global network of the third stage of capital" works. Not by concealing the inside but by concealing the outside. As legatees of modernism, we look into the mirror, expecting to see through the looking glass. As interpreters of a postmodernism that comes *before* that projective moment (in the sense of appearing before a judge), we must learn first to look *at* the mirror and not at the distorted images of our selves (or our "others") projected on its screens. Doing so gives us a better chance of looking beyond the screen or, really, behind it, into possible futures and possible pasts that may yet escape the entropy of reflection and rereflection that is approached by postmodernity's self-reflexive feedback loops.

Writing about Pittsburgh's Golden Triangle before the PPG complex was built, Tafuri observed that "[i]f Rockefeller Center represented the most complete 'disenchanted mountain' of the 1930s, renovated Pittsburgh was the maximum example of the 'disenchanted city' of the 1960s."[47] The Golden Triangle's showpiece was Gateway Center, a multi-architect, middle-class housing development that included a building by Harrison and Abramovitz. But shortly after Tafuri wrote, more than five acres of urban fabric within the Golden Triangle were declared "blighted" so that, under the same legislation that made Gateway Center possible, the city's Urban Redevelopment Authority (URA) could acquire them for resale to PPG in preparation for PPG Place, under an agreement it had made with the company in 1979.[48] In the context of the narrative of enchantment and disenchantment that Tafuri constructs around the American skyscraper, from Eliel Saarinen's Chicago Tribune Tower competition entry in 1922 to the SOM's John Hancock Center in 1968, it is important to recognize PPG Place as a project of *reenchantment*, or in the language of biopolitics, of "revitalization." As Tafuri said of the Golden Triangle, which also included the Alcoa and U.S. Steel buildings, "The capitalist city no longer hid its face beneath a romantic mask; no Mendelsohn would ever again photograph Pittsburgh as a mysterious forest; no Saarinen or Ferriss would be moved to 'sing' its force. The 'city without quality' created itself in Pittsburgh as the direct expression of the forces that actually manage it."[49] Maybe, or maybe not; but either way, there would be a Johnson to build a crystal cathedral in its heart.

Pittsburgh's public policy makers and their civil society counterparts had taken to calling the development of the Golden Triangle, which was underwritten by a new politico-economic model based on public/private partnerships, a "Renaissance." So when, as the city emerged from the fiscal crisis of the mid-1970s, the office occupancy rate approached 99 percent in the Central Business District (CBD), a new set of political and civic actors led by the city's mayor, Richard Caligiuri, decided to redevelop the CBD in a new "urban revitalization" project that they called "Renaissance II." Rebirth, followed by re-rebirth; like the reflections and rereflections in which they are materialized, these are the feedback loops of development in late capitalism. By the mid-1990s, Pittsburgh's public agencies, which during the 1980s had adopted a managerial approach to urban redevelopment that restricted the state's role to that of an initiator and facilitator of the partnerships with corporate capital, actively resolved to take a "customer-first approach" to the application of its instruments.[50]

This thinking, in turn, had been made possible by the perceived success of Renaissance II, in which, according to one historian,

The eruption of new downtown office towers generated by the restored public-private partnership (and favorable market conditions), the rapid transit projects, the cultural initiatives of the 1980s supported by the Caligiuri administration all provided tax revenues and employment. More important, they provided the office space, infrastructure, and quality of life improvements that Caligiuri hoped would facilitate Pittsburgh's transition from a paleotechnic nineteenth-century economy of coal and steel to a post-steel economy rooted in advanced technology, information processing, professional services, and cultural vitality.[51]

Such was the city's apparent dematerialization into "post-steel" that by 1989, the *New York Times Magazine* was calling Pittsburgh "America's most promising postindustrial experiment."[52]

Among the conditions set down in the "public/private partnership" between PPG and the city was that the City Planning Agency would redevelop the adjacent Market Square shopping district. Describing the changes undergone by the city's downtown shopping district during the 1970s, another historian came closer to naming the game:

> The department stores had begun to struggle in their competition with suburban malls as white flight accelerated, especially after the 1968 Martin Luther King riot in the [predominantly black] Hill District. The once vital retail corridor between the Horne's and Kaufmann's department stores began to look shabby and increasingly catered to lower-income African American shoppers, who had lost their neighborhood business district in the adjacent lower Hill District to urban renewal [i.e., Renaissance I].[53]

But an observer for *Architecture* magazine, the official organ of the American Institute of Architects, was most explicit. The firm of Hardy Holzman Pfeiffer (HHP) had been commissioned to renovate Market Square, a project that was never completed. In 1989, referring to what his title called "PPG's Unpopulated Places" at street level, Lawrence Houstoun Jr. wrote: "[T]he dormant [HHP] plan addresses the fear of 'undesirables' by creating outdoor spaces that attract more middle-class people, thus diluting the perceived impact of unwanted people."[54] Houstoun surmises that the HHP plan was conceived in the tradition of William H. Whyte's "Street Life Project," as documented in *The Social Life of Small Urban Spaces* (1980). Equally important, however, are the terms in which the reshaping of urban space according to the behaviorist precepts advocated by Whyte are recast here. As Michel Foucault once put it with reference to the (earlier) emergence of biopower in modernity, "It is at this moment that racism is inscribed as the basic mechanism of power, as it is exercised in modern states."[55] And now by capital, as well.

Foucault's argument is that a type of racism that is more practical than ideological, more a matter of the "technology of power" than of the "mentalities, ideologies, or the lies of power," took hold as a defining characteristic of modern sovereignty in the nineteenth century.[56] The old sovereign right to decide who dies was hence permeated with a new possibility: "the right to make live and to let die."[57] And racism "justifies the death function in the economy of biopower" by making the "health" or "purity" of one (normalized) race depend on the often violent elimination of the "threat" represented by another, the ultimate example of which is genocide.[58] But Foucault is not only speaking about limit cases, "[not] simply murder as such, but also every form of indirect murder: the fact of exposing someone to death, increasing the risk of death for some people, or, quite simply, political death, expulsion, rejection, and so on."[59] The "public/private partnerships" of "urban revitalization," dedicated as they are, and in such practical ways, to values like "quality of life" brought about through the injection of "cultural vitality," represent a migration of these processes of normalization into the sphere of capital. In "poststeel" Pittsburgh, as in so many de- and reindustrializing cities, suburbs, and ex-urbs around the world, capital, enabled by state policy, assumes previously important aspects of the state's biopolitical function.

If petrifaction, the turning of stone into glass, at PPG was one among many techniques of power that—indirectly but decisively—helped to divide the urban population into "desirables" and "undesirables" (i.e., inhabitants of "unpopulated" places), thereby condemning the latter to a sort of passive death, what of life? Four years earlier Johnson/Burgee had completed the Garden Grove Community Church (known as the "Crystal Cathedral") in Garden Grove, California. Of their client, the televangelist Dr. Robert H. Schuller, the architects report that the purpose of his project was "to help transmit his message through architecture." The sharp-cornered, star-shaped building for three thousand people was therefore required "to be inspiring, soothing, and was to bond the experience of religion with the experience of nature." The firm's monograph makes no mention of the surrounding city. Instead, it emphasizes the energy efficiency of the building's all-mirrored exterior, which "screens out 8 percent of the sunlight, creating a hushed, underwater atmosphere within."[60]

In this statement we can hear an echo of the 1973 oil crisis, in the aftermath of which it mattered far more, both economically and symbolically, to reduce energy consumption. But such echoes, too, reverberated between the mirrored glass surfaces that proliferated on the architecture of the multinational corporations during the late 1970s and early 1980s like so many rereflections. Johnson/Burgee's Crystal Cathedral confirmed the new mystique of the mirror, its new aura, even. The rigid, mechanical iterability of long-span trusses and glass visible in Mies's earlier, disenchanted project for a convention center in Chicago, a shed for the "mass ornament," had now turned its gaze back to nature. Not through

Philip Johnson and John Burgee, Garden Grove Community Church, Garden Grove, California, 1980. Photograph by Richard Payne, FAIA.

mimetic doubling but by materializing the discourse on "environment" that we have already encountered. In Johnson's own account of his building, glass is magically turned into water—and by extension at PPG, stone into reenchanted, "revitalized" glass. Such alchemical feats manage the risks that are posed by "the global network of capitalism" by screening them, and it, out.

In that sense, the Crystal Cathedral is the ultimate fetish: a religious artifact thought to possess special powers, marshaled in the name of— but also against—the invisible. Looked at directly, its glass makes the new, officially sanctioned environmentalism visible, while simultaneously blocking out the presence of the economic arrangement that had brought it into existence in the first place. Like its technological and aesthetic cousin, PPG Place, it performs a very particular magic trick: the restoration of meaning to the suburban strip and the inner city, respectively; *not* through figuration, though both are clearly figural, but through *materialization*.

Materialization and not dematerialization, in the complex sense of an immaterial materiality, or the illusion of an illusion. In a table summarizing the characteristics of "Fordist modernity" versus "Flexible postmodernity" David Harvey gave the distinction a peculiarly Christian cast, when he assigned to the paternalism of the former the attributes of "God the Father/materiality" and to the latter, "The Holy Ghost/ immateriality."[61] But Johnson/Burgee's Crystal Cathedral, as well as PPG Place, Transco, and in its own way, Pennzoil, were material evidence to the contrary; evidence less of a dialectical oscillation than of a strange simultaneity. For what these and so many other postmodern mirrors teach us is that it takes a real "global network" to support the illusion that there is nothing there.

Responding to questions from the historian Francesco Dal Co, Kevin Roche pointed out in 1985, "The interesting thing about mirror is that it is very inexpensive, almost as inexpensive as paint."[62] Elsewhere in the same interview he added: "Recent developments in the stone industry have made it possible to cut granite very thin, 3 centimeters thick, in large sheets. Also, the methods for making attachments and gluing stone together have made much progress, so it is now possible to consider granite as an economic alternative to glass."[63]

Here again, stone approaches glass as glass approaches stone. And not by chance, perhaps, mirrored glazing figures prominently in the work of Roche Dinkeloo Associates. In the city-within-the-city-within-the-world called United Nations Plaza, begun in 1966 (just as Roche Dinkeloo were completing the late Eero Saarinen's mirrored Bell Laboratories building in suburban New Jersey) but not completed until 1983, two faceted towers are set at right angles and clad entirely in reflective blue-green glass on a uniform, horizontally oriented module. The complex occupies the full length of two adjacent Manhattan blocks, its sides running east–west and north–south respectively, and its two volumes form a corner at a scale one notch larger than Pennzoil Place. The massing of each tower builds up toward a climactic street corner, where in plan the chamfered volume of one tower stands juxtaposed sharply against the square corner of the other. Like Pennzoil Place (and like PPG's facades), these two buildings reflect one another as, to borrow again from Walter Benjamin, "reproduction without original."

It is not surprising, then, to find Roche Dinkeloo designing two sets of twinned towers for Gerald Hines in 1981, one for Houston and the aforementioned one for Denver. Though neither project was realized, together they anticipate the technical—but also aesthetic—facts later reported to Dal Co: that as mirror approached paint, stone approached mirror. In the pair of towers designed to occupy a downtown Houston block, the effect of Pennzoil is visible, as a crevice is opened up between two offset shafts, each of which is topped with a shed roof. Between them is an atrium. Pennzoil's tinted glazing has been replaced here by mirror, now overlaid with a striped fabric of dark metal panels. In the second pair, for Denver, two identical towers are turned diagonally on a city block, their corners overlapping slightly. Like another unbuilt project done for another Houston developer the same year, they take up the problem of the skyscraper as overscaled architectural element, as it was first posed by Adolf Loos in his Chicago Tribune Tower competition entry of 1922 in the form of a

Kevin Roche John Dinkeloo and Associates, Project for Two Office Towers, Denver, 1981. Courtesy of Kevin Roche John Dinkeloo and Associates.

Kevin Roche John Dinkeloo and Associates, J. P. Morgan Headquarters, New York, 1989. Courtesy of Kevin Roche John Dinkeloo and Associates.

single Doric column that is recognizable now as proto-Pop. In this other Houston project, Roche Dinkeloo treat the skyscraper as a single, mirrored column split into four enormous pilasters running up the corners in support of a phallic top. While in Denver, in the project for Hines, the reflective glass shaft rises out of a granite-clad base to support an enormous four-sided gable above.

This basic diagram, in which mirrored glazing gives up its claim on uniformity to become incorporated into variegated patterns of glass and granite, is consummated in Roche Dinkeloo's Morgan Bank Headquarters on Wall Street in lower Manhattan, completed in 1989. There, a granite base (with atrium) transitions into a mirrored glass-and-granite shaft, topped off by a copper-clad mansard roof. Massive pilasters turn the corners, as glass and stone combine to materialize yet another node in the "global network." But as before, these materials do not simply represent the network; in combination with many others, they *are* the network, both as representations and as things. Like the processes that produce them, the exchanges that consume them, and the arrangements that organize them, they are concrete, tangible. The tricks with mirrors and other real materials performed by corporate globalization produce the illusion that there is an illusion; the illusion that their materiality is illusory, unreal, derealized. The illusion that there is an illusion—neither a double negative nor a tautology—also describes what a new stage in commodity fetishism might actually look like: the inability simply to look at something directly, rather than attempt to see through it. This mode of distraction draws us in even as it keeps us out.

The historical specificity of such buildings and the materials that they assemble is therefore not limited to their architectural style or to the politico-economic world order that they serve. It has to do with their particular relationship to what Jameson repeatedly refers to as the "totality" of that system. But to follow him here and to link Deleuzian deterritorialization, analogized to the fluid dynamics of finance capital, with the "ultimate dematerialization" of the territory of the city into speculative real estate, is to risk conflating materiality with locality.[64] In architecture, this ultimately correlates with a mysticism in which materials like "local stone" work another kind of magic, in the form of another, complementary (and compensatory) fetish to the fetishism of "oil" as pure liquidity, pure circulation. Such effects notwithstanding, the hardened materiality of architecture is not henceforth irretrievably condemned to absolute exchangeability in the echo chambers of global capital and its cultural adjuncts. On the contrary, the "logic" of late capitalism is relentlessly and irreducibly material. It is a product of the very objects that it seems to condemn to a shadow play of economic speculation. Or, to put it another way, what seems like a hall of mirrors is actually a highly organized shell game but one in which the shells themselves are all there is to the game. Now you see it, now you don't; now it's glass, now it's stone. This particular "world game" (to recall Buckminster Fuller) is not just a language game played with signifiers that float in thin air like balloons trailing their strings. It cannot be played without material assemblages like "oil," "stone," and "glass." It is a game of transubstantiation rather than of derealization. And its rules are eminently visible on the very surfaces of the very shells to which its architecture has only apparently been reduced.

6   SUBJECTS

Mass Customization

IF THE MIRROR IS ITS PARADIGMATIC OBJECT, who is the subject of postmodern architecture? Processes of subject formation at both the individual and the group level have been widely treated by theorists as central to comprehending postmodernity's scope and effects. Still, as we have seen, architecture proper has been taken up in this context largely as a set of symptomatic objects to which only vaguely do specific subject formations attach. Among the latter would be the catch-all category of "consumer society," to which postmodern architecture's imagistic character is often assumed to correlate. But such correlations, while plausible enough, are insufficient if we are to take a fuller measure of architecture's presumed function as a cipher for an emergent world-historical conjuncture. One important way—and in a theoretically rigorous sense, the *only* way—to do so is indirectly, by sorting through the mediating instruments whereby subjects and objects are arranged on the stage of history. That this stage itself is not objectively "given," and is in its own way a function of those same instruments (which are in their own way a function of the stage, and so on), introduces a certain reflexivity into the interpretative equation. It might help here to take as one of our coordinates Jacques Rancière's notion of a "distribution of the sensible" that includes, excludes, and arranges objects and phenomena as elements of aesthetic *and* historical experience; still, even then we find architecture oscillating between object and frame.[1] For in the particular distribution of the sensible that is postmodernism (a category that, we must note, Rancière finds unhelpful), architecture is arranged, or brought into view, in a particular way, even as it helps to do the arranging, the framing, and the occluding.

. . .

Taking a cue from cinema studies, architectural theory has periodically found it useful to refer to Jacques Lacan's notion of the "mirror stage" to describe this ambiguous state of affairs. In the mirror stage, the infant, recognizing her or his reflection in the mirror as a *gestalt* before having gained full motor control, is put in the paradoxical position of apprehending her or himself as an integrated body or "self" but only from the outside, and therefore as an object or body alienated from itself and subject to the controlling gaze of another.[2] For Lacan, this foundational *méconnaissance* and its corresponding psychic alienation anticipates modernity's constitutive social alienation. But I will not dwell here on Lacanian psychoanalysis as it may or may not bear directly on an analysis of postmodern architecture.[3] I will only suggest that, as we did above in our reflections on materiality, we keep our eye on the mirror itself, in order to discern its way of dividing up the world. This means confronting architecture as both an object and as a frame or a mediating instrument—in other words, as *both* an aesthetic medium *and* a component in a media apparatus.

The basic problem for postmodernism at this level is the constitutive possibility that there is nothing in the mirror. That is, as objects dissolve into imagistic play, so do subjects. This can be construed as a mimesis to the second degree, in which the aesthetic object does not merely reflect, in some mediated way, the "real" world of empirical objects but rather gestures toward the unrepresentable sublime or Real (in the Lacanian sense) of late-capitalist dissolution.[4] But with what techniques and with what material assemblages is this dissolution accomplished? And who, in the end, is this subject who disappears?

Surveying the architectural panorama of the 1980s, David Harvey condemns the fetishism of the surface that he finds characteristic of populist efforts to extend architecture's symbolic capital to many "taste cultures" at once. Behind the postmodern mirror reflecting consumerist strategies of product differentiation, Harvey finds a sharper divide: "Free-market populism, for example, puts the middle class into the enclosed and protected spaces of shopping malls and atria, but it does nothing for the poor except to eject them into a new and quite nightmarish landscape of homelessness."[5] Thus, the veil of commodity fetishism is stripped away to reveal the actualities of structural poverty, hidden from view by the urban spectacle. But this expulsion of the poor from the defensible, populist enclaves of the middle class is not only a matter of economic access. It also entails—indeed, it *requires*—a retraining of perception, a process of technical mediation in which architecture also participates, in an equally structural and perhaps reciprocal way. As with the illusion of an illusion we have watched circulate through architecture's hall of mirrors, this retraining yields the perceptual paradox of a certain visible invisibility.

Like other surveyors of the postmodern scene, Harvey is able to arrive at his conclusions regarding urban spectacle with the help of Charles Jencks, whom, together with Robert Venturi and Denise Scott Brown, he takes as exemplary of postmodernism's cynical, stylistic eclecticism. Whereas his reference to "taste cultures" can be read here as a desublimation, from within the rhetorical surfaces of Las Vegas, of the sociological analytic developed by Herbert Gans in relation to Levittown on which Venturi and Scott Brown rely for their "populist" appreciation. This, however, is hardly an adequate point of departure for aesthetic analysis, which is only marginally better served by Jencks. In the 1984 (fourth, revised) edition of *The Language of Post-Modern Architecture* that Harvey cites, he finds Jencks attributing to newly developed techniques in "computer modelling" and automated production a degree of instrumentality that makes it possible for architects to design "almost personalized products" for clients possessed of heterogeneous tastes and stylistic proclivities collected together into the "world village" of global communications.[6] According to Harvey, the public sphere is effectively squeezed out of the resulting "emporium of styles," and with it public amenity and the common good. But this is more than mere aesthetic privatization, a turning inward that favors those in possession of the means of production and reproduction. It is a matter of production, reproduction, and re-reproduction in and of itself, in which the technical reproducibility of the modern masses, who also constitute the well-counted population of Foucault's biopolitics, is further abjected by the glare and sparkle of a new category of technically produced humans, a new kind of mass subject who must now be called a "person."

Much has been said in recent years about the role of computers in the production of architectural objects while relatively little has been said, in architecture, about their role in the production of subjects. Exhibiting an inherited stake in disciplinary autonomy, the vanguard that coalesced around computers during the 1990s in the American academy positioned itself as an Oedipalized heir to the neo-avant-gardes of the 1970s and 1980s, frequently claiming to have replaced the collage-like, fragmented objects associated with that period with a formal language of seamless integration. In an even more revised version of his original book, *The New Paradigm in Architecture: The Language of Post-Modernism* (2002), Jencks has joined many other commentators in assigning paradigmatic qualities to the new, computer-generated biomorphism that has emerged out of this assemblage.[7] Reproducing a version of Ernst Haeckel's "ontogeny recapitulates phylogeny" axiom, this biomorphism often explicitly mimics evolutionary development as individual units reproduce and combine. The "species being" of a mass-produced object and its correspondence with extra-individual needs and desires is thereby tempered, though not entirely superceded, by a technical and aesthetic emphasis on the uniqueness of each unit within an overall system. Unlike in the antimodernist humanism of a Ruskin or a Geoffrey Scott, both of whom were recovered for postmodernist discourse, this aesthetic uniqueness does not spring from the hand of the artist-creator but rather from the machine. While initially experimental, so-called parametric or nonstandard digital design and production techniques have now made their way into the professional mainstream.[8] And in nearly all cases they have sought—sometimes explicitly, sometimes implicitly—to replace the mechanical, fragmented, and repetitive mass ornament that Siegfried Kracauer saw embodied in the coordinated gyrations of the Tiller Girls with the rudiments of variable yet unified product line.[9]

Far from representing the latest innovation, however, this proposition was dreamed in advance by experimental architecture's corporate unconscious. As a result, and Jencks notwithstanding, with respect to the *corporate* architecture of the 1970s and 1980s, the newer *digital* architecture appears more symptomatic than innovative. While conversely, that same corporate architecture, in failing fully to domesticate its own aesthetic surplus, ultimately fails—despite itself—to confirm the absolute closure of a techno-economic system that seems increasingly to co-opt alterity and differentiation in advance. The complex architectural geometries made possible by the new softwares and hardwares produced and administered by transnational corporations may be of only secondary importance here, since these new technologies have also borne an old aesthetic promise that architecture has, by definition, long defied: the promise of a one-to-one match between representation and constructed reality. That is, computers promise to *collapse* the various stages in the production of buildings, which have heretofore run from exploratory sketch to presentation drawings to physical models to construction drawings to technical (or "shop") drawings executed by the fabricator to assembly in the field. If architecture has in that sense traditionally been a multimedia practice, not only is it now possible to model an object digitally and to "print" a three-dimensional version of it; it is also possible to fabricate the pieces of a building directly from computer files, with no intermediary representations. Carried to a logical conclusion, the new media thus promise an end to mediation itself—a condition where, in the language of computer interface designers, What-You-See-Is-What-You-Get (WYSIWYG).

A more concrete accompaniment to this dream of technical transparency has been enhanced flexibility in fabrication, since adjustments made in the computer can be transferred to production on demand with a minimum of intermediary steps and with minimal retooling, in a process known as mass customization. Though to date mainly implemented at the level of assembly in manufacturing, and at the level of information extraction in nonmanufacturing industries such as data mining and profiling (i.e., surveillance, for both marketing and "homeland security" purposes), such techniques are gradually entering the international construction industry. In principle, mass customization makes available to the consumer a rainbow of aesthetic and/or technical choices within parametrically variable tolerances. These parameters can be adjusted in a digital model to suit ever more personal preferences in a cascade of what Theodor Adorno long ago called pseudo-personalization, thus making each version of each product distinct from every other version produced and sold.

Contemporary architectural experimentation diagrams this new stage in consumer capitalism with such propositions as Greg Lynn's no-two-are-the-same "Embryologic Houses" of 2000, a mass-customized remake of Buckminster Fuller's utopian, mass-reproducible Dymaxion house. In an uncanny repetition of Jencks's ideological association of new forms of production with global consumerism aided and abetted by a transnational culture industry, Lynn has described his project (with no hint of irony) as "engag[ing] the need for any globally marketed product to have brand identity and variation within the same graphic and spatial system allowing both the possibility for recognition and novelty," since, as he puts it, "with the progressive saturations of our imaginations by an advanced media culture . . . a more advanced generic identity is . . . necessary for advanced domestic space."[10] In other words, a consumer who now imagines herself as different from (yet identified with) every other consumer must have objects to match. Thus we are also given Lynn's

Alessi tea service (2003), prototyped for some fifty thousand uniquely similar variations, as well as the something-for-everyone family of serially differentiated skyscrapers dancing around the memorial campfire of the global village that was proposed for Ground Zero in New York by the team that called itself the United Architects, of which Lynn and other proponents of a market-theological approach to mass customization were key members. If Kracauer saw the mechanical movements of the Tiller Girls and of the mass ornament as "demonstrations of mathematics," the parametric variation celebrated in these recent designs can be summarized as what Lynn has aptly called sketching with calculus.[11]

Further, the new forms of digitally aided *heimlichkeit* comprising integrated families of teapots, houses, and skyscrapers correspond not so much with a *depoliticization* of vanguardist architectural discourse as with a *repoliticization* on the order of Francis Fukuyama's neoliberal "end of history" thesis. In architecture, this was for a time given the embarrassingly frank name of "post-critical." Simply put, the "post-critical" posture (of which the United Architects group was exemplary) has sought to disengage architecture from any form of *emancipatory* politics implicit even in Manfredo Tafuri's critical melancholy, but *not* in order to secure architecture's silent, defeated autonomy, as Tafuri once suggested of a previous generation of architectural formalists led by Lynn's early sponsor, Peter Eisenman.[12] Rather, the new, metaphysical "post-criticality" has promised—in the manner of a politician—an unmediated intimacy, a millenarian transparency of production to consumption and, at the aesthetic level, of object to subject. In that sense, under the regime of the postcritical's technical correlate, mass customization, the personal is apparently postpolitical, since, in the seamlessly pliable network of personal choices thus called forth, conflict and dissent are assimilated into a pluralistic, managerial utopia of the sort that Rancière has dryly characterized as nurturing a "type of individual who lives in a permanent universe of freedom, of choice and of relaxed and lighthearted attitudes toward choice itself," in other words, "a world of self-pacified multiplicity" that announces, in the specifically political form of a promise, an "end" to politics itself.[13]

Similarly, the technical effort to do away with technical mediation ultimately promises to do away with architecture, in the historical sense of an aesthetic practice that actively mediates social relations, including relations of production and consumption. In contrast, to posit architecture as a mass medium here is to insist on a paradoxical, internally differentiated specificity, an obdurate historicity that is reducible *neither* to the posthistorical and postpolitical promises of technological processes *nor* to the late-modernist autonomy of architecture-as-such, remaining instead the basis for its own socioeconomic immanence. This immanence, however, is secured by virtue of aesthetic and technical developments specific to the discipline and manifest in its objects, where architecture's mirror reflects itself even as it reflects the work of history on the socioeconomic and political registers. On either side of this double mirror, we can see both in and out at once. In the interest of activating such a vision, a brief prehistory of the turn outlined above can be sketched in the form of a single, architectural case study involving two corporate headquarters designed about twenty years apart for the same company, the Union Carbide Corporation, by different architects in relation to changing social, economic, and technological conditions.

In August 1955, the Union Carbide Corporation announced that it would build its new executive headquarters in midtown Manhattan, at Park Avenue between Forty-seventh and Forty-eighth streets. The architect was to be the firm of Skidmore, Owings & Merrill (SOM), with Gordon Bunshaft (who had recently completed Lever House, a few blocks north) as chief designer. The decision was noteworthy not only because of its architectural implications but because Union Carbide had been considering moving its headquarters to a suburban site north of the city. To remain in Manhattan was to remain visible, a function amply satisfied by SOM's new building, which was described in the architectural press as first and foremost a "striking 'corporate image.'"[14]

Completed in 1960, the Union Carbide headquarters was a fifty-three-story skyscraper comprising 1.5 million gross square feet of sheer office building. Its presence on Park Avenue is announced by an attenuated plaza that sets the building's facade off from the street line, while a lower extension fills out the block and presents a secondary street facade on Madison Avenue. On the face of it, the tower's looming height thus monumentalizes the pinnacles of power—America's multinational corporations—that were gradually transforming this part of the city during the 1950s.

Like Lever House and the Seagram Building nearby, the architecture of the Union Carbide Headquarters might also seem the apotheosis of massification—an "enormous file" filled with robotlike workers, as the

Gordon Bunshaft of
Skidmore, Owings &
Merrill, Union Carbide
Headquarters, New York,
1960. Photograph by Ezra
Stoller. Copyright Esto.

sociologist C. Wright Mills described the new, modern office buildings
being built during the period.[15] To be sure, it has all the telltale signs:
a gridded, modular curtain wall, an empty plaza adjacent to an equally
empty lobby, rows and rows of desks, a gridded luminous ceiling, and
interchangeable, standardized office partitions. In other words, the
Union Carbide Building was a fully integrated and apparently seamless
system, the very image of the administrative rationality which Kracauer

had already discerned in the mass ornament. Mesmerized by the promise of a "total architecture" underwritten by the corporations, Bunshaft and SOM extended the building's systematicity into its most intimate details, including its desks, its filing cabinets, its drinking fountains, and its light switches.

And yet, the imagined subject of corporate capitalism under construction here was already changing from the masslike, robotic automatons projected by Mills into a new kind of human, the prototypical subject of what managers had called, since the 1930s, "human relations." At Union Carbide, the primary indicator for this was the building's overdetermined flexibility, registered visually in the grids and technically in the moveable, standardized units. This flexibility was correlated both to the unpredictable needs of a changing market as reflected in ongoing changes in Union Carbide's internal organization, as well as to the functional adaptability demanded of the human module out of which this organization was assembled, the so-called organization man. Despite his standardization, the organization man was no mere cog in a machine. He was, instead, a stereotypically sentient, emotional being who identified with the corporation as though it were his family, while adapting himself to the changes undergone by both with the postwar expansion of corporate capitalism. As such, the organization man was also in a sense made visible—mirrored even—by the architecture of buildings like the Union Carbide headquarters, with its stilted "flexibility."[16]

Likewise, though the postwar suburbanization of the United States appeared to maintain rigidly separate spheres for work and for living (the city and the suburb), the distance between these too was already collapsing. Thus, in 1978, in the wake of New York City's fiscal crisis, Union Carbide announced that it would abandon its Park Avenue building and relocate its headquarters to a new suburban facility in Danbury, Connecticut. By this point, the company had grown into a massive multinational conducting approximately 33 percent of its business outside the United States, with over 130 subsidiaries and five hundred manufacturing facilities in thirty-six countries worldwide. In addition to reflecting heightened anxieties about urban life among the managerial classes, the move out of New York reflected a complex tendency toward invisibility that accompanied global growth. As *Fortune* magazine put it that same year, despite its Park Avenue presence Union Carbide had been "a corporate giant that has somehow managed to project the public profile of a midget."[17] At the time of the move, however, it was (again according

Kevin Roche John Dinkeloo and Associates, Union Carbide Headquarters, Danbury, Connecticut, 1982. Aerial view. Courtesy of Kevin Roche John Dinkeloo and Associates.

to *Fortune*) "striving to raise its profile to something like true size." But this did not necessarily mean brazen swagger. Instead, it meant stealth, or what *Fortune* called "advocacy in a low key," in an effort to establish Union Carbide as a "responsible corporate citizen" in the eyes of government regulators, legislators, and others whose actions directly affected the company's bottom line. Union Carbide's new public relations strategy was, therefore, "to try to discern the popular will and then see how it can tailor its own interests to that sentiment."[18]

The design of its new headquarters coincided with this strategy. The site, located about an hour's drive from New York but only about twenty minutes' drive from the suburban domiciles of many managers, consisted of 645 acres of thick, gently rolling woodlands. And in stark contrast to the Park Avenue original, this new headquarters was to be visible in its entirety only from the air, with its architecture and entry sequence actively preventing full apprehension from the ground. Often described as a skyscraper turned on its side, the new complex for thirty-five hundred Union Carbide employees, designed by Kevin Roche of Kevin Roche John Dinkeloo and Associates and completed in 1982, can be more accurately described as a skyscraper turned inside out.

The selection of Roche was the first sign of a cultural shift, to the extent that Union Carbide's management had, according to Roche, been taken by his assertion that "office design should come from the people."[19] In turn, Roche's design for the new headquarters was a self-conscious response to the earlier SOM building—an attempt to further "humanize" what, despite the inroads made by the human relations counselors into the organization man's soul, would still have appeared as a modular abstraction, its curtain-walled facade folded onto every surface and into every detail of its gridded interiors. Thus Roche began the design with an exhaustive analysis of the existing headquarters, including extensive employee interviews. One finding was that employees objected to the spatial hierarchies still allowed by the existing building. Despite its egalitarian pretensions, the flexible partition system had in fact enabled offices of different sizes to be distributed to workers of different rank, while the building's urban location and monolithic configuration yielded select corner offices with double views that could be likewise rationed.[20]

Roche's response was to develop a set of technical parameters based on the variable iterability of a single unit of space: an individual office. Regardless of rank, each worker would receive 180 square feet of private office space, with each unit possessing an equivalent but different view of the surrounding forest. Environmental control was likewise personalized, with each office for each employee equipped with separate lighting and temperature controls, so that each could surround him- or (significantly for the corporate imagination of the late 1970s) herself with the climate of choice. Thus the design problem became fundamentally topological: thirty-three hundred units of space had to be organized in relation to one another and to the outdoors to achieve a new, architectural parity.

Due to its incipient capacity to model with quantitative exactitude multiple variations of a given problem, the computer was called in as a design tool (a practice still relatively uncommon at the time).[21] A number of diagrams were tested and rejected, beginning with a 2.6-mile-long tube of continuously varying dimension, from minimum to maximum, which allowed proportional as well as dimensional variation in the individual offices and other (larger) program spaces arrayed along its length, while affording the requisite equality of view. Other rejected schemes included a spine with bristles in which offices would wind up facing each other instead of the trees, as well as a multiple courtyard scheme with a similar problem. The organization that was ultimately selected (and realized in modified form) had the fractal-like, crenellated perimeter of a snowflake. The units themselves were oriented at forty-five-degree angles to one

Kevin Roche John Dinkeloo and Associates, Union Carbide Headquarters, Danbury, Connecticut, 1982. Preliminary layout of office cluster. Courtesy of Kevin Roche John Dinkeloo and Associates.

another in clusters strung along the edge of the snowflake, thus affording the desired view without compromising privacy.

Dropped onto the site and surrounded by the requisite parking, however, the snowflake became a kind of alien spacecraft that would have exposed Union Carbide's new home to full public view. Alternative massing studies were thus undertaken, resulting in a gently curved bar that could be inserted surgically into a contoured open field with minimum disruption. The inside-out design of the building that had begun by equilibrating the views from within each office was completed with the internalization of the parking into a series of multilevel garages with access bridges matched to the office clusters, thus enabling workers to drive in and park adjacent to their offices. The office building was now effectively one terminal in a continuous interior, in which these knowledge workers could move almost seamlessly from their house to their garage to their car to their garage to their office, and back again, day after day. There was no need to go outside.

It should not be surprising, then, that the extent to which this design also *re*designed—indeed customized—the subject of corporate capitalism is measured most accurately on the interiors of the offices themselves. Roche Dinkeloo developed thirty different office styles ranging

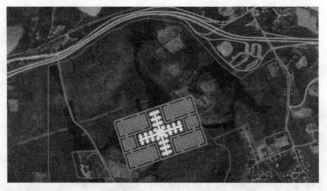

Kevin Roche John Dinkeloo and Associates, Union Carbide
Headquarters, Danbury, Connecticut, 1982. Preliminary site plan.
Courtesy of Kevin Roche John Dinkeloo and Associates.

Kevin Roche John Dinkeloo and Associates, Union Carbide
Headquarters, Danbury, Connecticut, 1982. Preliminary plan.
Courtesy of Kevin Roche John Dinkeloo and Associates.

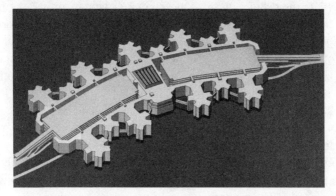

Kevin Roche John Dinkeloo and Associates, Union Carbide
Headquarters, Danbury, Connecticut, 1982. Axonometric.
Courtesy of Kevin Roche John Dinkeloo and Associates.

Kevin Roche John Dinkeloo and Associates, Union Carbide
Headquarters, Danbury, Connecticut, 1982. Office interior, mock-up.
Courtesy of Kevin Roche John Dinkeloo and Associates.

from what they called "very modern to traditional," with each set of furniture and accessories costing exactly the same, again to avoid any insinuation of class (whether on the basis of rank or of aspiration). Full-scale mock-ups of each office style were built, complete with simulated forest view (again: an apparently unmediated transparency, or WYSIWYG). These were displayed to three thousand employees, who were then interviewed for their choice of carpet, desk, counter, light fixture, plants, pens and pencils, and ashtrays. Each choice was input into a computerized purchasing database. A design was output. Thus also, fourteen categories of art were offered to decorate these thirty offices, from figurative to abstract. The final purchases were made on the basis of percentages drawn from the employee surveys. Roche himself asserted that "I felt, very strongly, that we should not impose our design aesthetic on people; let them choose as they wished," a strategy that was, as he put it, a "radical idea at the time."[22] As it turned out, no imposition was necessary. The furniture set designed in-house by the Roche office was reportedly the most popular selection, with second place going to an office with what Roche called a "very conservative desk," while least popular of all was the "contemporary" office with glass tabletop and chrome legs (too flashy, it seems).[23]

This level of detail is relevant here only to insist on the systematic, inside-out nature of this reinvention of Union Carbide's corporate identity, since not only does the new personalization reach into every detail of corporate life but it involves at every step a biopolitical refashioning of employees themselves into "persons" equipped with variable tastes, individual lifestyles, and eventually, personal computers. Thus did Union Carbide announce, in its annual report of 1981 as the building was nearing completion at the height of an economic recession, its new "emphasis on people," otherwise known as "human resources" or, in the terms in which Foucault reads American neoliberalism, "human capital."[24] As the company's chairman and CEO Warren M. Anderson put it in his letter to stockholders: "Union Carbide is a good place to work, and we are determined to make it an even better one, with opportunity and incentive for every employee to become *personally involved* in our objectives and our progress."[25]

But it is equally clear that Union Carbide did not regard all of its constituents as "persons," and perhaps not even as humans. On the night of 2 December 1984, two years after Roche's building was completed, forty-five tons of the lethal gas methyl isocyanate (MIC) leaked from a poorly maintained storage tank at the Union Carbide battery and pesticide manufacturing plant in Bhopal, India. The body count remains indeterminate. Though the Indian authorities stopped counting at 1,754, official government estimates put the immediate death toll at approximately thirty-eight hundred (roughly equivalent to the number of well-maintained persons housed in Union Carbide's Danbury headquarters).[26] Unofficial estimates of the death toll run to more than three times that much, and the consensus among activists and survivors groups hovers between seven thousand and ten thousand in the immediate aftermath and twenty thousand in the years that followed.[27] An estimated half a million people were injured, many severely and permanently. Most of the victims, including an unknown number of Union Carbide employees (so-called human resources), lived in the shadow of the plant and were overcome by the gas as they slept. Many were from the poorest classes of Indian society and lacked identification documents such as citizenship papers, marriage certificates, or land deeds, and were often omitted from official census counts.[28] Mass burials and mass cremations left fewer bodies accessible to officials, which meant that such records were often the only available evidence that someone had existed in the first place.

Union Carbide and its affiliates never stood trial in India. Anderson, the CEO who had announced Union Carbide's new "emphasis on people," was arrested upon his arrival in Bhopal but released on bail. In 1986 he retired, and he has never returned to India to face the criminal charges against him, despite a formal extradition request from the Indian government. Unsuccessful efforts in the United States to sue on behalf of the victims for a sum of U.S. $15 billion were met by the argument from the company's lawyers that, as one observer put it, "an American court was not competent to assess the value of a human life in the third world. 'How can one determine the damage inflicted on people who live in shacks?' asked one member of the legal team. 'An American life is worth approximately five hundred thousand dollars,' wrote the *Wall Street Journal*, 'taking into account the fact that India's gross national product is 1.7 percent of that of the United States, the court should compensate for the decease of each Indian victim proportionately, that is to say with eight thousand five hundred dollars.'"[29]

In 1985, the government of India passed the Bhopal Act, which consolidated all claims against Union Carbide and authorized the state to represent the interests of the victims, who were declared incompetent by virtue of their suffering and whose voices were thereby disallowed. In 1989, the government, which harbored its own conflicts of interest regarding the risks and rewards of multinational "development," settled out of court with Union Carbide for U.S. $470 million. The first round of compensation occurred in the early 1990s, and by late 2004, on the twentieth anniversary of the catastrophe, each affected family expected to receive between one hundred thousand and two hundred thousand rupees—about U.S. $2,150–$5,300 (including fifteen years of interest) or roughly 5 percent of the American "standard."[30] According to activists, by 2006 compensation had been made for only about six hundred deaths, while approximately half a million disability claims had been filed, with an average compensation of U.S. five hundred dollars each.[31] But beyond the grossly diminished numerical value placed on the lives of the victims, the larger point here has to do with the extraordinary fragility of this elementary form of representation—counting—as a dimension of the epistemic violence that we have seen reproduced in the apparently humane architecture at Danbury.

Evidence suggests that the "persons" in Danbury were aware in advance of the risks to the rather more abstract corporate subjects in Bhopal, where Union Carbide had minimized its own economic exposure through cost-cutting in the event the plant was nationalized under Indian legislation.[32] The global outrage, however, did not reach the fever pitch that became familiar in the United States in the wake of 11 September 2001, demanding instant, total, and personalized commemoration of each and every victim. The company erected no memorials, listed no names, published no pictures. Instead, it circulated sabotage theories while divesting itself of its assets to protect against litigation. Thus, in 1987 the company sold its already invisible Danbury headquarters and adjacent development rights to the Related Companies, a real estate group, becoming a leaseholding tenant in its own building.[33] In 1999, Union Carbide itself disappeared, though not because it was bankrupted by the relatively scant settlement but because it too was assimilated into an even larger network operating in 168 countries and employing forty-nine thousand people, having been bought by Dow Chemical.

What, then, of architecture here? Back in Danbury circa 1990, a Union Carbide executive noted that the company's response to what he called the "shock" of Bhopal was to reemphasize its social responsibilities, while also noting that the move to Danbury had itself succeeded in converting Union Carbide managers from alienated commuters to active members of the local community, for whom "diversity is the new name that's creeping into everybody's language."[34] Roche had already accommodated this diversified corporate community in, for example, a cafeteria divided into six unique sections dedicated to six different lifestyles, including a back room modeled on a men's club and a singles bar. But in commenting on his firm's design practices Roche seems to see a ghost in the ubiquitous mirrored surfaces adorning these pseudo-public interiors, or "living rooms," as he called them. For him, these mirrors were "constantly alive" as they reflected both the "sparkle" and "dark spots" of the "real world."[35] Designed by an architect who, as an associate of Eero Saarinen, had produced the first mirrored-glass curtain wall at Bell Laboratories in Holmdel, New Jersey, in 1962, the mirrors thereby distill architecture's paradoxical, noncommunicative specificity as mass medium, as they move from exterior (at Bell Labs) to interior (at Union Carbide).

Kevin Roche John Dinkeloo and Associates, Union Carbide Headquarters, Danbury, Connecticut, 1982. Cafeteria. Courtesy of Kevin Roche John Dinkeloo and Associates.

Initially, the mirrors may be interpreted as a response to Roche's teacher Mies, whose Federal Center in Chicago had been described by Tafuri and Francesco Dal Co as a mirror "reflecting images of the urban chaos that surrounds the timeless Miesian purity."[36] But in contrast to Mies, the mirrors at Union Carbide promise—again, in the manner of a politician—to make visible (indeed, to reflect) the new corporate subject, a person at home in the domestic interior of the office. Here is Roche: "[W]e tried to deinstitutionalize the building so that it seemed lively or more domestic, in a character appropriate to a corporate family."[37] But as in the curtain wall at Bell Laboratories, in these interiors there remains— rather literally, as Roche implies—nothing in the mirror, only agitated blurs and glancing highlights that refuse to coalesce. Thus, where Kracauer had found in the unconscious "surface-level" expressions of the mass ornament what he took to be "unmediated access to the fundamental substance of the state of things," we might discover something like the reverse at work in Union Carbide's mirrored halls: a barely discernible gap or hole in the surface giving access to otherwise invisible mediations and to an actively produced exclusion on the supposedly unmediated *interior* of a diversified corporate self.[38]

Here too we might also glimpse an inadvertent perceptual denaturalization, a momentary yet persistent estrangement that is also an internal multiplication. To see such a depersonalization is indirectly to see those in Bhopal whose "bare life" was not opposed to but *constitutive of* the well-adorned personhood cultivated in Danbury. And I again use Giorgio Agamben's terminology advisedly here, recalling that we have already explored the topologies that it implies. *Homo sacer*, the ambiguous figure from ancient Roman jurisprudence who may be killed with impunity but not sacrificed, is Agamben's name for all those who live without the protections of the law, a state of affairs for which the death camp is the defining instance.[39] And while Union Carbide's plant and its surroundings were not a camp, and the catastrophe was widely publicized, the all too visible invisibility of the Bhopal victims and the partial suspension of what might be termed their political right to be *counted* as dead, dying, or permanently impaired locates them—in only a slightly less literal sense—tendentiously in the space of *Homo sacer*, the subject of "bare" or "naked" life.

Under such conditions, unseen/uncounted also describes a subjectivity that is not unmediated but rather inaccessible to the spectacular mediation that is scaled down to the personal level under mass customization. And though their own lives are thereby constrained (again tendentiously) by relative exteriority, the labor of those who are quite visibly invisible to the spectacle remains necessary for the consumer-masses of mass customization to come into view—indeed, to enter the field of visibility as "persons." In "incidents" such as the Bhopal catastrophe, the act of counting thus approaches the limit case of deaths that are counted abstractly (as calculated risk) while remaining uncounted in actuality; as such, they are inextricably linked to the predatory expansion of multinational capital. These deaths cruelly rehearse the logic of the "life that does not deserve to live" uncovered by Agamben, a cruelty that is underpinned by a structural, technologically enabled blindness (a consequence of Rancière's "distribution of the sensible") that must itself be brought into view.[40]

Conversely, the architectural trajectory followed by the two Union Carbide headquarters actively consolidates what Gilles Deleuze called the "dividuation" (or infinitely divisible, distinguishable coding) that increasingly characterizes a mode of subjectivity immanent to global capital.[41] To this we can add that the "dividual" further appears as a subject converted into a numerical variable in a new form of mass—or now, mass-customized—ornament. This visibility imposes itself in a manner comparable to that of universal computation (or universal computability, as Alan Turing would have it). Like the mass ornament before it, the parametrically regulated technical means by which this is achieved in architecture and other domains begins and ends with numbers. The historical difference with respect to modernism is that, rather than marking an optimized standard to which design and production must conform, the new postmodern numbers enumerate and serialize difference itself. But in its new figuration as an instrument of choice under mass customization, the computer's supposed universality, translated into a capacity to register near-infinite differentiation, already contains within it something like a built-in limit case in the form of a constantly shifting horizon of visibility and of counting.

What cannot be seen or heard cannot be counted, except as a calculated risk. Whereas, at the other pole, what *can* be seen reveals a threshold also built into Kracauer's notion of the mass ornament. As an organized figure "composed of elements that are mere building blocks and nothing more," Kracauer attributed to the mass ornament a rationality closed off from reason that reflects the calculability demanded by capitalist production. This leads, among other things, to a "blurring of national characteristics and to the production of worker masses that can be employed equally well at any point on the globe."[42] Its precondition (as well as its endpoint) is the socioeconomic and technological process of massification, whereby "only as parts of a mass, not as individuals who believe themselves to be formed from within, do people become fractions of a figure."[43] Under mass customization, massification has been scaled down to the level of the "person." But this person is no longer understood in classically humanist terms as a bounded individual in possession of a unique and unassailable soul, a figure that Kracauer had already judged anachronistic with respect to the earlier phase of modernity he was describing. A person, now, is a techno-economic figure composed of numbers inside and out.

In biopolitical terms, such a figure is theoretically customizable under a computationally intensive human genomics as well as under a computationally enabled, expansionist corporate consumerism and the subjectivities it proliferates. Similarly, outward industrial expansion, exemplified in this case by India's chemically enhanced "green revolution," of which the Union Carbide pesticide plant was a part, is now accompanied by an expansion inward, into the interiority of the self. So even as the "mass ornament" might still be useful to describe the homogenizing reach of industrial capital into new global frontiers, it reaches its limit case internally as those frontiers begin to turn inward. For this, a complementary figure—the "person," a modified incarnation of *homo œconomicus* whom Foucault calls an "entrepreneur of himself"—must be articulated alongside the mass ornament. Such an articulation makes visible the spectacle of (in)dividuation inside the corporate self made possible by numerical abstraction, as well as that spectacle's dependence on its blind spots, the plainly visible invisibility of others whose deaths remain effectively uncounted, even as those same deaths are incorporated as a variable in the spreadsheets of global capital.[44]

Thus we arrive at a somewhat counterintuitive formulation. At one level, the subjective by-product of the cybernetic revolution is not a faceless, digital automaton, but a hyper-individuated, spectacularized quasi-singularity, composed of ever finer (and potentially incommensurable) data sets that profile personal taste, personal habits, personal opinion, and so on. While at another level, a complementary by-product of informatization is ultimately the heterogeneous subject of "bare life" whose death is not counted and therefore does not count. This is the horror of Bhopal and of so many other such catastrophes. In these, the biopolitical machinery of computational equivalence—enumeration, that is, and with it, interpolation into Deleuze's control society as a mathematical variable otherwise known as a "person"—functions increasingly via a symmetrical exclusion from counting and indeed from visibility, as an exception that has become internalized or rather *incorporated* as a norm. The relative invisibility of the deindividuated Bhopal victims (stripped of even the mass ornament of enumeration) has thus helped foreclose their access to jurisprudence while also helping, along with the company's own invisibility at the level of the cultural imaginary, to ensure Union Carbide's survival under the sign of Dow Chemical.

Still, as a biopolitical machine designed to make the personalized subject of global capital visible to itself, and thereby to rehearse the process of narcissistic self-identification, architecture here cannot help but register a kind of splitting open that releases a depersonalized remainder. This comes in the form of an outside marked on the inside by a shimmering blind spot, whose spectral presence organizes the deepest interiors of corporate domesticity. In that sense, the Union Carbide headquarters in Danbury was from beginning haunted by the ghosts of Bhopal, on behalf of whom, as an act of counter-memory, we may now claim it as a kind of inverted memorial—a memorialization in advance. This haunting, this commemoration in the future anterior tense, takes the form of an irreducible abstraction that, in effect, transcends the numerical abstraction of the mass ornament that is sublimated into mass customization. This other, postmodern abstraction is most directly visible in the mirrored surfaces that line the building's interior. But it is also discernible elsewhere: in the mechanical emptiness of the parking garages, for example (which offer a kind of final resting place for the mass ornament in their rows of empty machines), as well as in the less obvious emptiness of the office itself, to say nothing of the view out the window and today into the windows of the personal computer. As seen in these surfaces, the "person" called forth by mass customization is him/herself doubly spectral: first, in the Derridean sense read out of Shakespeare via Marx, of a fetishized commodity in which the social relations among things associated with industrial capital have been transformed into social relations among images; and second, in the sense of a having incorporated an otherwise invisible, and only apparently silent, counterpart.

To see or to hallucinate a ghost in the empty halls of the transnational corporate edifice is hardly to excuse the blind and systematic enthusiasm with which architecture continues to service a hegemonic world order. On the contrary, it is to locate strategically its internal aporias, the holes in the screen of mass-customized bliss. We cannot claim, with paternalistic sanctimony, to speak directly through these holes on behalf of a subaltern, or even to offer an equivocal opening onto visibility per se. "Please come here and count us." How, then, might we hear this appeal made by a Bhopal survivor to the judges of the Supreme Court of India who upheld the state's authority to represent those whom, like this woman, it deemed incapable of representing themselves.[45] As the muffled cry of a distant "other"? Or as an echo reverberating through the very headquarters of empire that marks the blind spots necessary for the apparatus to reproduce itself with ever-greater efficiency?

Today, this reproduction occurs most perversely in the name of a postpolitical multiplicity, a pseudopersonalization embraced by corporate global villagers and computer-aided architects alike. Yet what we see in these mirrored interiors, which perhaps mark the end of corporate architecture's mirror stage, is not our *selves* projected outward—customized masses converted into persons—but the names and faces of unrecognizable strangers within, for whom the personal remains political, both out there and in here.

. . .

The bourgeois interior was for Kracauer, as for Walter Benjamin, at once a last refuge for authentic individuality and a warehouse of empty memories cut out of lived time, most vividly in the photographs that lined its shelves. One branch of the historical arc followed by this spatial type has taken it into the suburban American living room, decoded in the mid-1970s by Venturi and Scott Brown for its "signs of life," and simultaneously back out into the ex-urban corporate office complex, where it has functioned less as a shell than as a screen. An inside-out mirror: that is how we can describe such a space—but also as Leibniz's "windowless monad," reflecting, in Adorno's trenchant analysis, the unremitting chaos of capitalist disharmonies, now inverted to reflect nothing at all. That this "nothing" is also very much *something,* a life, a population of humans under erasure, is what I have tried to show in the brief history that runs through two office buildings within one hundred miles of each other and a factory that, for the organizational complex to which it was nevertheless hardwired, might just as well have been on another planet.

This is also a way of touching something of the sublime that Fredric Jameson, with Lyotard audible in the distance, has identified as central to the aesthetic experience of postmodern space. But just as postmodernist pastiche mocks whatever might qualify as "beautiful" in architectural form, so too does the postmodern sublime invert the natural threat that both Burke and Kant posited as its origin. In Bhopal, as in Don Delillo's "airborne toxic event" in *White Noise,* as well as in the gas chambers that both distantly recall, the ominous cloud, unrepresentable as it is, is in the first instance a product of human calculation, and in Bhopal in particular of calculated environmental risk. It is a metonymic product of the difficult (but not impossible) to visualize "networks of multi-national capitalism" that are the ultimate target of Jameson's analysis. And among this new sovereign's (perhaps unwilling) subjects are those who, it must be said, are subjected to its threats *without a choice.* This subjection is founded on a certain *Existenzminimum* not only at the level of biological needs but also at the level of representation. That this form of unfreedom is both a consequence of and a precondition for the technologically mediated "freedom" to choose from among a surplus of mass-customized lifestyles prototyped on the supermarket shelves of culture is among the cruelest ironies of the current conjuncture.

7 ARCHITECTURE
Utopia's Ghost

WHAT IS TO BE DONE? Start from the beginning and reopen the "housing question."[1] Recall the example of public housing as emblematic of the allegedly failed modernist utopia par excellence. Recall also that this corresponds with a boundary problem that summarizes the discursive economy of postmodernism—the ostensible problem of distinguishing what is real from what is not. Historical attempts to confront real irrationalities such as the failure of the state adequately to house its population are, time and again, converted discursively into phantasms, such as the straw figure called "Pruitt-Igoe." These, in turn, are summoned as "realistic" cautions against too-ambitious plans to address the ongoing failures. In this way, cultural postmodernism has continued to serve as a training manual for the systematic abjection of human life accomplished in other spheres. A plausible response might therefore be to derealize the real. Derealization, however, must be accomplished at two levels. First, by interrogating critically the "givens" assumed by anticritical realisms. And second, by restoring the "unreal"—i.e., Utopia—to its proper status as a kind of performative. In other words, derealization means learning to think at the intersection of representation and production. And it means doing so through the mediation of cultural forms, including architecture.

Not in order to build utopias but to live with their ghosts. As discursive figures, ghosts embody a host of boundary problems of their own. Corollary to the postmimetic mirror, the ghost poses the question of projection, which can be defined as crossing the line that separates what exists from what does not. At first, projection may seem a simple enough matter of making projects, that is, of inventing still-unrealized (and perhaps unrealizable) alternatives to what exists, and thrusting them forward into the future as a kind of ideal target or negatively, as a dystopian or apocalyptic warning. In practice, however, projection of any sort entails far more complex rearrangements of past, present, and future. An architectural project is therefore any work in which what may once have been threatens, in the present, to return transfigured at some unspecified future time. Utopia is a special type of project, since it threatens to replace what exists in its entirety. Thus the messianic overtones of many utopianisms, as well as the barely disguised nostalgia for some long-lost wholeness or state of nature that they often exhibit. But in the same sense that spectrality is also a functional property of finance capital oriented toward the management of the future, there is no guarantee that projection entails systemic transformation. For just on the other side of the line, in the realm of everyday practice, lies the professionalization of projection, and its consequent setting aside as an instrument of critical thought.

Utopian projection has been part of the architect's tool kit since the European eighteenth century, having theretofore largely been the domain of literature and, to some extent, painting.[2] In the nineteenth and early twentieth centuries, it was amplified with the assimilation of a Romantic melancholy, a process that reached symbolic maturity in the United States in the figure and work of Frank Lloyd Wright and, in Europe, in that of Le Corbusier. During the first half of the twentieth century, the architect as professional melancholic was diversely characterized by compensatory meditations on the loss and reconstitution of nature under modernization (Wright), or by the choice—forced by Le Corbusier—between the reform of everyday life ("architecture") and the overthrow of its structures ("revolution"). Either way, these were all-or-nothing propositions, the totality of which was figured less in the intricate detail with which so many of the resulting utopian "solutions" were endowed than in the panoramic dimensions of their original, binary configuration: nature *or* culture, architecture *or* revolution.

In the West (but also, for example, in Japan), the latter part of the twentieth century saw the gradual and uneven replacement of this professional melancholy with an almost manic playfulness. Whether in the neofuturism embodied in the 1960s megastructures, in the helpless sarcasm of the Italian *architettura radicale,* or in Pop attempts to reground architectural "communication," this playfulness would seem already to correspond with the agonistic play of one language game off of another and thereby to exhibit a key symptom of the "postmodern condition" more generally.[3] The search for a ludic authenticity found its complement in the archaism of an eternal present, from the organic gemeinschaft sought in various "vernacular" and non-Western milieux (by Team X and others) to symbolic expeditions into the standing reserve of history itself. The past (or, for the environmental movement, nature) was no longer irretrievably lost to aesthetic re-presentation; rather, history was made newly available as a simulacrum, in the form of recombined citational elements, just as nature reappeared indexically through compilations of data, whereas futurology and its many popular and technical variants, which as we have seen were encapsulated in the epistemologies of risk analysis, systematically recast the future as merely one (albeit, potentially catastrophic) scenario among others, rather than as a unifying ideal.

In this respect, if there was something like an epistemological crisis associated with the emergence of the postmodern in and around archi-tecture, it entailed a transformation of the (modernist) crisis of represen-tation into a *crisis of projection*. This is somewhat different than suggest-ing, with Manfredo Tafuri, that architectural postmodernism played out a crisis of the *project*.[4] To put it as succinctly as possible, a *project* is an ideological phantasm, while *projection* is a concrete historical and dis-cursive practice, with utopian thought as one of its by-products. And so my analysis shifts attention away from the ideological claims and counterclaims made by architects and their apologists vis à vis the duty (or the capacity) of architecture to make yet another "knight's move" on the chessboard of modernity.[5] Instead, I focus on the rules admitted by that chessboard itself, which evolved to prohibit certain acts of imagina-tive projection while permitting other, new ones. All of which produced new problems for architecture and for architectural knowledge, though often in the form of ideological pseudosolutions to old ones.

Among these rules are those of projection itself, which, as Erwin Panofsky showed as early as 1927, are eminently historical and therefore subject to revision.[6] Without really setting out to do so, Panofsky's essay on perspective demonstrates the technical contingencies by which any attempt to construct a "picture" of a possible future is necessarily con-strained. For it should not be forgotten that those melancholic futurisms that were later subject to the postmodern totality/totalitarian elision, metonymically captured in Le Corbusier's Ville Contemporaine (1922) or in Wright's Broadacre City (1932), were most compellingly represented in panoramic, perspectival visualizations. Nor should it be forgotten that underlying these representations was the Cartesian grid, which became the very emblem of modernist "rationality" as the latter came under postmodern attack. In short, the grid as a unifying and coordinating device, whether of pictorial or planimetric space (and allowing for the differences between the two), was simultaneously reified and displaced in a series of discursive moves that reconfigured the postmodern playing field into something that could now only be grasped as an unstable matrix composed of a thousand plateaus.

Under these conditions, the projection of radical alternatives to the status quo was not merely ideologically tainted. It was technically impossible. Utopia was *made* impossible by the new configuration of the playing field, the new instrumentation, and the new rules of engagement. But what I hope to show here is something like the survival of the old rules and the old techniques in the shell or skin of the new, which combine with this skin in surprising and possibly underdeveloped ways. This is the first dimension of a spectrality with which the apparent arbitrariness and abruptness of an epistemic modulation is infused. Given my (and our) relative embeddedness within this discursive formation, I have been willing to accept for the moment the overall proposition that it entails a shift from one (modern) regime to another (postmodern) one. But for no reason other than historical accuracy I am also compelled to note the incompleteness of this supposed shift, and the persistence or afterimage of a specific form of modernist vision—the act of projection—within postmodernism's games, whether they are semantic, technological, or formal.

On the order of discourse, the possibility of a still-utopian imagination, half alive (or at least, to speak in the terminology of the ghost, undead) within the postmodern edifice, suggests a very peculiar set of options. Any attempt at revival, whether historiographical or actual, would seem as "unrealistic" (or really, as "postmodern") as any attempt at exorcism, since what is specifically *real* about a ghost is its constitutive unreality. Instead, the one positive option before us would seem to be, to paraphrase Jacques Derrida, to learn to live with modernism's ghosts, preeminent among which I count the ghost of Utopia itself.[7] That particular ghost occupies the site of projection in which past, present, and future meet at a single threshold. Also at this site, power, knowledge, and art mix to form new compounds with new possible outcomes. In that sense, Utopia is one among many ghosts that appear here like so many uninvited visitors to the postmodern scene.[8] Such visitations suggest that, with architecture's help, we might yet discover postmodernism's paradoxical modernity. Today, at a moment when there also seems increasingly less likelihood of an exit from the cul-de-sac that we call globalization and its crises, as managed by transnational corporations, empire-building nations, and even well-meaning NGOs, there can indeed be no more urgent task than to learn to live with—and to think—Utopia once again. This is another way of saying: to begin the hard work of learning to imagine again that, in a favorite slogan of the new social movements, "another world is possible."

"Learning to live with ghosts" also defines a limit case, in the form of the horizon of (in)visibility within which the implied constituents or subjects of any project are confined, and from which those without access to its promises are excluded. This dynamic of inclusion and exclusion maps a topology of projection with which any effort to rethink the postmodern impasse must also grapple. But even the term *horizon,* with its perspectival overtones, is inadequate to describe the reconfiguration of inside and outside that is at stake here. More than mere trespassers, ghosts are poised on what we must recognize as the biopolitical threshold of life and death. Hence, they haunt the premises of any self-satisfied interior, including some of the actual spaces we have already encountered— domestic interiors, corporate offices, gated communities, and so on. But even more, *Utopia's* ghost haunts the presumed interior of a discourse in which, as Tafuri notoriously said of his contemporaries and their historical revivals, architects have been content to "gather round the hearth and listen to the fables of the new grannies."[9]

And so we begin again with a short trip backward in time, to Venice circa 1980: "A spectre is roaming through Europe: The Postmodern."[10] This is how the Italian architect and critic Paolo Portoghesi introduced his book on postmodernism in architecture, which was subtitled *The Architecture of the Postindustrial Society* and published in Italian in 1982 and in English in 1983. Portoghesi's introductory sentence was a double quotation. It was the title of an article published in the French newspaper *Le Monde* on the occasion of the traveling exhibition known as *La Strada Novissima* (The New Street). Unlike Disneyland's Main Street, which leads to Fantasyland and to a mythical, stereotyped future, the Strada Novissima appears to lead nowhere in particular; but more precisely, as we shall see, it leads inward and outward at once. Still, it was an important document in the production of the postmodernist imaginary: a full-scale, multi-architect "street" replete with historical quotations. It served as the centerpiece of the first official architecture biennale in Venice, which was curated by Portoghesi in 1980 and later traveled to both Paris and San Francisco. While the *Le Monde* headline, of course, was itself a historical quotation, or really, a paraphrase, of the oft-cited opening line of *The Communist Manifesto,* which was translated into English (with the approval of Engels) as follows: "A specter is haunting Europe—the specter of Communism."[11]

The stated theme of the 1980 Biennale, "The Presence of the Past," was intended to evoke a burgeoning interest in historical citation on the part of architects on both sides of the Atlantic as well as in Japan. By the early 1950s, a hegemonic international modernism, expressed by such enigmas as "functionalism," was thought to have relegated architectural styles like Beaux Arts classicism to the dustbin of history. But by 1980, following the political, economic, and technological cataclysms of the 1960s and the early 1970s, modernism itself was thought by many to belong to that same dustbin, with its utopian aspects reduced to historical curiosities if not Faustian nightmares. And so in Venice "The Presence of the Past" referred to the proclivity among architects to scavenge history's dustbin for obsolescent languages and styles, sometimes earnestly and sometimes irreverently but always against the prohibitions enforced by modernist dogma.

Needless to say, neither the Strada Novissima nor any other manifestation of such tendencies succeeded in restoring the historical "past" to full presence in architectural terms. Arguably, this was never the intention in the first place, though certainly many claims were made on behalf of a return to past architectures for their restorative moral capacity, especially in the face of traumas visited upon both urban form and civic representation by the rigors of functionalism and associated doctrines. Still, the 1980 Biennale's "historicism" emphatically *did not* result in a simple resurrection of historical styles. Instead, visitors were presented with a cacophony of pseudoevents, pseudorestorations, and pseudorevivals— in a word, pastiche.

But to describe these as pastiche does not exhaust their meaning. More recently, Marx and Engels's famous line provided a subtext for Derrida's conjurations of the undead spirits of German idealism that haunt Marx's historical materialism, while at the same time conjuring the spirits of Marx and Marxism that neoliberalism, especially after 1989, claimed finally to have exorcised. Derrida calls this logic of haunting a "hauntology" (as distinct from an ontology), which he means us to take

Venice Biennale, La Strada Novissima, 1980. From Paolo Portoghesi, *Postmodern: The Architecture of the Postindustrial Society,* trans. Ellen Shapiro (New York: Rizzoli, 1983).

fairly literally. To illustrate, he begins with a reading of Hamlet, concentrating not on the characters but on the stage props, in this case the suit of armor in which the father's ghost appears (or seems to appear) onstage, his face concealed by the helmet's visor. Derrida calls this the "visor effect," in which a specter appears indirectly, through its concealment under a visor—as a stage prop, that is—and looks at us. With the scenographic, stage-set qualities of the Strada Novissima in view (and noting that its facades were actually constructed in the Italian cinematic dream factory Cinecittà), I hope therefore to make visible, indirectly, the specters of Utopia as they stare us in the face through the visor of architectural postmodernism.

The great majority of modern and protomodern utopian architectural propositions from Ledoux to Le Corbusier have entailed making a picture of an idealized world—a project, that is—and then launching it like a projectile into the future. Oddly enough, the entry of this utopian image into the real, its moment of impact as it were, necessarily marks the millennial—or apocalyptic—end of history, in the sense of an ongoing historical dialectic: when and if Utopia actually arrives, it's all over. Postmodernism and modernism thus share aspects of the "end of history" endgame, though they approach this end from opposite directions: modernism through the messianic realization of redemptive metanarratives (whether utopian or otherwise), and postmodernism through the exhaustion of all such narratives, which now seem to have broken up into a thousand little stories.[12] These are no longer represented in panoramic perspectives and all-or-nothing master plans but rather in two reciprocal forms of incompleteness: narrative fragments and statistical, probabilistic tendencies.

Consider again the faux-historical "timeline" of postmodernism included by Charles Jencks in *The Language of Post-Modern Architecture*. The teleological, from–to narratives of the modernist avant-gardes, conditioned by a Hegelian zeitgeist, have been replaced here with an image of architectural history going nowhere in particular. This "evolutionary tree," branching out into a pointless ecology of architectural styles, is organized around a series of image-based feedback loops tending toward the entropy of "radical eclecticism," a kind of pluralistic equilibrium in which everything is different from everything else, and is therefore the same.[13] To this day, Jencks continues to insist on the emergence of discernible patterns out of this media-ecological soup, in the form of secondary formations or groupings. But these too are going nowhere in particular, emerging from the soup only to disappear back into it, to be replaced by new and equally meaningless groupings, ad infinitum, in a kind of dynamic, swirling stasis.[14] Where could the utopian spirit of decisive historical change possibly be found here, except as one irrelevant little story among many? To explore this question, I want to begin by tracking this sense of going nowhere, of a kind of exhausted dynamism, in its most explicit form possible: what the Congrès International d'Architecture Moderne (CIAM) simply called "circulation."

Recall the figural role played by the *promenade architecturale* in the work of an architect like Le Corbusier. In the Villa Savoie at Poissy, for example, the passage through the building was no mere functionalist means to get from bottom to top. Instead, the cinematic ramp materializes the very sense of historical progress to which I have been alluding, as it weaves upward through the building's various functional zones and lands dramatically on the roof, where the user is presented with a framed view of the pastoral landscape in which the Corbusian *machine à habiter* has decisively landed. The ramp thus succinctly summarizes what we can call a Corbusian teleology, in the form of a space-time vector leading inexorably toward the mechanico-arcadian future captured in great detail by the Swiss architect's utopian master plans of the same period.

Compare this sense of purpose, allegorized in a linear circulation system, with the equally classical—and, we can say, still Corbusian—*promenade architecturale* passing through the Neue Staatsgalerie in Stuttgart designed by the British architect James Stirling, completed in 1983. Widely considered a key monument of postmodernism, this architectural icon was added to a deindustrializing city in part to generate tourism, and so must also be considered a precursor to Frank Gehry's Guggenheim Museum in Bilbao. But in Stuttgart, in what was then West Germany, entrants to the architectural design competition won by Stirling's office had to contend with the geopolitical requirement to include a

James Stirling, Neue Staatsgalerie, Stuttgart, 1983. Approach. Photograph by John Donat. Courtesy of Royal Institute of British Architects, Library Photographs Collection.

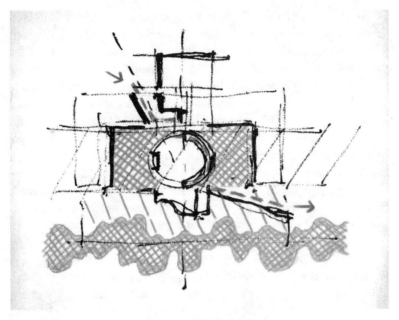

James Stirling, Neue Staatsgalerie, Stuttgart, 1983. Sketch of main circulation. James Stirling / Michael Wilford Fonds, Collection Centre Canadien d'Architecture/Canadian Centre for Architecture, Montréal.

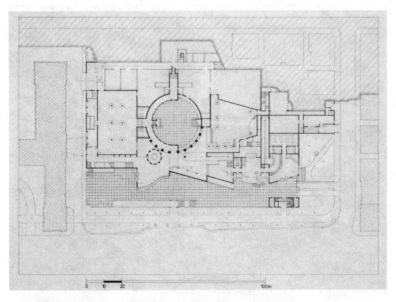

James Stirling, Neue Staatsgalerie, Stuttgart, 1983. Plan, entry level. James Stirling / Michael Wilford Fonds, Collection Centre Canadien d'Architecture/Canadian Centre for Architecture, Montréal.

"democratic" path, or a public passage that was commonly required through the site of major West German civic institutions.[15] In these waning days of the cold war, this path was not required to lead the pedestrian anywhere in particular, except to the degree that it led toward all that was ambiguously "western" and democratic about West Germany. Thus its presence, and with it, the sense of accessibility and approachability generously accommodated by Stirling's scheme, declared between its lines that, whatever could be said of West German public institutions, they were emphatically *not* of the East—as in *East* Germany and *East* Berlin and the authoritarian overtones carried in the West by those locales.

Follow the path through Stirling's building. Where does it lead? Zigzagging through a series of layers, it reaches no climax. Instead, it stages a narrative of passage with no end, sliding across the forecourt, establishing an axis only to displace it, skirting the "metaphysical" voided central court and leaking out the back, with a tangential escape into the museum itself near the front. In contrast to the informality of this entry sequence (and this is one of Stirling's many playful juxtapositions in the building), the galleries consist of discrete rooms arranged *enfilade* in the nineteenth-century manner, rather than the drifting, loftlike expanses characteristic of many other twentieth-century museum interiors.

The ambiguous anticlimax of Stirling's *promenade architecturale* in Stuttgart can be compared to that of another museum designed (but not built) in 1975, for another West German city. This is the entry submitted by the German architect Oswald Mathias Ungers to a competition in which Stirling also participated, for the Wallraf-Richartz Museum in Cologne.[16] The Ungers project, situated on the riverbank adjacent to the Cologne cathedral and flanked by the train station, attempts to reconcile these disparate urban elements by inserting a comprehensive, gridded matrix of infrastructure, out of which emerge the individual components of the museum. An apparently direct entry sequence is cut into this matrix, in the form of a linear axis that begins at the plaza surrounding the cathedral, extends onto an above-grade terrace, and then descends to a dock on the river. The axis is another instance of the "democratic" path, passing from public plaza to public waterfront. But at another, more allegorical, level it is also something else entirely. Three architectural episodes, or scenes, are arranged sequentially along this axis, each as inconclusive as the one before it.

As is made clear by Ungers's three-part perspective drawing of the sequence, the aesthetic references are to surrealism and its precursors, from De Chirico to Magritte. The first scene presents an empty forecourt

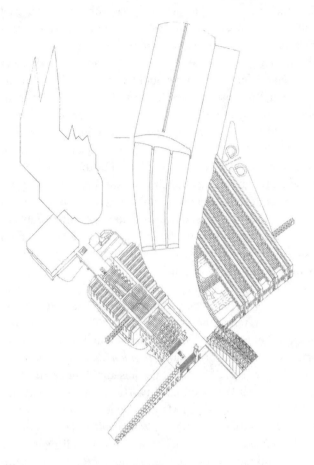

Oswald Mathias Ungers, Wallraf-Richartz Museum,
Cologne, 1975. Competition entry, axonometric.
Courtesy of Oswald Mathias Ungers Archive.

populated, in the drawings, by a De Chirico mannequin and spherical
trees; the second presents a ramp leading from an empty "street" with
diagrammatic facades through a series of squared-off archways, off of
which are arranged gridded antechambers that serve the galleries; and
the third, a sculpture garden with cubic trees arranged in a grid and
large-scale sculptures posed abjectly in niches on either side. An otherwise minor detail in the plan, which is emphasized in the perspectives, is
instructive. Where the central axis, marked in the drawings by a hovering

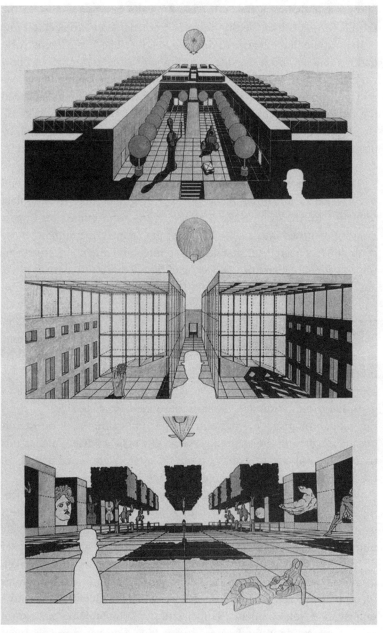

Oswald Mathias Ungers, Wallraf-Richartz Museum, Cologne, 1975. Competition entry, perspectives. Courtesy of Oswald Mathias Ungers Archive.

blimp, expands into a space of passage in the first two scenes, in the third it contracts into the thinness of a line, marked by the central row of trees in the floating grid. And so the Magritte-like "scale figure," who had first entered from the side and climbed the central ramp, has now been shuffled off to the side again by the rather unaccommodating tree grid and condemned to a degree of abjection equivalent to that afforded the reclining protosurrealist figure opposite. I emphasize this because Ungers could have accommodated the passage all the way through, by utilizing a grid consisting of four rows of trees rather than three. But he did not, and he made a point of it in every detail of the drawing.

Though Ungers's stated intentions emphasize place-making, the end result is that we are presented here with an enigmatic, allegorical subject of history (in the form of the Magritte figure—who in another Ungers drawing is turned into a self-portrait of the architect), a human whose centrality has been displaced, in this architectural dream, by an anachronistic, highly schematized dialectic of nature and culture: trees, grids, and a blimp. So, in sharp contrast to whatever classical precedent on which Ungers's symmetries may have drawn, the humanist human who started out as the central character in the narrative of the "democratic" path has, by the inconclusive "end," been relegated to a supporting role. In this way, Ungers effectively *extended* rather than interrupted the post-humanist tendencies of functionalism à la Mies, Gropius, and Hilber-seimer, with their serialities and their grids. He has not, in other words, deployed a more "humane," well-proportioned, axial classicism *against* the indeterminate geometries of modernism but *with* them, by extend-ing their logic into the standing reserve of classicism itself, just as this pseudoclassical anti-axis emerges out of the gridded infrastructures of the museum, adjacent and below.

To give some indication of the refractory nature of such displace-ments, I want to pay a brief visit to a house designed by an architect whose humanity, as well as that of his architecture, has gone largely unquestioned. That architect is Charles Moore, the self-appointed maker of "places" in opposition to the non-places of modernism—a maker, in other words, of destinations, safe havens, or even homes, antidotes to what Georg Lukàcs long ago called, with reference to modernity's upheavals, a "transcendental homelessness."[17] The building that I want to visit is a condominium complex that Moore designed in Los Ange-les in 1978 for himself and two of his friends. Linguistically it leans sol-idly toward the eclectic, another supposed hallmark of postmodernism,

Charles W. Moore with Richard Chylinski and Urban Innovations Group, Moore, Rogger, Hofflander Condominium, Los Angeles, 1978. Courtesy of Charles Moore Foundation.

with its awkward combination of vernacular, regional, and even modernist references. While on the interior, the three units are simultaneously woven together and separated by a sequence of irregular stairways, along which fragments of space are distributed to the left and to the right but also above and below.

Where do these stairways lead? Again, they lead nowhere in particular, but with great precision. As such, they exemplify Moore's predilection for what he calls "leaky" space, interior space that breaks open in unsystematic ways, often to allow light in through irregular cracks, diagonal views, or apparently ad hoc functional connections. As realized even at a small scale in Moore's houses, such space has been called Piranesian, though at first glance this would appear to be a domesticated Piranesi, especially in view of the quaint encrustations of bric-a-brac with which Moore habitually adorned it. But something of the sinister, Piranesian sublime does remain nevertheless, not so much in the fragmentation of interior space but rather in the frustrations brought on by the fragmented passages up and through this space, as they fail to connect up in any cognitively transparent way, much like the archways and bridges to nowhere in Piranesi's prison etchings.

To be sure, unlike the civic drama played out in the public spaces of a museum, there is no self-evident reason why the circulation in a house should lead anywhere in particular. But we can be equally sure that the

Charles W. Moore with Richard Chylinski and Urban Innovations
Group, Moore, Rogger, Hofflander Condominium, Los Angeles,
1978. Interior. Courtesy of Charles Moore Foundation.

erudite Moore was well aware of the history of the *promenade architecturale* when he was designing his houses, including its heroic iterations
in Le Corbusier's domestic architecture. Indeed, unlike the examples we
have just encountered with Stirling and Ungers, Moore's irregular stairways and passages cannot even convincingly be said to correspond to
discrete episodes in an inconclusive architectural narrative. They are,
in a sense, pure events, one after the other. A pastiche not so much of

architectural styles as of the notion of historicity and of historical progress itself, Moore's little domestic episodes are events that occur outside of the time and space of any narrative whatsoever, despite—or perhaps even *because of*—the architectural histories to which they and their enclosing volumes refer.

So, in architectural terms, the bad copies of historical elements visible in these examples matter less than the way in which they are assembled, especially (as in the case of Moore) when the attempt is to produce the effect of casual juxtaposition—the effect, in other words, of pastiche itself. In all three of these cases, this is achieved by manipulating the architecture of circulation. And the fact that the supposed narratives played out along the way say almost nothing about architecture's relationship to its own histories—whether past, present, or future—does seem to suggest that this architecture has been content to exchange the master narratives of modernism for any number of inconclusive, episodic, and noncommittal micronarratives that add up, exactly, to nothing.

But what if it is also the other way around? What if, in direct contradiction to the claims made by so many protagonists on all sides of the postmodern debates in architecture, there is something specifically and helplessly *utopian* about this failure to add up? I do not mean this in the sense of a conciliatory pluralism, in which each competing micronarrative and each competing style is given equal time and space in a pseudo-democratic cacophony perfectly adapted to the demands of a bland multiculturalism coincident with globalization. I mean it in the sense of a project that refuses to take the form of a project—a kind of inadvertent or accidental project that appears indirectly, in an almost unrecognizable return of the repressed. For if we were truly and fully postmodern we would not experience even a twinge of frustration when confronted by the failure of these built-in architectural narratives to add up. But I think we do. Why?

Perhaps it is because in staging different forms of frustration or exhaustion, they cannot help but also stage its antithesis—the forever-deferred possibility of arrival, of a break, of irreversible and maybe even revolutionary historical change. In that sense, these frustrated passages, which might also be seen as ghosts of the arcaded, phantasmagoric passages of nineteenth-century Europe artfully explored by Walter Benjamin, might still harbor, despite themselves, what Benjamin called a "weak messianic power." It is just that the changes they announce look different than we might have thought. Or, to put it another way, we are no longer able to recognize ourselves or our histories in them. After all, ghosts do not show up in mirrors.

If these frustrated architectural passages lead anywhere, it is back to the stage set, to its props, and to the visor effect. That is, they lead back inside, to architecture and only architecture, or to what Tafuri described as a Piranesian prison house of linguistic play to which a nonredemptive, autonomous architecture-as-such was thenceforth supposedly condemned.[18] But even out in the city, far from restoring humanity to a dehumanized modernism by reintroducing categories like "place," "the street," "human scale," and so on, much so-called postmodern architecture actually internalized Utopia's otherworldliness. There is, for example, a certain inhuman scale that reappears across the postmodern spectrum. Sometimes, as in the case of Michael Graves's Portland Building (especially in its original versions), this gigantism masquerades as a sensitivity to multiple scales, from sidewalks to supergraphics. That these scales fail to add up, however, is normally not noticed, except in such rare instances as that recorded in *The Charlottesville Tapes*, where Kevin Roche (himself a master of gigantism) is to be found ironically congratulating Graves on the inflation of another such office building to "elephantine" proportions.[19]

Here we can agree with Fredric Jameson that the rhetorical inflation of architectural scale in such projects constitutes an aesthetic response to the inflation of building footprints under the speculative premises of late capitalism and its real estate markets.[20] But with this gigantism, and its accompanying miniaturization of the architectural object as a consumable in various coffeepots and tableware, also comes a displacement of human scale, the humanist rhetoric of "place" and "proportion" again notwithstanding. Peter Eisenman's 1978 Cannaregio project in Venice acknowledges as much, with its fractal logic of "scaling" in place of the modular "measure of man" inscribed into the unbuilt hospital designed by Le Corbusier for the adjacent site, on which Eisenman draws for his own grids. In these and other scalar displacements, the human subject of late capitalism has been effectively dehumanized, ghosted. But is this in fact the ghost of Utopia (the ultimate humanist project) lurking within these empty shells, or merely the abstract inhumanity—the spectrality, that is—of capital itself?

Consider another even more typical postmodernist trope: that of a kind of linguistic babble, a free play of signs materialized on the Strada

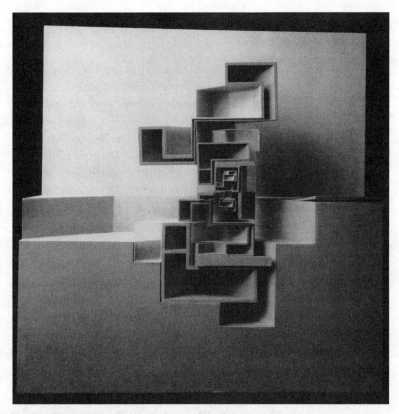

Peter Eisenman, competition entry for the International Seminary of Design, Cannaregio-West, Venice, 1978. Sectional model. Peter Eisenman Fonds, Collection Centre Canadien d'Architecture/Canadian Centre for Architecture, Montréal.

Novissima in what Portoghesi called the "end of prohibition." On the one hand, the new plurality was nothing more than a consumerist response to the global marketplace of cultures. But despite its overall reverence for the Western classical tradition, and its Eurocentrism, the architecture lining the Strada Novissima is surely pastiche, defined by Jameson as "speech in a dead language." And with dead languages come more ghosts, especially when that death occurs in Venice. Not just the ghost of the classical res publica as summoned up by an architect like Léon Krier but the ghost of both Europe and its recently decolonized others, on the other side of the Mediterranean and the other side of the world, whose own architectural languages were at that very moment both fetishized and condemned as "regional" in parallel, postmodern forums such as the journal *Mimar,* which began publication in 1981. A specter is haunting Europe, indeed.

By 1984 even Jencks, in a new introduction to the *The Language of Post-Modern Architecture,* counted regionalism among postmodernism's defining features.[21] In this light, the pseudocontroversy of the 1980 Biennale as to whether the American camp was under- or overrepresented was more symptomatic than axiomatic. For behind the problem of the "old world" versus the "new" was the complicated history of the new world figured as Utopia. The best evidence of this is obtained by scratching the surface of one of the stage-set facades built in Venice, a negative Doric column designed by Ungers. As his Austrian (and Strada Novissima) neighbor Hans Hollein and many other Europeans had also done in the 1960s, Ungers had for some time taken the United States as a reference point. But rather than look to America for its counterculture or its popular culture, Ungers looked to America for its historical experiments with Utopia. This took the form of research done in collaboration with his wife, Liselotte, and collected together in a little volume published in 1972 as *Kommunen in der Neue Welt* (*Communes in the New World*), excerpts of which were published under the title "Utopische Kommunen in Amerika 1800–1900" (Utopian Communes in America) and in English (in *AD*) as "Early Communes in the USA."[22]

Basically an inventory of utopian experiments in the United States from Moravia in the 1740s to New Haven in the 1970s, *Kommunen in der Neue Welt* presents itself as a scientific document that records "new [i.e., protomodern] forms of living together" often initiated in the eighteenth and nineteenth centuries by European immigrants. As such, it surely provided raw material for Ungers's own typological and linguistic experiments. But the very definition of Utopia is that it is foreign, which is also what connects it with colonialism. So let Ungers's coauthored little book stand as evidence not only of a utopian consciousness right there in the middle of the Strada Novissima but also of a kind of closure, whereby the bipolar relationship between "old" and "new" worlds—Europe and the United States, classicism and modernism—is allowed to stand in for (and thus occlude) actually existing decolonizations and globalizations, circa 1980.

But even as the Strada Novissima leads outward, to a world divided between histories visible and invisible, remembered and forgotten, it also leads inward, to Architecture (or architecture with a capital A). Consider, for example, another Ungers museum, a museum of architecture itself, the Deutsches Architekturmuseum in Frankfurt of 1984. Here Ungers inserts his typeforms into an existing nineteenth-century villa, alternating (as he did in Cologne) between an emphasis on the gridded matrix and on the figural pavilions that fit one within the other, in a cascade of houses-within-houses, or architecture-within-architecture. By the mid-1980s the archetypal house form, polemically stated by Robert Venturi in his mother's house of 1964, was well established as a cipher for architecture-as-such and had already been set off into a mise en abyme by Moore, in the house-within-a-house he designed for himself in California in 1962. And so it would have seemed entirely appropriate for Ungers to put the house form (i.e., Architecture) on display in an architecture museum, even as he used it as scaffolding for the museum's exhibits. But as before, the actual architecture he designed abounds with ambiguities. Central among these is the ghostliness of the archetypal "house"

Oswald Mathias Ungers, Deutsches Architekturmuseum, Frankfurt am Main, 1984. Axonometric, final version. Courtesy of Oswald Mathias Ungers Archive.

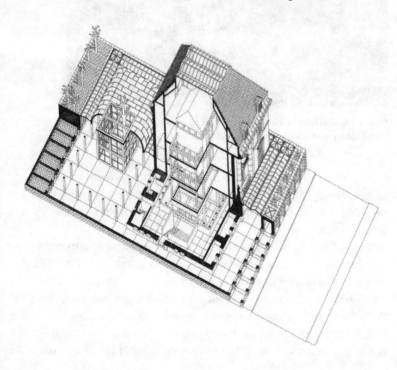

Oswald Mathias Ungers, Deutsches Architekturmuseum, Frankfurt am Main, 1984. Interior. Courtesy of Oswald Mathias Ungers Archive.

itself in its multiple iterations. Perhaps a distant relative of Venturi's own, rather literally ghosted house museum for Benjamin Franklin in Philadelphia (1976), this museum house designed by Ungers is, strictly speaking, haunted.

First, it is haunted in the conventional sense that we might attribute to a project like Aldo Rossi's monument to the partisans at Segrate of 1965, which makes even starker use of the triangular archetype in the form of an abstracted, extruded pediment. As with all museums, there is something funerary and commemorative about Ungers's project, which like Rossi's work more generally can be thought ultimately to be dedicated not to architecture-as-such but to its memory. But this house museum is also haunted by the city, on which it turns its back. As manifest in its own self-referential emptiness, the building also remembers, and in a sense mourns, a collective future from which the entire assemblage now recoils, looking inward rather than outward.

Such claustrophobia repeats in other Ungers projects, including that for the Hotel Berlin (1980), with its buildings-within-buildings sequence pausing on the interior at a little atriumlike glass "house" and on the exterior at a rigorous extrusion of the typical Berlin perimeter block. The hotel's nested topologies return us to the disorienting, nested interiors of John Portman's Bonaventure Hotel in Los Angeles, which Jameson has famously read as a diagram of nothing less than "postmodern space." Surely Jameson was right in calling for new cognitive maps to navigate the labyrinths of late capitalism. But we also need new forms of projection, maps that lead to an exit from such spaces. Rather than projecting outward, from the architectural object to the city and to the world, such maps might lead to an exit or exits deep *inside* our postmodern nightmares. Built-in trap doors concealed in the architecture itself that, like visors, open onto other, possible worlds, rather than onto one more solipsistic prison cell to which one is forever condemned, like a Russian matryoshka doll.

This sense of absolute closure with hidden holes reproduces Utopia's island function. Take, for example, the original competition entry submitted by Charles Moore's office for a mixed-use development in the Tegel Harbor district of West Berlin in 1980, an example of the "critical reconstruction" undertaken in the 1980s under the direction of Josef Paul Kleihues and the Internationale Bauausstellung (IBA).[23] At its center is a shiplike island accommodating public recreational functions, and on the surrounding shores, housing. Only the housing and an adjacent library were built. The island remained an island, with nothing on it. Though the original scheme translates rather faithfully Moore's earlier commitments to the public realm as mediated through Disney, the empty island even more faithfully registers the fate of the actual public realm under "critical reconstruction." In the decade or so that followed, this emptiness was poignantly revealed by the marketing of a reunified Berlin as a center of the new Europe. Not as a capital city, despite the relocation of the seat of government from Bonn, but as a city of capital, a monument to the demise of the welfare state and to the privatization of the public realm.

Take another project from the IBA: John Hejduk's Berlin Masque of 1981. It is, in fact, a gated community, but one so otherworldly that

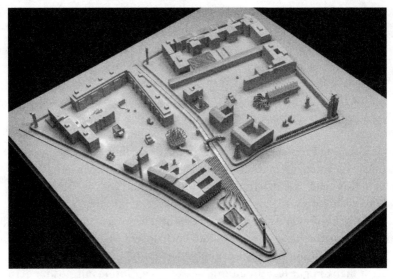

John Hejduk, Berlin Masque, 1981. Model. John Hejduk Fonds, Collection Centre Canadien d'Architecture/Canadian Centre for Architecture, Montréal.

regardless of whether it were built or not (and it was not) the threshold or limit that sets it off from the real world of (East and West) Berlin becomes a primary focus. This threshold is controlled by a twelve-foot-high hedge surrounding each of the two blocks that make up the site, which are connected by a "cross-over bridge" made of steel. Inside this hedge is, among other things, another stage set: a setting for a masque, a type of courtly theater originating in the sixteenth century but also a masquerade. At the eastern end of this theater within a theater is a single male inhabitant selected, according to Hejduk, by the nonexistent "city of Berlin."[24] This figure gazes from the past toward the future. Opposite him is a single female inhabitant (again selected by the "city") who, like Benjamin's melancholy angel of history, gazes from the future toward the past.

Especially when seen next to the Berlin Masque's inverted twin, Hejduk's Lancaster/Hanover Masque, an equally enigmatic staging of rural community on the order of the New England utopias explored by Ungers, this and other highly schematic, self-negating symmetries built into the figures that populate Hejduk's stage set reinforce an overall sense of futility. The play has either just ended or has yet to begin. If it performs anything at all, the Berlin Masque therefore performs another version of the story about going nowhere, about standing in place, despite the

John Hejduk, Lancaster/Hanover Masque, 1982. Plans and elevations
of elements. John Hejduk Fonds, Collection Centre Canadien
d'Architecture/Canadian Centre for Architecture, Montréal.

vehicles that house its nomadic inhabitants. And if, as Louis Marin says,
the pseudo-utopic character of Disneyland also consists in situating visitors as actors in a scripted performance "like rats in a maze," Hejduk's
Berlin Masque is a sort of anti-Disneyland, an enigmatic, overscripted
performance in which characters drift, waiting.[25]

We can also read the cold war in Hejduk's project: Berlin as a kind of
split island, scaled down into two city blocks populated by two paradigmatic characters: islands within islands within islands. For other such
nested topologies, think of the island-worlds brought inside in Hans
Hollein's artificial palm tree–filled travel agencies, themselves internal-
izations of a raft with palm trees that Hollein installed in the 1972 Venice
Biennale. Is not the ubiquitous palm tree a sublimated index, etched into
the Western imagination, of decolonized space made newly available to
the global tourist, as well as to the cold war imaginary à la James Bond?
And then there is Aldo Rossi's melancholy world-within-a-world of the
Teatro del Mondo: Is this a universal symbol, the last gasp of a Eurocen-
tric humanism, or the beginning of some science-fiction voyage toward
an ungraspable posthumanity? And of course, there is Rossi's San Cataldo
Cemetery in Modena (1982), an islandlike city of the dead with an empty

Aldo Rossi with Gianni Bragheri, San Cataldo Cemetery, Modena, 1982.
Bird's-eye perspective, n.d. Aldo Rossi Fonds, Collection Centre Canadien
d'Architecture/Canadian Centre for Architecture, Montréal.

Aldo Rossi with Gianni Bragheri, San Cataldo Cemetery, Modena,
1982. Ossuary. Photograph by Barbara Bergh and Oliver Schuh.

housing block at its center that, in a sense, collapses two very powerful images drawn from European modernity, the factory and the concentration camp, thereby confirming the basic ambivalence of the island figure that we discussed earlier in Rossi's writings. This ambivalence accounts for the underlying implication of centrist critiques from Rowe to Jencks, that modernist utopianism shades dangerously close to totalitarianism in its commitment to world-historical transformation. Thus it must be held in abeyance, if not abolished entirely. Still, ghosts have an uncanny way of showing up unannounced, and in the strangest places.

Probably the most comprehensive diagram of postmodernism's topological cascades was drawn in 1977 with Cities within the City, a project for the reurbanization of West Berlin (which even then was a "shrinking" city) by a group of faculty and students from Cornell led by Ungers, in collaboration with Hans Kollhoff, Rem Koolhaas, and others.[26] The project proposed that a "green archipelago" of parklike islands be extracted out of the existing fabric as a way to deal with the city's depopulation. This arrangement would be punctuated by an equivalent archipelago of built "islands" modeled on precedents as diverse as the radial plan of Karlsruhe and Ivan Leonidov's linear city design for Magnitogorsk. To mediate between these urban scale insertions and the scale of the individual building, and to counter the persistent tendency of residents to prefer the individuality of detached houses to the anonymity of large apartment blocks, the urban villa, a detached collective dwelling made up of four to eight units, was proposed as a prototypical residential building.

Both Ungers and Koolhaas had already been exploring this proposition in their own work, Koolhaas in his reading of the Manhattan grid as an infrastructure that supported individual expression in each of its blocks, diagrammed as a museum of architectural history by his collaborator Zoe Zenghelis in The City of the Captive Globe of 1972, and Ungers in such projects as his Marburg housing competition of 1976, in which the urban villa prototype was projected onto an entire city block broken down into five residential units, each given its own distinct form, in recognition of the predilection for variety and individuality on the part of the consumers for whom the project was designed.

At the level of its polycentric urban organization, the Cities within the City model recognized and sought to reinforce certain characteristics

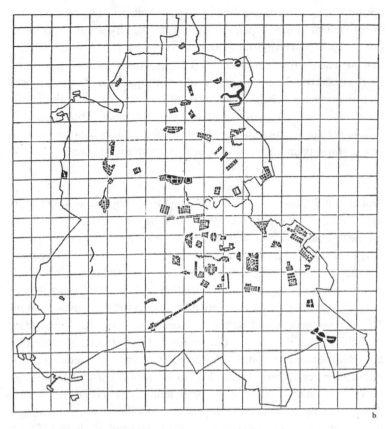

Oswald Mathias Ungers, Rem Koolhaas, Peter Riemann, Hans
Kollhoff, and Arthur Ovaska, *Cities within the City,* Berlin, 1977. Urban
archipelago. Courtesy of Oswald Mathias Ungers Archive.

that were emerging in cities across the northern transatlantic in response
to the decentralizing pressures of suburbanization and deindustrializa-
tion. The resulting archipelago, with its attempt to maintain in its components "as wide an architectural spectrum as possible," was offered not
as a utopia but as a conciliatory anti-utopia or, as its authors put it, as an
"improvement of what is already there." Proposed, as were so many modernist utopias before it, as a scientific solution to objective problems, the
project was published with the following comment: "There is no need for
a new Utopia but rather to create a better reality."[27]

Interestingly enough, Jameson too has suggested that the political
model of a federated archipelago might offer an alternative map capable

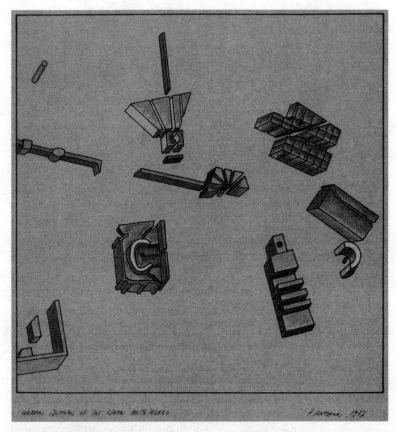

Oswald Mathias Ungers, Rem Koolhaas, Peter Riemann, Hans
Kollhoff, and Arthur Ovaska, *Cities within the City,* Berlin, 1977. Urban
archipelago, detail. Courtesy of Oswald Mathias Ungers Archive.

of grasping and to some extent managing the multiple displacements
of postmodernism and by extension, we might add, of globalization. He
offers Yona Friedman's *Utopies réalisables* of 1975 as an example, with
its proposal for a "multitude of non-communicating communities," or
an archipelago of autonomous islands wrapping the globe and linked by
a shared infrastructure, where it is the inalienable right of every inhabitant of every "island" to leave behind their homeland and migrate.[28] A
proposal like Friedman's, and to a lesser extent the Ungers/Koolhaas project for Berlin, seems at first glance to have the virtue of acknowledging
the individuality of its mass subjects, who like the inhabitants of metropolitan Berlin had been treated as standardized stereotypes by earlier

generations of architect/planners. Both projects recognize multiple and conflicting identities and desires, by essentially refracting Utopia itself into a multitude of little Utopias—many little islands rather than just one big one. That, in Cities within the City, Karlsruhe and Magnitogorsk are chosen as models further suggests that, despite the contentions of the plan's authors, Utopia's ghost had hardly been exorcised by the supposed realism of their plan; instead, it had multiplied.

But this multiplicity, this splitting of the ghost into a ghostly multitude, is not without its own problems. Taken to a logical conclusion, and without the architecture of the urban villa as a semicollective stopgap, it finally accedes to the atomization and fragmentation of the entire postindustrial consumerist landscape, by imagining a series of individual, private futures in place of a single, collective one. Or, in another possible extension, it risks simply replacing the homogenizing universalism that guided earlier efforts to build for the stereotyped masses, with a logic of diversified enclaves that rapidly begin to resemble the "neighborhood" or other forms of supposedly local, organic "community," whether gated or otherwise, to say nothing of the accompanying "archipelagoes of exception" à la Agamben.[29] Nevertheless, in its refraction, in its splitting up, Utopia's ghost has also managed here to preserve something of its otherworldliness, its sense of being nowhere. It does so to the extent that in the project nowhere is to be found almost everywhere, though in a different form in each case.

Finally, a negative example that helps us double back on the positive consequences implied by this state of affairs. In the late 1970s, at around the same time that many of the works we have just discussed were being designed and/or built, three cities—Brussels, Strasbourg, and Luxembourg—were being considered for the parliamentary seat of the European Union, which would hold its first direct election in 1979. The French architect Roger Taillibert was therefore commissioned to produce a plan for Luxembourg that integrated the new institutions into the city center. The project, called Centre 300, was presented to the public in February 1978, amid a sense of urgency that it be swiftly approved in order to be realized by 1979, in time for the elections. It consisted of a Brasilia-like platform on which the new monuments would sit, poised like very large abstract sculptures, ready to accept the organs of the new European legislative body.[30]

Also in 1978, the Luxembourgian architect Léon Krier prepared a counter project in response. Here again was the "city-within-a-city" archipelago model, though this time in the form of what Krier called the "city as a federation of quarters," or pedestrian-scaled neighborhoods in the form of reconstructed streets flanked by a pseudovernacular, low-rise, mixed-use urban fabric and punctuated by neoclassical monuments.[31] The plan's ideal, imagined subject was neither an industrial worker nor a postindustrial manager but rather a preindustrial artisan who lived down the block from where he worked. Thus in many ways Krier is the most rigorously utopian of the many architects commonly designated as "postmodern," to the point that in the dogmatic, preindustrial purism and absolutism characteristic of his work in the late 1970s he sometimes seems hardly to have encountered modernism at all.

But I want to suggest that Krier's manifest and unmediated utopianism, pure as it may be, works on the contrary to *exorcise*—rather than to conjure—the many ghosts of Utopia that we have been tracking in other works from this period. For in proposing what he calls a "city of stone" to counter the willfulness and artificiality of the city of concrete, steel, and glass, Krier attempts a revivification, a bringing back to life, rather than a conjuration. A nostalgia for modernity's ultimate lost object—the home, or in this case, the home*land,* at the very moment of its deterritorialization in the "new" Europe of postcolonial migrations—runs so deep in his architecture as to force a comparison with the violent nostalgia for a nonexistent, glorious past brought back to life in the work of Albert Speer, an architect whose reputation Krier has been singularly devoted to rehabilitating.[32] In contrast, like Georg Simmel's metropolitan stranger, ghosts are effectively homeless. That is, they are *of* a place only in the sense of returning to haunt it without ever quite fitting in. And so it is here, of all places, in the heart of "old Europe" as it reorganizes itself in response to new historical conditions, that Krier's ultimately xenophobic project puts the question in the starkest terms possible: critical cosmopolitanism, or provincialism? An unconditional hospitality and an as-yet-unrealized openness to strangers, or a purified "European" identity, built in stone?

As we have seen, there are many examples of haunted urban islands that point in a different direction, to the outside on the inside of "old Europe": cities within cities such as Rossi's Modena cemetery, or Hejduk's Berlin Masque. These and other projects may finally mark an end but also a new beginning for that humanist enterprise that wanted desperately to link architecture to the city, and thereby to society, so beautifully summarized by Leon Battista Alberti in his dictum: "The city is like some large house, and the house is in turn like some small city."[33] Cut off from the

Oswald Mathias Ungers, *La Strada Novissima,* Venice Biennale, 1980. Exhibit facade. Courtesy of Oswald Mathias Ungers Archive.

city like an isolated house on a deserted street on a deserted island, these enclosures may seem only to converge, like Ungers's museum, on architecture, autonomous and useless. But inside we might be surprised to find that same street, leading back to that same house—in short an entire city and an entire world, refracted through the minutest of details like the turn of a corner, the modulation of a grid, or a voided Doric column.

There may indeed be no escape from this hall of mirrors. But in this realm of materialized spirits, which is a realm of real conflicts and real solidarities, also lurks the potential for a new kind of project, in which the specter that once haunted Europe finally goes global. By this I mean a form of thought that neither attempts narcissistically to render its own pasts present nor mourns their passing. Instead, in looking back it reorients its gaze toward futures yet to come. It does this by probing its own claustrophobic interiors, its many histories, not as some kind of defeat but in search of a strategic, topological reversal, where the further inside you go the further outside you get. With such a turning of the tables, history itself, far from having come to an end, would also turn and return in the feedback loops of a slightly offset periodicity. Caught in these loops, we may eventually realize that if the "post" in postmodernism means anything, it means learning to live with ghosts, including the ghosts of futures past and present, the ghosts of others alive and dead, and with them, the ghosts of our former selves. It means, in other words, learning to think the thought called Utopia once again.

NOTES

Introduction

1 Among the many accounts of the scope and interrelation of postmodernity and postmodernism, Perry Anderson's *The Origins of Postmodernity* (New York: Verso, 1998) remains particularly useful.

2 The term *postmodernism* has an ambiguous genealogy in architecture. By most accounts, it was first used, in a somewhat different sense, by Joseph Hudnut in "The Post-Modern House," *Architectural Record* 97 (May 1945): 70–75, reprinted in *Royal Architectural Institute of Canada Journal* 22 (July 1945): 135–40. Robert Venturi's *Complexity and Contradiction in Architecture* (New York: Museum of Modern Art, 1966) and Aldo Rossi's *The Architecture of the City*, trans. Diane Ghirardo and Joan Ockman (Cambridge, Mass.: MIT Press, 1984), represent important initial (though hardly exhaustive or definitive) formulations of key postmodernist themes. Key exhibitions include *Rational Architecture* at the 1973 Milan Triennale, the Venice Biennales of 1978 and 1980, titled *Utopia and the Crisis of Anti-Nature* and *The Presence of the Past*, respectively, the 1984 *Post-Modern Visions* exhibition at the new Deutsches Architekturmuseum in Frankfurt, and the *Internationale Bauausstellung* (IBA) in Berlin of the mid-1980s. Arthur Drexler's 1975 exhibition at the Museum of Modern Art in New York, *The Architecture of the École des Beaux-Arts,* was also an important reference. Important critical surveys include Charles Jencks, *The Language of Post-Modern Architecture* (London: Academy Editions, 1977); Paolo Portoghesi, *Postmodern: The Architecture of the Postindustrial Society*, trans. Ellen Shapiro (New York: Rizzoli, 1983); and Heinrich Klotz, *The History of Postmodern Architecture*, trans. Radka Donnell (Cambridge, Mass.: MIT Press, 1988). Jencks historicizes his own use of the term *postmodern* in an appendix added to the introduction of *The Language of Post-Modern Architecture*, 2d rev. ed. (London: Academy Editions, 1978), 8. See also the collection of essays in the *Harvard Architecture Review* 1, special issue "Beyond the Modern Movement" (Spring 1990).

3 In architecture, the most influential of these was probably Fredric Jameson's essay, "Postmodernism, or The Cultural Logic of Late Capitalism," *New Left Review* 146 (July–August 1984): 53–92. Another landmark is *New German Critique* 33, spe-

cial issue on modernity and postmodernity (Fall 1984). An early review of post-modernist developments that concentrates on literature and the visual arts is Andreas Huyssen, "The Search for Tradition: Avant-Garde and Postmodernism in the 1970s," *New German Critique* 22, special issue on modernity (Winter 1981): 23–40.

4 An example would be the "critical regionalism" of Alexander Tzonis and Liane Lefaivre, which was also taken up in a slightly different register by Kenneth Frampton. See Tzonis and Lefaivre, "The Grid and the Pathway: An Introduction to the Work of Dimitris and Susana Antonakakis. With Prolegomena to a History of the Culture of Modern Greek Architecture," *Architecture in Greece* 15 (1981): 164–78, and Frampton, "Towards a Critical Regionalism: Six Points for an Architecture of Resistance," in *The Anti-Aesthetic: Essays on Postmodern Culture,* ed. Hal Foster (Port Townsend, Wash.: The Bay Press, 1983), 16–30.

5 This is an argument made in general terms by Fredric Jameson in *Postmodernism: Or, The Cultural Logic of Late Capitalism* (Durham, N.C.: Duke University Press, 1991); see in particular 122–29, 208–17, 401ff. Corresponding arguments run throughout Jameson's *Archaeologies of the Future: The Desire Called Utopia and Other Science Fictions* (London: Verso, 2005), including the introduction, "Utopia Now," xi–xvi, and the republished essay of 1982, "Progress versus Utopia, or Can We Imagine the Future?" 281–95. For two versions of what Manfredo Tafuri called a "crisis of Utopia" operating already within modern architecture, see Tafuri, *Architecture and Utopia: Design and Capitalist Development,* trans. Barbara Luigia La Penta (Cambridge, Mass.: MIT Press, 1976), and Colin Rowe and Fred Koetter, "Utopia: Decline and Fall?" in *Collage City* (Cambridge, Mass.: MIT Press, 1978), 9–31.

6 Michel Foucault, *Security, Territory, Population: Lectures at the Collège de France 1977–1978,* ed. Michel Senellart, trans. Graham Burchell (New York: Palgrave Macmillan, 2007); and Michel Foucault, *The Birth of Biopolitics: Lectures at the Collège de France 1978–1979,* ed. Michel Senellart, trans. Graham Burchell (New York: Palgrave Macmillan, 2008). See also Sven-Olov Wallenstein, "Foucault and the Genealogy of Modern Architecture," in *Essays, Lectures* (Stockholm: Axl Books, 2007), 361–404, and Sven-Olov Wallenstein, *Biopolitics and the Emergence of Modern Architecture* (New York: Buell Center for the Study of American Architecture/Princeton Architectural Press, 2009).

7 One set of coordinates for this argument is supplied in Michael Hardt and Antonio Negri, *Empire* (Cambridge, Mass.: Harvard University Press, 2000). In particular, see chapter 3.4, "Postmodernization, or the Informatization of Production," 280–303. See also Maurizio Lazzarato, "Immaterial Labor," trans. Paul Colilli and Ed Emory, in *Radical Thought in Italy: A Potential Politics,* ed. Paolo Virno and Michael Hardt (Minneapolis: University of Minnesota Press, 1996), 133–47.

8 Ernest Mandel, *Late Capitalism,* trans. Joris De Bres (New York: Verso, 1978), 9.

9 Reinhold Martin, *The Organizational Complex: Architecture, Media, and Corporate Space* (Cambridge, Mass.: MIT Press, 2003).

10 One such attempt to codify the architecture of the postwar period can be found in

Sarah Williams Goldhagen and Réjean Legault, *Anxious Modernisms: Experimentation in Postwar Architecture Culture* (Montreal: Canadian Centre for Architecture; Cambridge, Mass.: MIT Press, 2000).

11 Jean-François Lyotard, "Answering the Question: What Is Postmodernism?" in *The Postmodern Condition: A Report on Knowledge*, trans. Geoff Bennington and Brian Massumi (Minneapolis: University of Minnesota Press, 1984), 71. For the aforementioned citations see, respectively, Jameson, "Postmodernism, or The Cultural Logic of Late Capitalism," 54; and Jameson, *Postmodernism*, 2, as well as Fredric Jameson, *A Singular Modernity: Essay on the Ontology of the Present* (New York: Verso, 2002), and Andreas Huyssen's review of this book, "Memories of Modernism," *Harvard Design Magazine* 20 (Spring/Summer 2004): 90–95; Andreas Huyssen, *After the Great Divide: Modernism, Mass Culture, Postmodernism* (Bloomington: Indiana University Press, 1986), 183–88; and David Harvey, *The Condition of Postmodernity* (Oxford: Oxford University Press, 1990), 4–6.

12 On neo-Kantianism and the revision of modernist historiography beginning in the 1950s, see Anthony Vidler, *Histories of the Immediate Present: Inventing Architectural Modernism* (Cambridge, Mass.: MIT Press, 2008), 17–105.

13 Manfredo Tafuri, "Les cendres de Jefferson," *Architecture d'aujourd'hui* 186 (August–September 1976): 53–72; revised and reprinted as "The Ashes of Jefferson" in Tafuri, *The Sphere and the Labyrinth: Avant-Gardes and Architecture from Piranesi to the 1970s* (1980), trans. Pelligrino d'Acierno and Robert Connolly (Cambridge, Mass.: MIT Press, 1987), 291–303. On the collector as an archetype see Walter Benjamin, "Eduard Fuchs, Collector and Historian," trans. Michael W. Jennings and Howard Eiland, in *Walter Benjamin: Selected Writings*, vol. 3, *1935–1938* (Cambridge, Mass.: Harvard University Press, 2002), 260–302. For a summary of the mutual imbrication of past, present, and future in Benjamin's notion of collecting, see Ackbar Abbas, "Walter Benjamin's Collector: The Fate of Modern Experience," *New Literary History* 20, no. 1 (Autumn 1988): 217–37.

14 Conrad Fiedler introduced the notion of "pure visibility" in his *Über die Beurteilung von Werken der bildenden Kunst* (1876) (On Judging Works of Visual Art), trans. Henry Schaefer-Simmern and Fulmer Mood (Berkeley: University of California Press, 1949). His lone excursion into architectural theory, "Bemerkungen über Wesen und Geschichte der Baukunst" (1878), reproduces some of the earlier essay's premises in an analysis of the Romanesque. Conrad Fiedler, "Observations on the Nature and History of Architecture," trans. Harry Francis Mallgrave and Eleftherios Ikonomou, in *Empathy, Form, and Space: Problems in German Aesthetics, 1873–1893*, ed. Harry Francis Mallgrave and Eleftherios Ikonomou (Santa Monica: Getty Center for the History of Art and the Humanities, 1994), 125–46. See also Mallgrave and Ikonomou, "Introduction," 29–35.

15 On modernism's ambivalent endgames, see in particular Felicity D. Scott, *Architecture or Techno-Utopia: Politics after Modernism* (Cambridge, Mass.: MIT Press, 2007), and Vidler, *Histories of the Immediate Present*.

16 Kenneth Frampton suggests the connection to Stalinism in "Towards a Critical Regionalism," 19. It is Manfredo Tafuri's singular contribution to have demonstrated

tirelessly the assimilation of Utopia into capitalist development, beginning with *Architecture and Utopia.*

17 Andreas Huyssen, "Introduction: Modernism after Postmodernity," *New German Critique* 99 (Fall 2006): 1–5.

1. Territory

1 According to his biographers, in 1911, while still a manager at National Cash Register (NCR), Thomas J. Watson wrote the directive "THINK" on a board during a presentation to capture the attention of his sales team. NCR's founder, John Henry Patterson, then had the slogan placed on signs in each of the company's departments. Hired in 1914 by the financier Charles Flint to run the Computing-Tabulating-Recording Company (CTR), which had earlier merged with Herman Hollerith's Tabulating Machine Company, Watson brought the slogan with him, placing it in every room in the company. In 1924, he changed the company's name to International Business Machines (IBM). Thomas Graham Belden and Marva Robins Belden, *The Lengthening Shadow: (The) Life of Thomas J. Watson* (Boston: Little, Brown, 1962), 157–59. By the early 1930s, "THINK" had become the company's unofficial slogan. Identifying productive thought with loyalty and conformism even as it seems to encourage intellectual autonomy, the slogan performs a double bind that corresponds with the consolidation of "immaterial production" as a defining characteristic of late-twentieth-century corporate capitalism. On immaterial production and its correlates, see in particular Lazzarato, "Immaterial Labor," 133–47.

2 Daniel Bell, *The Coming of Post-Industrial Society: A Venture in Social Forecasting* (New York: Basic Books, 1973); Gilles Deleuze, "Postscript on Control Societies," in *Negotiations 1972–1990,* trans. Martin Joughin (New York: Columbia University Press, 1995), 177–82; Hardt and Negri, *Empire;* Alain Badiou, *The Century,* trans. Alberto Toscano (Malden, Mass.: Polity Press, 2007).

3 I do not use the term *territory* in a scalar sense but in the sense of a variously demarcated or bounded space. Nor do I distinguish between city and territory, a distinction that is familiar to students of urban debates since the 1960s, which Pier Vittorio Aureli has reintroduced in a discussion of the Italian scene during that period. Rather than associating (as Aureli does) "territory" with an emphasis on urban infrastructure or open-ended networks, and "city" with discrete urban artifacts or islands of architectonic form, I argue below that networks and islands cannot be understood independently of one another. In the postmodern city, the two terms are not opposed but, rather, conjoined to produce complex topologies in which insides and outsides are multiply enfolded. For Aureli's position, see *The Project of Autonomy: Architecture and the City within and against Capitalism* (New York: Buell Center for the Study of American Architecture / Princeton Architectural Press, 2008).

4 Robert Venturi, Denise Scott Brown, and Steven Izenour, *Learning from Las Vegas* (Cambridge, Mass.: MIT Press, 1972). The book was reissued in a second, revised

edition in 1977. For an insightful, close reading of *Learning from Las Vegas*, see Aron Vinegar, *I Am a Monument: On Learning from Las Vegas* (Cambridge, Mass.: MIT Press, 2008). See also the essays collected in Aron Vinegar and Michael J. Golec, eds., *Relearning from Las Vegas* (Minneapolis: University of Minnesota Press, 2009).

5 Jürgen Habermas's 1980 Adorno Prize address was first translated by Seyla Benhabib as "Modernity versus Postmodernity," *New German Critique* 22 (Winter 1981): 3–14; it was republished as "Modernity—An Incomplete Project," in Foster, *The Anti-Aesthetic*, 3–15. The quotation is from the latter publication, 9.

6 Jürgen Habermas, "Modern and Postmodern Architecture," in *The New Conservatism: Cultural Criticism and the Historians' Debate*, ed. and trans. Shierry Weber Nicholsen (Cambridge, Mass.: MIT Press, 1989), 3–21. The essay was originally delivered as a lecture at the opening of the exhibition *The Other Tradition: Architecture in Munich from 1800 to the Present* in November 1981.

7 See Jameson, *Postmodernism*, cf. Introduction; Huyssen, *After the Great Divide*; Seyla Benhabib, "Epistemologies of Postmodernism: A Rejoinder to Jean-François Lyotard," *New German Critique* 33 (Autumn 1984): 103–26; Harvey, *The Condition of Postmodernity*; Ihab Hassan, *The Postmodern Turn: Essays in Postmodern Theory and Culture* (Columbus: Ohio State University Press, 1987); Lyotard, "Answering the Question: What Is Postmodernism?" 71–82; Terry Eagleton, *The Illusions of Postmodernism* (Malden, Mass.: Blackwell, 1996); Alex Callinicos, *Against Postmodernism: A Marxist Critique* (London: St. Martin's Press, 1989). For a succinct history of postmodernist theory, see Anderson, *The Origins of Postmodernity* .

8 See, for example, Fredric Jameson, "Periodizing the 60s," in *The Ideologies of Theory: Essays 1971–1986*, vol. 2, *The Syntax of History* (Minneapolis: University of Minnesota Press, 1989), 178–208.

9 See in particular Harvey, *The Condition of Postmodernity*, chapter 9, "From Fordism to Flexible Accumulation," 141–72.

10 In addition to a certain topological mindset (that owes much to structuralism) running through much of the cultural and political theory that I cite below, topology was a common tool for architectural speculation during the 1950s and 1960s, in both Europe and the United States. For an account of its impact in France, see Larry Busbea, *Topologies: The Urban Utopia in France, 1960–1970* (Cambridge, Mass.: MIT Press, 2007). For some earlier examples from architecture and the visual arts in the United States, see Anna Vallye, "The Strategic Universality of *trans/formation*, 1950–1952," *Grey Room* 35 (Spring 2009): 28–57.

11 See, for example, Jameson's remarks on Venturi and Jencks in relation to the commercialized "populism" of postmodern architecture, which he measures against the oppositional populism of earlier political movements. Jameson, *Postmodernism*, 2, 62–64.

12 Venturi, Scott Brown, and Izenour, *Learning from Las Vegas*, 107. In the book's second edition, this was emended to read "the aspirations of almost all Americans, including most low income urban dwellers." Venturi, Scott Brown, and Izenour, *Learning from Las Vegas*, 2d ed. (Cambridge, Mass.: MIT Press, 1977), 161.

13 Ibid., 106. Nixon had used the construction "great silent majority" in a speech on 3 November 1969, ostensibly in reference to those who did not oppose the war in Vietnam, although it was also understood by many in racial terms. Responding to a piece by Venturi and Scott Brown on the Co-op City housing development in the Bronx in *Progressive Architecture* in February of 1970, Ulrich Franzen wrote, in a letter to the editor, that "In tune with the present era, the Co-op City survey by Robert Venturi *[sic]* raises the ghost of a 'silent majority' architecture," Franzen, Letter to the Editor, *Progressive Architecture* (April 1970): 8. He is referring to Robert Venturi and Denise Scott Brown, "Co-op City: Learning to Like It," *Progressive Architecture* (February 1970): 64–72. Shortly thereafter Kenneth Frampton asked, in a polemic with Scott Brown conducted under the auspices of the Institute for Architecture and Urban Studies in New York, with reference to Scott Brown and Venturi's urban theory: "Should designers like politicians wait upon the dictates of a silent majority, and if so, how are they to interpret them?" Kenneth Frampton, "America 1960–1970: Notes on Urban Images and Theory," *Casabella* 25–36, 359–60 (May–June 1971): 31. To which Scott Brown replied in the same issue: "One can be totally committed to civil rights, social progress and the needs of the poor without having to hate the lower-middle classes who face injustice too. But the concept of a hard-hat majority to be scorned will legitimize and expose a lot of now repressed upper-middle-class prejudice." Denise Scott Brown, "Reply to Frampton," *Casabella* 25–36, 359–60 (May–June 1971): 43. In the architectural debates, the term *silent majority* only appears to have been racialized (as "silent white majority") with the publication of *Learning from Las Vegas* in 1972.

14 According to Foucault, the "apparatuses of security" are to be distinguished from their accompanying disciplinary apparatuses, such as prisons and asylums, as follows: "[I]n the disciplines one started from a norm, and it was in relation to the training carried out with reference to the norm that the normal could be distinguished from the abnormal." While in the case of apparatuses of security, "The normal comes first and the norm is deduced from it." Foucault, *Security, Territory, Population*, 63. On the relation between disciplinary apparatuses and territorial sovereignty, see also Michel Foucault, *"Society Must Be Defended": Lectures at the Collège de France 1975–1976*, ed. Mauro Bertani and Alessandro Fontana, trans. David Macey (New York: Palgrave Macmillan, 2003), 35–40, and on the articulation of disciplinary power and biopower, 239–61. For a fuller account of the latter, see Foucault, *The Birth of Biopolitics*.

15 Max Horkheimer and Theodor W. Adorno, *Dialectic of Enlightenment: Philosophical Fragments*, ed. Gunzelin Schmid Noerr, trans. Edmund Jephcott (Stanford: Stanford University Press, 2002), in particular, "The Culture Industry: Enlightenment as Mass Deception," 94–136; Marshall McLuhan, *Understanding Media: The Extensions of Man* (New York: McGraw-Hill, 1964). For an overview of the American debates on the subject in the mid-1950s, see Bernard Rosenberg and David Manning White, eds., *Mass Culture: The Popular Arts in America* (New York: The Free Press, 1957). Adorno and Horkheimer use the term *mass culture* to denote the content of the "culture industry." In contrast, Raymond Williams omits *mass*

culture from his *Keywords*, though he does include proximate terms such as *mass society* and *mass media*. He also notes the persistence into the 1980s of a dual meaning within the term *popular culture*: both positive, in the sense of "well-liked by many people" (as in "popularity") as well as of "the people," and negative, in the sense of "inferior kinds of work" and "work deliberately setting out to win favour." This duality of meaning also carries into the political sense of "populism." Williams, *Keywords: A Vocabulary of Culture and Society*, 2d ed. (New York: Oxford University Press, 1983), 237–38. For an incisive discussion of Adorno's attitudes toward mass culture in relation to postmodernism, see Huyssen, *After the Great Divide*, chapter 2, "Adorno in Reverse: From Hollywood to Richard Wagner," 16–43.

16 Venturi, *Complexity and Contradiction in Architecture*, 22–23.

17 Aldo Rossi, *The Architecture of the City*, 162–63.

18 Harvey, *The Condition of Postmodernity*, 83–85.

19 Peter Eisenman, "The Houses of Memory: The Texts of Analogy," editor's introduction to Rossi, *The Architecture of the City*, 10.

20 Ibid.

21 Ibid., 9–11. The definitive translation of the passage in Alberti is "The city is like some large house, and the house is in turn like some small city." Leon Battista Alberti, *On the Art of Building in Ten Books*, trans. Joseph Rykwert, Neil Leach, Robert Tavernor (Cambridge, Mass.: MIT Press, 1998), 23.

22 Eisenman, "The Houses of Memory," 11.

23 Here is the passage from Foucault's notes, as published in *Naissance de la biopolitique: cours au Collège de France 1978–1979*, ed. Michel Senellart (Paris: Gallimard, 2004), 266: "Non pas un individualization uniformisante, identificatoire, hiérarchisante, mais une *environmentalité* ouverte aux aléas at aux phénomès transversaux. Latéralité." Emphasis added. Though the English translation renders "*environmentalité*" as "environmentalism," I have retained the more literal translation, which resonates with Foucault's notion of governmentality. See Foucault *The Birth of Biopolitics*, 261. In a related passage, Foucault also refers to "environmental technology" and "environmental psychology" as elements of "a society in which there is an optimization of systems of difference," 259.

24 See for example Paul Virilio, *Lost Dimension*, trans. Daniel Moshenberg (New York: Semiotext(e), 1991), particularly chapter 1, "The Overexposed City," 9–27.

25 Venturi, *Complexity and Contradiction in Architecture*, 89. Venturi is quoting from Herbert A. Simon, "The Architecture of Complexity," *Proceedings of the American Philosophical Society* 106, no. 6 (12 December 1962): 467–82.

26 Venturi, *Complexity and Contradiction in Architecture*, 102.

27 Hardt and Negri, *Empire*, 336–37.

28 Giorgio Agamben, *Homo Sacer: Sovereign Power and Bare Life*, trans. Daniel Heller-Roazen (Stanford: Stanford University Press, 1998), 37.

29 Ibid., 169–70.

30 Aldo Rossi, *A Scientific Autobiography*, as quoted in Eisenman, "The Houses of Memory," 10. As published in 1981, Lawrence Venuti's translation of Rossi's passage reads slightly differently: ". . . cities, even if they last for centuries, are in reality

great encampments of the living and the dead where a few elements remain like signals, symbols, warnings." Aldo Rossi, *A Scientific Autobiography*, trans. Lawrence Venuti (Cambridge, Mass.: MIT Press, 1981), 20. In the Italian version, published in 1999, Rossi writes: ". . . la città, anche se durano se durano secoli, solo in realtà dei grandi accampamenti di vivi e di morti dove restano alcuni elementi come segnali, simboli, avvertimenti." Aldo Rossi, *Autobiografia Scientifica* (Milan: Nuova Pratiche Editrice, 1999), 31. As is made clear by the remainder of the passage as well as by the text that precedes it, Rossi is referring to holiday encampments such as the one in Seville that he describes as "rigorously laid out like a Roman city" (*Scientific Autobiography*, 20). However, I retain Eisenman's translation as, at minimum, circumstantial evidence of the elision between two different kinds of encampments, for leisure and for confinement, on which I elaborate below.

31 Harvey, *The Condition of Postmodernity*, 85.

32 Stephen Graham and Simon Marvin, *Splintering Urbanism, Networked Infrastructures, Technological Mobilities and the Urban Condition* (London: Routledge, 2001).

33 Teresa Caldeira's work on São Paulo is particularly relevant here. See Teresa P. R. Caldeira, *City of Walls: Crime, Segregation, and Citizenship in São Paulo* (Berkeley: University of California Press, 2000).

34 Agamben, *Homo Sacer*, 38.

35 Ibid., 175. His examples of provisional (yet increasingly permanent) *zones d'attentes*—the stadium in Bari into which illegal Albanian immigrants were herded in 1991; the velodrome in which the Vichy authorities gathered Jews destined for the camps; the Hôtel Arcades in Roissy, in which Somali asylum seekers were detained in 1992—indirectly highlight the relational character of the inside-outside paradigm (174). For example, the Hôtel Arcades is near the Paris-Orly airport and was therefore available for authorities to designate as a de facto extension of the airport's juridically indeterminate "international zone." Many have followed Agamben's lead by associating the camp-as-biopolitical-diagram—understood in the Foucauldian sense of an organizing virtuality like the panopticon—with a host of actualities such as refugee camps, prison camps, and other holes in the contemporary politico-juridical landscape, with varying results. For an overview, see Richard Ek, "Giorgio Agamben and the Spatialities of the Camp: An Introduction," *Geografiska Annaler, Series B: Human Geography* 88, no. 4 (2006): 363–86. See also Zygmunt Bauman, *Society under Siege* (Malden, Mass.: Blackwell, 2002), and Bülent Diken and Carsten Bagge Lausten, *The Culture of Exception: Sociology Facing the Camp* (New York: Routledge, 2005).

36 Giorgio Agamben, "What Is a Camp?" in *Means without Ends: Notes on Politics*, trans. Vincenzo Binetti and Cesare Casarino (Minneapolis: University of Minnesota Press, 2000), 42. On the camp and the gated community, see in particular Diken and Lausten, *The Culture of Exception*, 79–100. See also Bauman, *Society under Siege*, 114–17.

37 Agamben, "What Is a Camp?" 41.

38 For a brief history of the gated community in the United States, see Setha Low,

Behind the Gates: Life, Security and the Pursuit of Happiness in Fortress America (New York: Routledge, 2003), 13–16. See also, Dolores Hayden, *Building American Suburbia: Green Fields and Urban Growth, 1820–2000* (New York: Pantheon Books, 2003).

39 For a comprehensive review of the discourse of "urban decline" with which practices of "renewal" were associated in the United States, see Robert A. Beauregard, *Voices of Decline: The Postwar Face of U.S. Cities,* 2d ed. (New York: Routledge, 2003).

40 Katharine G. Bristol, "The Pruitt-Igoe Myth," *Journal of Architectural Education* 44, no. 3 (May 1991): 163–71. See also Lee Rainwater, *Behind Ghetto Walls: Black Families in a Federal Slum* (Chicago: Aldine Publishing Co., 1970).

41 Oscar Newman, *Defensible Space: Crime Prevention through Urban Design* (New York: Macmillan, 1972), 3.

42 Jencks, *The Language of Post-Modern Architecture,* 9. This same photograph was also reproduced without comment by Colin Rowe and Fred Koetter in the introduction to *Collage City,* 7, the opening chapter of which is titled "Utopia: Decline and Fall?" 9–31.

43 Newman, *Defensible Space,* 207.

44 Ibid., 56–58.

45 Ibid., 203.

46 Ibid., 195.

47 Ibid., 197.

48 Ibid., 203.

49 Ibid., 205–6. On the emergence of risk as an epistemological category (and a dimension of capital) in the nineteenth century, see François Ewald, "Insurance and Risk," in *The Foucault Effect: Studies in Governmentality,* ed. Graham Burchell, Colin Gordon, and Peter Miller (Chicago: University of Chicago Press, 1991), 197–210.

50 This division, and its accompanying "ghettoization" of crime, can also be interpreted as marking a transition away from an anthropology of the criminal and the rational and absolute elimination of criminality that Foucault associates with early nineteenth-century panopticism and other reformist practices, and toward the toleration of a certain degree of criminality judged to be acceptable according to the economic rationality of risk-reward formulas, as in the crime rates that Newman cites. See Foucault, *The Birth of Biopolitics,* 248–60.

51 Ibid., 259–60. In particular Foucault refers here to the "market milieu" as the specific environment in which subjectivization takes place under neoliberal "environmentality."

52 On the centrality of the notion of "human capital" in American neoliberalism, and in particular its distinction from a Marxian notion of labor power, see Foucault, *The Birth of Biopolitics,* 219–33. This is borne out further by other, synchronic developments, such as the progressive interdependence of work and pleasure analyzed by Jacques Donzelot in the emergent, post-Taylorist "corporate" state: "a principle of continuity, an unbroken circularity . . . between the register of pro-

duction and productivity, and that of the sanitary and social administration of society." Jacques Donzelot, "Pleasure in Work," in Burchell, Gordon, and Miller, *The Foucault Effect*, 279.

53 Thomas More, *Utopia*, trans. Robert M. Adams (New York: W. W. Norton, 1975), 50–52, 74.

54 Jameson, *Postmodernism*, 127. On postmodernism and biopower, see Hardt and Negri, *Empire*, 146–54, 187–90, 280–303.

55 Jameson cites Gehry's house for what he calls its "attempt to think a material thought" while in the process damning Gehry with faint praise, by suggesting that, though the house effectively models the contradictions of postmodern hyperspace, the question as to whether it is capable of generating what Jameson calls a "new Utopian spatial language" remains unanswered. Jameson, *Postmodernism*, 128–29.

56 For a collection of Jameson's writings on utopian science fiction, see Jameson, *Archaeologies of the Future*.

57 See Bauman, *Society under Siege*, 116–17.

58 Louis Marin, *Utopics: The Semiological Play of Textual Spaces*, trans. Robert A. Vollrath (Amherst, N.Y.: Prometheus Books, 1984). The diagrams are to be found on page 117.

59 Ibid., 103.

60 On the dialectic of the two American "utopias," see Tafuri, *Architecture and Utopia*, 30–40. On "hypermodernism," see Manfredo Tafuri, "'L'Architecture dans le boudoir': The Language of Criticism and the Criticism of Language," *Oppositions* 3 (May 1974): 55, and also Manfredo Tafuri, *Interpreting the Renaissance: Princes, Cities, Architects*, trans. Daniel Sherer (New Haven: Yale University Press / Harvard University Graduate School of Design, 2006), xxvii.

61 Marin, *Utopics*, 240.

62 Charles Moore, "You Have Got to Pay for the Public Life," *Perspecta* 9–10 (1965), 57–87.

63 Ibid., 59.

64 Marin, *Utopics*, 246.

65 The work of Mike Davis remains indispensable here. On the city-as-gated community, see his early classic, *City of Quartz: Excavating the Future in Los Angeles* (New York: Verso, 1990); on slums as a structural component of postmodern urbanization, see *Planet of Slums* (New York: Verso, 2006). For a more subtle case study on the interrelationships of walled or gated enclaves and *favelas* in São Paulo (including a comparison with Los Angeles), see Caldeira, *City of Walls*. On the antinomies of postmodernity, see Fredric Jameson, *The Seeds of Time* (New York: Columbia University Press, 1994), 1–71. Replacing the traditional opposition of utopia to dystopia with that of Utopia/anti-Utopia as one such antinomy (which I modify here by linking it to the modern), Jameson reminds us of an important distinction between dystopian texts, which are generally narrative in form, and utopian ones, which are descriptive. In the latter, the description tends to pivot around some

sort of "Utopian machine" or mechanism, of which Jameson uses Rem Koolhaas's account of the twin inventions of the elevator and the urban grid in *Delirious New York* as an example (55–58).

66 This is among Jameson's major themes in *Archaeologies of the Future.*

67 Michel Foucault, "The Thought of the Outside," trans. Brian Massumi, in *Michel Foucault: Aesthetics, Method, and Epistemology,* ed. James D. Faubion (New York: New Press, 1998), 147–69.

68 Michel Foucault, "Different Spaces," trans. Robert Hurley, in Faubion, *Michel Foucault,* 175–85. On the topological character of Foucault's thought, see Gilles Deleuze, *Foucault,* trans. Seán Hand (Minneapolis: University of Minnesota Press, 1988), "Topology: 'Thinking Otherwise,'" 45–123.

69 For an elaboration of the utopian boundary or limit as "frontier" see Louis Marin, "Frontiers of Utopia: Past and Present," *Critical Inquiry* 19, no. 3 (Spring 1993): 397–420. For Marin, Utopia is "the figure of the horizon," a kind of infinite inbetween or threshold, "the figure of the limit and of the distance, the drifting of frontiers within the 'gap' between opposite terms, neither this one nor that one," 412. The inside outness of Utopia for which I argue here is a spatially paradoxical condition, rather than merely an ambiguous or ambivalent one.

70 On the choice "not to be governed like that" see Michel Foucault, "What Is Critique?" trans. Lysa Hochroth, in *The Politics of Truth,* ed. Sylvère Lotringer (New York: Semiotext(e), 1997), 41–81.

2. History

1 Tafuri, "Les cendres de Jefferson," 53–72; revised and reprinted as "The Ashes of Jefferson" in Tafuri, *The Sphere and the Labyrinth,* 291–303. Tafuri repeated the same statement in another version of this text published in 1976 as "'European Graffiti': Five × Five = Twenty-five," trans. Victor Caliandro, *Oppositions* 5 (Summer 1976): 57.

2 Francis Fukuyama, *The End of History and the Last Man* (New York: Avon Books, 1992), chapter 9, "The Victory of the VCR," 98–108. For a detailed treatment of Fukuyama's "end of history" thesis, see Perry Anderson, *A Zone of Engagement* (London: Verso, 1992), 279–375.

3 Though Fukuyama does not use the term *postmodernism,* he does identify cultural relativism as one of the properties of the "end of history." Fukuyama, *The End of History and the Last Man,* 306–7.

4 Jacques Derrida, *Specters of Marx: The State of the Debt, The Work of Mourning, and The New International,* trans. Peggy Kamuf (New York: Routledge, 1994), 69.

5 Though the original, Italian title of Manfredo Tafuri's *Architecture and Utopia* is *Progetto e utopia: Architettura e sviluppo capitalistico* (Bari: Laterza, 1973), Tafuri's frequent use of the term *progetto* is, as Andrew Leach puts it, "elastic" in its connotations. Andrew Leach, *Manfredo Tafuri: Choosing History* (Ghent: A & S Books, 2007), 249.

6   Georg Simmel, *The Philosophy of Money*, ed. David Frisby, trans. Tom Bottomore and David Frisby (New York: Routledge, 1990). In particular chapter 6, "The Style of Life," 429–512.

7   See Michel Serres, *Hermes: Literature, Science, Philosophy*, ed. Josué V. Harari and David F. Bell (Baltimore: Johns Hopkins University Press, 1982), chapter 7, "The Origin of Language: Biology, Information Theory, Thermodynamics," 71–83, on a "sheaf of times" organized around feedback.

8   Jameson, *Postmodernism*, 90.

9   Tafuri, *The Sphere and the Labyrinth*, 302. Emphasis in original.

10 The campaign saw a group called Swift Boat Veterans for Truth sponsor a series of unsubstantiated attack advertisements against the candidacy of Kerry, the Democratic presidential nominee, who had commanded a U.S. Navy swift boat during the Vietnam conflict.

11 Jameson discusses Tafuri's "absolute pessimism" in *Postmodernism*, 60–62.

12 For an overview of post-theory (or "post-critical") discourse in architecture, see George Baird, "'Criticality' and Its Discontents," *Harvard Design Magazine* 21 (Fall 2004–Winter 2005): 16–21. See also Reinhold Martin, "Critical of What? Toward a Utopian Realism," *Harvard Design Magazine* 22 (Spring–Summer 2005): 104–9.

13 Tafuri, *The Sphere and the Labyrinth*, 300.

14 Paul N. Edwards, *The Closed World: Computers and the Politics of Discourse in Cold War America* (Cambridge: MIT Press, 1996), chapter 4, "From Operations Research to the Electronic Battlefield," 113–45.

15 Lyotard, *The Postmodern Condition*, 55–56.

16 R. Buckminster Fuller, "World Game: How It Came About," in *Fifty Years of the Design Science Revolution and the World Game* (Carbondale: World Resources Inventory, Southern Illinois University, 1969), 114.

17 See Scott, *Architecture or Techno-Utopia*, 202–4.

18 Fuller, "World Game," 111.

19 Jameson, *Postmodernism*, 105.

20 Ibid., 117.

21 Ibid., 127.

22 Manfredo Tafuri and Francesco Dal Co, *Modern Architecture*, vol. 2, trans. Robert Erich Wolf (New York: Rizzoli, 1986), chapter 17, "The Activity of the Masters after World War II," 309–14.

23 See Martin, *The Organizational Complex*.

24 Venturi, Scott Brown, and Izenour, *Learning from Las Vegas*, 65, 100.

25 Jameson, *Postmodernism*, 38–45.

26 Colin Rowe, introduction to *Five Architects: Eisenman Graves Gwathmey Hejduk Meier* (New York: Wittenborn & Company, 1972), 4. On the Chicago School, see Colin Rowe, "Chicago Frame: Chicago's Place in the Modern Movement," *Architectural Review* 120 (November 1956): 285–89.

27 For a reading of the Seagram Building that extends Tafuri's interpretation further in the direction of Adorno and Horkheimer, see K. Michael Hays, "Odysseus and

the Oarsman, or Mies's Abstraction Once Again," in *The Presence of Mies*, ed. Detlef Mertins (New York: Princeton Architectural Press, 1994), 235–48.

28 See "Five on Five," response to Five Architects organized by Robert A. M. Stern, *Architectural Forum* 138 (May 1973): 46–576. The articles included were Stern, "Stompin' at the Savoye," 46–48; Jaquelin Robertson, "Machines in the Garden," 49–53; Charles Moore, "In Similar States of Undress," 53–54; Allan Greenberg, "The Lurking American Legacy," 54–55; and Romaldo Giurgola, "The Discreet Charm of the Bourgeoisie," 56–57. See also Peter Eisenman and Robert A. M. Stern, eds., "White and Gray: Eleven Modern American Architects," *Architecture and Urbanism* 4 (April 1975): 25–180.

29 Vincent J. Scully Jr., *The Shingle Style and the Stick Style: Architectural Theory and Design from Richardson to the Origins of Wright*, rev. ed. (New Haven: Yale University Press, 1971), xix–xx.

30 J. G. Ballard, *The Atrocity Exhibition* (London: Jonathan Cape Ltd., 1969), 23.

31 Ibid., 68.

32 Further, as Crary puts it, a mass medium like television now becomes primarily a "switching device" optimizing and thereby intensifying such flows, "while at the same time imposing intricate circuitries of control." Jonathan Crary, "Eclipse of the Spectacle," in *Art after Modernism: Rethinking Representation*, ed. Brian Wallis (New York: New Museum of Contemporary Art and Boston: David R. Godine, 1984), 293.

33 Ballard, *The Atrocity Exhibition*, 107.

34 Friedrich Kittler has formulated a schematic genealogy of "media war" in terms of the "strategies of the Real" associated with different technical media, from the storage media of World War I, to the transmission media of World War II, to the universal computing media of Reagan's Strategic Defense Initiative (SGI). Kittler, "Media Wars: Trenches, Lightning, Stars," in *Literature, Media, Information Systems: Essays*, ed. John Johnston (Amsterdam: G + B Arts International, 1997), 117–29.

35 Ulrich Beck, *Risk Society: Towards a New Modernity*, trans. Mark Ritter (London: Sage Publications, 1992); Anthony Giddens, *The Consequences of Modernity* (Stanford: Stanford University Press, 1990); Ulrich Beck, Anthony Giddens, Scott Lash, *Reflexive Modernization: Politics, Tradition and Aesthetics in the Modern Social Order* (Stanford: Stanford University Press, 1994).

36 Jameson, *A Singular Modernity*, 29.

37 Fredric Jameson, "'End of Art' or 'End of History'?" in *The Cultural Turn: Selected Writings on the Postmodern, 1983–1998* (New York: Verso, 1998), 90. On *posthistoire*, see Anderson, *A Zone of Engagement*, chapter 13, "The Ends of History," 279–375.

38 There are some affinities between what I am describing as an anachronistic "asynchronic periodicity" and the notion of "nonsynchronous" temporalities that Ernst Bloch developed to explain the appeal of fascism to the working class, but in reverse. Though potentially as technocratic as the rationally planned utopias that

Bloch regards as inauthentic, the periodicity built into the feedback loop also carries within it an "anticipatory illumination" that is closer to that elaborated by Bloch in *The Principle of Hope* and elsewhere. On "nonsynchronous" temporalities, see Ernst Bloch, "Nonsynchronism and the Obligation to Its Dialectics," trans. Mark Ritter, *New German Critique* 11 (Spring 1977): 22–38; see also Anson Rabinbach, "Ernst Bloch's Heritage of Our Times and the Theory of Fascism" in the same issue, 5–21. On the "anticipatory illumination," see Ernst Bloch, *The Principle of Hope*, 3 vols., trans. Neville Plaice, Stephen Plaice, and Paul Knight (Cambridge, Mass.: MIT Press, 1986); see also Ernst Bloch, "The Artistic Illusion as the Visible Anticipatory Illumination," in *The Utopian Function of Art and Literature: Selected Essays*, trans. Jack Zipes and Frank Mecklenburg (Cambridge, Mass.: MIT Press, 1988), 141–55. For Bloch's views on architecture, see "Building in Empty Spaces," in *The Utopian Function of Art and Literature*, 185–99.

39 David Joselit explores related strategies of critical art practice in the age of network television in *Feedback: Television against Democracy* (Cambridge, Mass.: MIT Press, 2007).

40 Cited in Marilyn B. Young, *The Vietnam Wars 1945–1990* (New York: HarperCollins, 1991), 190.

41 Ibid., 191.

42 Skidmore, Owings & Merrill, "Saigon South Master Plan," www.som.com. See also Richard Marshall, *Emerging Urbanity: Global Urban Projects in the Asia Pacific Rim* (London: Routledge, 2002), as well as the Central Trading & Development Group Web site, at www.saigonsouth.com, and Kristen Bole, "Cushman & Wakefield Invades Vietnam," *San Francisco Business Times* (25 July 1997), http://sanfrancisco.bizjournals.com.

43 On Operation Igloo White, see Edwards, *The Closed World*, 3–6, 142.

44 Huntington cited in Michael E. Latham, "Knowledge at War: American Social Science and Vietnam," in *A Companion to the Vietnam War*, ed. Marilyn B. Young and Robert Buzzanco (Malden, Mass.: Blackwell, 2002), 435.

45 Ibid.

3. Language

1 Michel Foucault, *Naissance de la biopolitique*, 266. *Environmentalité* is translated as "environmentalism" in Foucault, *The Birth of Biopolitics*, 261.

2 Richard M. Nixon, "Statement about the National Environmental Policy Act of 1969," 1 January 1970, The Richard Nixon Library and Birthplace Archives (RNLBA). Available from http://www.nixonfoundation.org.

3 Richard M. Nixon, "Special Message to the Congress on Environmental Quality," 10 February 1970, RNLBA. Available from: http://www.nixonfoundation.org.

4 Ibid.

5 Ulrich Beck, *Risk Society*, 21. Emphasis in the original. On the biological notion of the milieu, see Georges Canguilhem, "The Living and Its Milieu," trans. John Savage, *Grey Room* 3 (Spring 2001): 7–31. On the representation of the mileu, see also

Edward Eigen, "Dark Space and the Early Days of Photography as a Medium," *Grey Room* 3 (Spring 2001): 90–111.

6 Michel Foucault, *The Order of Things: An Archeology of the Human Sciences* (London: Tavistock Publications, 1970), 382.

7 Beck, *Risk Society*, 74.

8 National Environmental Policy Act of 1969, Sec. 102(A) (42 USC 4332).

9 Gyorgy Kepes, "Art and Ecological Consciousness," in *Arts of the Environment*, ed. Gyorgy Kepes (New York: George Braziller, 1972), 4–5. Kepes adds that "artists have come to recognize that their creative imagination and sensibilities are neither self-generated nor self-contained: they belong to the larger environmental field of nature and society" (5). Thus, the list of contributors he compiled to articulate art's regulatory, homeostatic role within this "total system" included microbiologist Rene Dubos, physicist Dennis Gabor, anthropologist Edward T. Hall, psychologist Erik H. Erikson, historian Leo Marx, planner Kevin Lynch, architect Dolf Schnebli, architecture critic James T. Burns Jr., computer scientist Jay W. Forrester, architect Eduardo Terrazas, environmental artists Pulsa, artist Robert Smithson, and biochemist Albert Szent-Gyorgi.

10 Leo Marx, "American Institutions and the Ecological Ideal," in Kepes, *Arts of the Environment*, 78–97. What was unique about the entry of "environment" into this arena—in the American context in particular—was that it coincided with resistance to government intervention in the wake of the New Deal and Johnson's Great Society. Indeed, Marx considered the limited capacity of government to respond to what he called the "ecological ideal" and was skeptical of the willingness of the Nixon administration actually to allocate funds to support its rhetoric.

11 Ibid., 93.

12 According to Marx, the ecological perspective "calls into question the controlling purposes of all the major institutions which actually determine the nation's impact on the environment: the great business corporations, the military establishment, the universities, the scientific and technological elites, and the exhilarating expansionary ethos by which we all live." Ibid., 96.

13 Tomás Maldonado, *Design, Nature, and Revolution: Toward a Critical Ecology*, trans. Mario Domandi (New York: Harper & Row, 1972), 133–34, n. 3.

14 Ibid., 76.

15 Ibid., 133–34, n. 3. And as did Leo Marx, Maldonado observed the determinate role of history: "The ferocious sack of nature carried out in the last two centuries would be incomprehensible without a careful examination of the operative modalities of these historical factors. In practice that means that the question concerning the scandal of society must precede the question concerning the scandal of nature" (76). That this notion presupposes the internal consistency of the system and does not see the production of that consistency (or normalcy) as itself a political process is not surprising, because it derives in part from the conservative and specifically antirevolutionary (i.e., anti-Marxist) sociology of Vilfedo Pareto, whose thought informed the sociobiological hypotheses of L. J. Henderson, Parsons's mentor at Harvard. Maldonado's effort, then, to clarify the popular use of

the term *system* by referring to von Bertalanffy's distinction between closed systems (for Maldonado, authoritarian ones) and properly open ones, is limited by this assumption. Because within his discourse, a discourse of the integrated ecosystem, nothing is outside "the system" as such. There are only choices between open and closed systems. In other words, environmental degradation marked a scandal of the system of systems, in which humanity's balance sheet showed two accounts, one with nature and one with society, in mutual interdependence and mutual crisis.

16 Ibid., 60–61. The extension of environment from the biological to the social realm was not lost on Nixon, who noted from his retreat in San Clemente that "It doesn't involve just air, water, and traffic, which are the obvious ones, but it also involves open space, leisure time. What are people going to do?

"As we drove along, for example, we saw a sign pointing to Leisure World. I don't know whether any of you have been there. I was there a few years ago, fifteen years ago. This is one of several very exciting projects that are being developed for older people, where they live. The people live longer if they retire sooner, if they have longer vacations. There is the question of what we are going to do with them, where they are going to go. This is why we are looking into these problems in terms that are much broader than simply the immediate ones of air, water, and so forth." Richard M. Nixon, "Remarks on Signing the National Environmental Policy Act of 1969," 1 January 1970, RNLBA. Available from: http://www.nixonfoundation.org.

17 Maldonado, *Design, Nature, and Revolution*, 119–20, n. 2.

18 Gyorgy Kepes, *Language of Vision* (Chicago: Paul Theobald, 1944). Kepes thanks Morris for his comments on the manuscript in the book's acknowledgments, 4.

19 Whereas Venturi had also cited Kepes on the interplay of organism and environment, in the context of his own Gestalt-psychological reading of figural ambiguity in *Complexity and Contradiction in Architecture*. See Venturi, *Complexity and Contradiction in Architecture*, 85.

20 Kevin Lynch, *The Image of the City* (Cambridge, Mass.: MIT Press, 1960).

21 Gyorgy Kepes, cited in Princeton University, *Planning Man's Physical Environment*, Series 2, Conference 5 (Princeton: Princeton University, 1946), 21. Kepes added that "[t]he world man has constructed is without sincerity, without scale, without cleanliness—twisted in space, without light, and cowardly in color. It combines a mechanically precise pattern of the details within a formless whole. It is oppressive in its fake monumentality, it is degrading in its petty fawning manner of decorative face lifting. Man living in this false environment and injured emotionally and intellectually by the terrific odds of a chaotic society, cannot avoid having his sensibilities, the foundation of his creative faculty, impaired" (21).

22 Colin Rowe and Robert Slutzky, "Transparency: Literal and Phenomenal," *Perspecta* 8 (1963): 45.

23 Colin Rowe and Robert Slutzky, "Transparency: Literal and Phenomenal . . . Part II," *Perspecta* 13–14 (1971): 389.

24 The paragraph in Kepes immediately following the one cited by Rowe and Slutzky reads: "The order of our time is to knead together the scientific and technical

knowledge acquired, into an integrated whole on the biological and social plane. Today there are hardly any aspects of human endeavor where the concept of interpenetration as a device of integration is not a focus. Technology, philosophy, psychology, and physical science are using it as a guiding principle. So do literature, painting, architecture, motion picture and photography, and stage design. Furthermore, it is a commonplace technical knowledge in our everyday life. Radio waves are the clearest example of this." Kepes, *Language of Vision*, 77. Rowe and Slutzky, "Transparency: Literal and Phenomenal . . . Part II," 398.

25 This subject is engaged, as Rowe and Slutzky point out, not in a simple stimulus-response relation with an environment, visual or otherwise, but in what perceptual psychologist George W. Hartmann describes as a relation that proceeds in three steps: "Constellation of Stimuli-Organization-Reaction to Results of Organization." Ibid., 29, n. 14.

26 Peter Eisenman, in "Contrasting Concepts of Harmony in Architecture: Debate between Christopher Alexander and Peter Eisenman," *Lotus* 40 (1984): 60.

27 Peter Eisenman, "From Object to Relationship: The Casa del Fascio by Terragni," *Casabella* 34 (January 1970): 38.

28 Ibid. Eisenman draws the notion of a technologically embedded shift in space conceptions from Colin Rowe's "Chicago Frame" essay of 1956.

29 Ibid.

30 Ibid.

31 Kepes, *Language of Vision*, 13.

32 S. I. Hayakawa, "The Revision of Vision," preface to Kepes, *Language of Vision*, 9–10.

33 Peter Eisenman, "Notes on Conceptual Architecture: Toward a Definition," *Casabella* 35 (December 1971): 57, n. 26.

34 Charles W. Morris, *Foundations of the Theory of Signs* (Chicago: University of Chicago Press, 1938), 8.

35 Eisenman, "Notes on Conceptual Architecture," 51.

36 Ibid.

37 Noam Chomsky, *Cartesian Linguistics: A Chapter in the History of Rationalist Thought* (New York: Harper & Row, 1966), 33.

38 Eisenman, "Notes on Conceptual Architecture," 49.

39 Peter Eisenman, "From Object to Relationship II: Giuseppe Terragni Casa Giulani Frigerio," *Perspecta* 13–14 (1971): 39.

40 Ibid.

41 This notion of a common, unifying environment *internal* to architecture-as-language also effectively inverts that invoked by Kepes in *Arts of the Environment* when he refers to the *externalities* of a "new common—the potential complex, total system now being made possible by our scientific technology" (8).

42 Peter Eisenman, "The Big Little Magazine: *Perspecta* 12 and the Future of the Architectural Past," *Architectural Forum* 131, no. 3 (October 1969): 74–75, 104.

43 Peter de Bretteville and Arthur Golding, "About *Perspecta* 11," *Perspecta* 11 (1967): 7. The editors introduce their issue specifically through the lens of historical per-

spective, acknowledging, as does Eisenman, a renewed interest in early modernism. But they also describe a shift in interest away from the artifacts being produced by a "third generation" of modern architects who were seeing their works realized during the 1960s and toward the ideas that informed them. Among these they find "the conviction that art is coming to play a more diffused and direct role in the environment," as well as a "new concern with the whole synthetic and natural environment in terms of the interconnected processes that shape it and result from it" (7). In that sense, far from representing an ahistorical or nonpolemical survey of the contemporary scene, *Perspecta* 11, with its mirrored cover, sought deliberately to reflect outward—toward that *terrain vague* called "environment"—certain concepts immanent to architectural discourse at the time.

44 Marshall McLuhan, "The Invisible Environment: The Future of an Erosion," *Perspecta* 11 (1967): 167.

45 Ibid.

46 Peter Eisenman, "Cardboard Architecture," *Casabella* 37 (February 1973): 24.

47 Ibid.

48 Tafuri, "'European Graffiti,'" 47.

49 Ibid., 48–49.

50 For Tafuri, "the syntactic laboratory, as it is invoked through objects which are perfectly locked in a mutual dialogue of signs, accepts no intruders." But in superimposing a value-laden real/virtual schism over a relation that Eisenman has taken care to hold in suspension in the closed system of his theory-practice feedback loop, Tafuri is thus forced to infer not only the incapacity of these objects to ascend to the heights of a communicative "*architecture autre*" but also the superfluity of every inhabitant, every subject, "scandalously" condemned to interrupt the endgame with the restoration of "substance" to cardboard "intangibles." Tafuri, "'European Graffiti,'" 49.

51 Ibid., 71.

52 See Noam Chomsky, *Aspects of the Theory of Syntax* (Cambridge, Mass.: MIT Press, 1965), 3–9.

53 Noam Chomsky and Michel Foucault, "Human Nature: Justice versus Power," in Arnold I. Davidson, ed., *Foucault and His Interlocutors* (Chicago: University of Chicago, 1997), 131–32.

54 Ibid., 136.

55 Tafuri, *The Sphere and the Labyrinth*, 301.

56 Richard M. Nixon, "Address to the Nation Outlining a New Economic Policy: 'The Challenge of Peace,'" 15 August 1971, RNLBA. Available from: http://www.nixon foundation.org.

57 Gilles Deleuze and Félix Guattari, *A Thousand Plateaus: Capitalism and Schizophrenia*, trans. Brian Massumi (Minneapolis: University of Minnesota Press, 1987), 82.

58 Ibid., 76, 82, 101.

59 See Benjamin Lee and Edward LiPuma, "Cultures of Circulation: The Imaginations of Modernity," *Public Culture* 14, no. 1 (Winter 2002): 191–213; as well as Benjamin

Lee and Edward LiPuma, *Financial Derivatives and the Globalization of Risk* (Durham, N.C.: Duke University Press, 2004).

60 Richard M. Nixon, "Statement about Signing the United Nations Environment Program Participation Act of 1973," 17 December 1973, RNLBA. Available from: http://www.nixonfoundation.org.

61 Hardt and Negri, *Empire*, 269–72.

62 See Jameson, "'End of Art' or 'End of History'?" 90–91.

63 The World Trade Center in New York, designed by Minoru Yamasaki and Emery Roth & Sons, officially opened in 1973. Its destruction on 11 September 2001 provided the occasion for a series of speech acts by then–U.S. president George W. Bush that effectively bypassed congressional authority in declaring an open-ended "war on terror."

4. Image

1 Fredric Jameson, foreword to Lyotard, *The Postmodern Condition*, xvii.

2 See in particular the essays collected in Part 2 of Jameson, *Archaeologies of the Future*.

3 Theodor W. Adorno, *The Jargon of Authenticity*, trans. Knut Tarnowski and Frederic Will (Evanston: Northwestern University Press, 1973), 5–6.

4 Ibid., 9–10. Adorno is referring to Benjamin's famous essay, "The Work of Art in the Age of Its Technological Reproducibility" of 1936. The essay, as translated by Edmund Jephcott and Harry Zohn, can be found in *Walter Benjamin: Collected Writings*, vol. 3, *1935–1938*, 101–33.

5 Adorno, *The Jargon of Authenticity*, 160, 168.

6 See Sigfried Giedion, *The Eternal Present: A Contribution to Constancy and Change*, 2 vols. (New York: Bollingen Foundation / Pantheon Books, 1962–64). There is some irony in the fact that Giedion's earlier work on architecture and technology was a source for Benjamin in the *Arcades* project. In terms of architecture's version of an explicitly Heideggerian "jargon," I am thinking of the work of Christian Norberg-Schulz in particular. Kenneth Frampton's "critical regionalism" also makes use of such terminology in a slightly different sense.

7 Venturi, Scott Brown, and Izenour, *Learning from Las Vegas*, 65–71. Intriguingly, Aron Vinegar argues that the "duck" and the "decorated shed" are less mutually exclusive than they are intertwined. See Vinegar, *I Am a Monument*, chapter 3, "Of Ducks, Decorated Sheds, and Other Minds," 49–92.

8 Venturi, Scott Brown, and Izenour, *Learning from Las Vegas*, 65–66.

9 Ibid., 66.

10 Ibid., 68.

11 Jencks, *The Language of Post-Modern Architecture*, 87–88.

12 Morris was also involved with the New Bauhaus/Institute of Design in Chicago, where Kepes taught. See James Sloan Allen, *The Romance of Commerce and Culture: Capitalism, Modernism, and the Chicago-Aspen Crusade for Cultural Reform* (Chicago: University of Chicago Press, 1983), 59–60. The behavioral psychologist

Edward C. Tolman is generally credited with originating the term *cognitive mapping* in the 1940s. Though Lynch himself does not use the term, and Tolman's study of rats in a maze is not among the many psychological works he lists in his appendix, he does include Morris's *Foundations of the Theory of Signs* (1938). Lynch, *The Image of the City.*

13 Jameson, *Postmodernism,* 54.

14 Ibid., 2–3.

15 Michael Herr, *Dispatches* (New York: Knopf, 1977), 9, as quoted in Jameson, *Postmodernism,* 45.

16 Jameson, *Postmodernism,* 44.

17 Ibid., 27.

18 Ibid., 37.

19 Jencks, *The Language of Post-Modern Architecture,* 35.

20 Ibid., 79.

21 See also Martin, "Pattern-Seeing," *The Organizational Complex,* 42–47.

22 Jencks, *The Language of Post-Modern Architecture,* 127.

23 Ibid.

24 Ibid., 10–15.

25 Jameson, *Postmodernism,* 207.

26 Charles Jencks, *Architecture 2000: Predictions and Methods* (New York: Praeger, 1971), 32.

27 Ibid., 21.

28 Ibid., 118.

29 Ibid., 120.

30 Ibid., 123. Jencks's charts, both here and in *The Language of Post-Modern Architecture,* also bear a loose (if metaphorical) resemblance to the tree diagrams characteristic of Chomsky's generative grammar.

31 Fredric Jameson, "The Brick and the Balloon: Architecture, Idealism and Land Speculation," in *The Cultural Turn,* 185.

32 Jencks, *Architecture 2000,* 33.

33 Horkheimer and Adorno, *Dialectic of Enlightenment,* 117. Jencks's source for the notion of "frameworks for speculation" and "surprise free" projections is Herman Kahn and Anthony J. Wiener, *The Year 2000: A Framework for Speculation on the Next Thirty-three Years* (New York: Macmillan, 1967).

34 Niklas Luhmann, *Art as a Social System,* trans. Eva Knodt (Stanford: Stanford University Press, 2000), especially chapter 2, "Observation of the First and of the Second Order," 54–101, and chapter 6, "Evolution," 211–43. Jameson compares Luhmann's notion of differentiation with the differential expansion of capital in *A Singular Modernity,* 89.

35 Lyotard, *The Postmodern Condition,* 61–62.

36 Jameson, *Postmodernism,* 127.

37 Ibid., 378–79. The chart is from Bruno Latour, *The Pasteurization of France,* trans. Alan Sheridan and John Law (Cambridge, Mass.: Harvard University Press, 1988), 207.

38 Bruno Latour, *We Have Never Been Modern*, trans. Catherine Porter (Cambridge, Mass.: Harvard University Press, 1993), 2.

39 Ibid., 64–65.

40 Ibid., 20–22. Latour is referring to the discussion of the constitution of scientific facts with respect to the controversy between Thomas Hobbes and Robert Boyle regarding the results of Boyle's "air pump" experiment during the 1660s, in Steven Shapin and Simon Schaffer, *Leviathan and the Air Pump: Hobbes, Boyle, and the Experimental Life* (Princeton: Princeton University Press, 1985).

41 Latour, *We Have Never Been Modern*, 21.

42 Bruno Latour and Steve Woolgar, *Laboratory Life: The Social Construction of Scientific Facts* (Beverly Hills: Sage Publications, 1979).

43 Louis Kahn, *What Will Be Has Always Been: The Words of Louis I. Kahn*, ed. Richard Saul Wurman (New York: Access Press / Rizzoli, 1986), 216.

44 Latour and Woolgar, *Laboratory Life*, 43–88.

45 Venturi, Scott Brown, and Izenour, *Learning from Las Vegas*, 64.

46 Robert Venturi, "Thoughts on the Architecture of the Scientific Workplace: Community, Change, and Continuity," in *The Architecture of Science*, ed. Peter Galison and Emily Thompson (Cambridge, Mass.: MIT Press, 1999), 390.

47 Ibid., 391.

48 Bruno Latour, *Politics of Nature: How to Bring the Sciences into Democracy*, trans. Catherine Porter (Cambridge, Mass.: Harvard University Press, 2004), 132.

49 Ibid., 136–61.

50 Ibid., 165, 161.

51 Ibid., 220.

52 Ibid., 163.

53 See Beck, *Risk Society*.

54 Jameson, *Postmodernism*, 156.

55 Fredric Jameson, "World Reduction in Le Guin: The Emergence of Utopian Narrative," *Science Fiction Studies* 2, no. 3 (November 1975), 230. This essay is also included in Jameson, *Archaeologies of the Future*, 267–80.

5. Materiality

1 Amitav Ghosh, "Petrofiction," first published in *The New Republic*, 2 March 1992, and reprinted in Ghosh, *Incendiary Circumstances: A Chronicle of the Turmoil of Our Times* (New York: Houghton Mifflin, 2005), 138–51.

2 Frank D. Welch, *Philip Johnson and Texas* (Austin: University of Texas Press, 2000).

3 Jameson, "The Brick and the Balloon," 164.

4 Ibid., 181–83. Jameson is referring to Rem Koolhaas, *Delirious New York: A Retroactive Manifesto* (Oxford: Oxford University Press, 1998) and to Manfredo Tafuri, "The Disenchanted Mountain: The Skyscraper and the City," in Giorgio Ciucci et al., *The American City: From the Civil War to the New Deal*, trans. Barbara Luigia La Penta (Cambridge, Mass.: The MIT Press, 1979), 389–503.

5 Jameson, "The Brick and the Balloon," 184–85. Also David Harvey, *The Limits to Capital* (Oxford: Blackwell, 1982), 265, 347.

6 Jameson, "The Brick and the Balloon," 186.

7 Ibid.

8 Ibid., 187.

9 Ibid., 183.

10 An example of the treatment of "oil" as a mythic cultural object, or fetish, is Daniel Yergin, *The Prize: The Epic Quest for Oil, Money and Power* (New York: Free Press, 1991). The principle of commodity fetishism to which I am alluding here is explicated by Marx in *Capital*, vol. 1. See Karl Marx, "The Fetishism of the Commodity and Its Secret," in *Capital*, vol. 1., trans. Ben Fowkes (New York: Vintage Books, 1977), 163–77. On semischolarly, epic histories of commodities, see Bruce Robbins, "Commodity Histories," *PMLA* 120, no. 2 (March 2005), 454–63.

11 *Arbusto* means "bush" in Spanish. On George W. Bush's early career in the energy business, see George Lardner Jr. and Lois Romano, "Bush Name Helps Fuel Oil Dealings," *Washington Post*, 30 July 1999, A1. In his 2006 State of the Union speech, Bush declared that "America is addicted to oil, which is often imported from unstable parts of the world." George W. Bush, "State of the Union Address by the President," 31 January 2006, http://www.cnn.com/2006/POLITICS/01/31/sotu.transcript/.

12 Herbert S. Parmet, *George Bush: The Life of a Lone Star Yankee* (New York: Scribner, 1977), 82–86.

13 Peter Papademetriou, "Is 'Wow!' Enough?" *Progressive Architecture* 58, no. 8 (August 1977): 66, and William Marlin, "Pennzoil Place," *Architectural Record* 160, no. 7 (November 1976): 106–7.

14 Philip Johnson, "The Seven Crutches of Modern Architecture," *Perspecta* 3 (1954): 40–44.

15 Philip Johnson, quoted in John Pastier, "Evaluation: Pennzoil as Sculpture and Symbol," *American Institute of Architects Journal* 71, no. 7 (June 1982): 42.

16 Papademetriou, "Is 'Wow!' Enough?" 68.

17 Johnson, "The Seven Crutches of Modern Architecture," 42.

18 With reference to Pennzoil Place and other commercial developments, Hines said of his firm, "We are in the business of building not only successful buildings but also *exciting* ones. The two go together, as I have come to see it." Gerald Hines, quoted in Marlin, "Pennzoil Place," 110. For more general comments on the relationship between developers and architects in this context, see "Interview: Gerald D. Hines and Peter Eisenman," *Skyline* (October 1982): 18–21.

19 Johnson, "The Seven Crutches of Modern Architecture," 43.

20 Papademetriou, "Is 'Wow!' Enough?" 66–68.

21 Johnson, "The Seven Crutches of Modern Architecture," 43.

22 Marlin, "Pennzoil Place," 106. Papademetriou, "Is 'Wow!' Enough?" 66.

23 Philip Johnson, "Schinkel and Mies" [1961], in Johnson, *Philip Johnson Writings* (New York: Oxford University Press, 1979), 171.

24 Marlin, "Pennzoil Place," 109.

25 Ibid., 110.

26 Hal Weatherford of S. I. Morris, quoted in Marlin, "Pennzoil Place," 110.

27 Frank Gehry's observations are noted in Pastier, "Evaluation," 42.

28 Juan Pablo Pérez Alfonzo, cited in Terry Lynn Karl, *The Paradox of Plenty: Oil Booms and Petro-States* (Berkeley: University of California Press, 1997). This quotation is the basis for Watts's title, below.

29 Michael J. Watts, "Oil as Money: The Devil's Excrement and the Spectacle of Black Gold," in *Money, Power, and Space*, ed. Stuart Corbridge, Nigel Thrift, and Ron Martin (Oxford: Blackwell, 1994), 406–45. I am grateful to Brian Larkin for bringing this work to my attention.

30 Marlin, "Pennzoil Place," 110.

31 Ibid., 107.

32 Harvey, *The Condition of Postmodernity*, 344. On "economics with mirrors," see 329–35; on "Fordist Modernity" versus "Flexible Postmodernity," see 338–42; on the "crisis of historical materialism," see 353–55.

33 Ibid., 345.

34 Ibid., 337. Compare here also Mary McLeod, "Architecture and Politics in the Reagan Era: From Postmodernism to Deconstructivism," *Assemblage* 8 (February 1989): 22–59.

35 See Sabine Melchoir-Bonnet, *The Mirror: A History*, trans. Katharine H. Jewett (London: Routledge, 2001).

36 Georges Teyssot has analyzed the mirror as a paradigmatic device for the production of an interior/exterior threshold in the eighteenth and nineteenth centuries. See Georges Teyssot, "A Topology of Thresholds," *Home Cultures* 2, no. 1 (2005): 89–116; and Georges Teyssot, "Mapping the Threshold: A Theory for Design and Interface," *AAFiles* 57 (2008): 3–12. One well-known example of a seventeenth-century hall of mirrors is the *cabinet des glaces* at Versailles.

37 Harvey, *The Condition of Postmodernity*, 260–323.

38 Jameson, *Postmodernism*, 42.

39 Ibid., 37.

40 Ibid., 14.

41 Ibid., 27–28.

42 Ibid., 42.

43 Friedrich Kittler, "Romanticism – Psychoanalysis – Film: A History of the Double," in Johnston, *Literature, Media, Information Systems*, 85–100. Here is Kittler, with reference to the literary-Romantic, fantastical figure of the Double: "The empirical-transcendental doublet Man, substratum of the Romantic fantastic, is only imploded by the two-pronged attack of science and industry, of psychoanalysis and film. Psychoanalysis clinically verified and cinema technically implemented all of the shadows and mirroring of the subject. Ever since then, what remains of a literature that wants to be Literature is simply *écriture*—a writing without author," 95. See also Marcel O'Gorman, "Friedrich Kittler's Media Scenes. An Instruction Manual," *Postmodern Culture* 10, no. 1 (September 1999) http://muse.jhu.edu/journals/pmc/.

44 Jameson, *Postmodernism*, 38. See also Mike Davis, "Urban Renaissance and the Spirit of Postmodernism," *New Left Review* 1, no. 151 (May–June 1985): 106–13, for a critical response to Jameson's reading of John Portman's Westin Bonaventure Hotel and urban redevelopment in Los Angeles in relation to capitalism's "stages."

45 Philip Johnson and John Burgee, *Philip Johnson/John Burgee Architecture 1979–1985* (New York: Rizzoli, 1985), 63.

46 Ibid.

47 Tafuri, "The Disenchanted Mountain," 493.

48 Roy Lubove, *Twentieth-Century Pittsburgh*, vol. 2, *The Post-Steel Era* (Pittsburgh: University of Pittsburgh Press, 1996), 74, 304, n. 50.

49 Tafuri, "The Disenchanted Mountain," 493.

50 Brian Jacobs, *Strategy and Partnership in Cities and Regions: Economic Development and Urban Regeneration in Pittsburgh, Birmingham and Rotterdam* (London: St. Martin's Press, 2000), 90–91. See also Shelby Stewman and Joel A. Tarr, "Public-Private Partnerships in Pittsburgh: An Approach to Governance," in *Pittsburgh—Sheffield: Sister Cities*, ed. Joel A. Tarr (Pittsburgh: Carnegie Mellon University, 1986), 141–81.

51 Lubove, *Twentieth-Century Pittsburgh*, 2:61.

52 Vince Rause, *New York Times Magazine* (26 November 1989), cited in Lubove, *Twentieth-Century Pittsburgh*, 2:295, n. 4.

53 Edward K. Muller, "Downtown Pittsburgh: Renaissance and Renewal," in *Pittsburgh and the Appalachians: Cultural and Natural Resources in a Postindustrial Age*, ed. Joseph L. Scarpaci with Kevin J. Patrick (Pittsburgh: University of Pittsburgh Press, 2006), 13.

54 Lawrence Houstoun Jr., "PPG's Unpopulated Places," *Architecture* 78 (December 1989): 61.

55 Michel Foucault, "*Society Must Be Defended*," 254.

56 Ibid., 258.

57 Ibid., 241.

58 Ibid., 258.

59 Ibid., 256.

60 Johnson and Burgee, *Philip Johnson/John Burgee Architecture 1979–1985*, 16.

61 Harvey, *The Condition of Postmodernity*, 339 (Table 4.1).

62 Kevin Roche, "Kevin Roche on Design and Building: Conversation with Francesco Dal Co," in Francesco Dal Co, *Kevin Roche* (New York: Rizzoli, 1985), 85.

63 Ibid., 41.

64 Fredric Jameson, "Culture and Finance Capital," in *The Cultural Turn*, 153–54.

6. Subjects

1 Jacques Rancière, *The Politics of Aesthetics: The Distribution of the Sensible*, trans. Gabriel Rockhill (London: Continuum, 2004).

2 Jacques Lacan, "The Mirror Stage as Formative of the Function of the I as Revealed

in Psychoanalytic Experience," in *Écrits: A Selection,* trans. Alan Sheridan, (New York: W. W. Norton, 1977), 1–7.

3   In explicating his notion of an "architectural uncanny," Anthony Vidler has drawn on the underlying spatiality of psychoanalysis to reveal a whole host of psycho-spatial instabilities latent in architectural modernism and its successors; see in particular his reading of the project for the French national library in Paris by Rem Koolhaas and OMA for an articulation of Lacan's mirror stage with an architecture of transparent/reflective indeterminacy. Anthony Vidler, *The Architectural Uncanny: Essays in the Modern Unhomely* (Cambridge, Mass.: MIT Press, 1992), 216–25. In passing, Fredric Jameson has also noted analogies between psycho-analytically oriented film theory and the imagistic preoccupations of postmodern architecture and criticism, in *Postmodernism,* 124.

4   Jameson, *Postmodernism,* 94.

5   Harvey, *The Condition of Postmodernity,* 77.

6   Ibid., 76. Harvey is citing from Charles Jencks, *The Language of Post-Modern Architecture,* 4th rev. ed. (London: Rizzoli, 1984), 5.

7   Charles Jencks, *The New Paradigm in Architecture: The Language of Post-Modernism* (London: Verso, 2002), 211–27.

8   There is a growing literature on digitally aided design and fabrication in architecture. For a summary of the initial experiments in what has been called "nonstandard" design, see the exhibition catalog edited by Frederic Migayrou, *Architectures non standard* (Paris: Centre Pompidou, 2003). See also "Versioning: Evolutionary Techniques in Architecture," a special issue of *Architectural Design* 72, no. 5, guest edited by SHoP/Sharples Holden Pasquarelli (September–October 2002).

9   Siegfried Kracauer, "The Mass Ornament" (1927), in *The Mass Ornament: Weimar Essays,* trans., ed. with and introduction by Thomas Y. Levin (Cambridge, Mass.: Harvard University Press, 1995), 75–86.

10 Greg Lynn, "Embryologic Houses," *Domus* 822 (January 2000): 11.

11 Kracauer, "The Mass Ornament," 76. Greg Lynn, *Animate Form* (New York: Princeton Architectural Press, 1999), 17.

12 On the "post-criticality" debate see Baird, "'Criticality' and Its Discontents," and Martin "Critical of What?"

13 Jacques Rancière, *On the Shores of Politics,* trans. Liz Heron (New York: Verso, 1995), 22.

14 "Union Carbide's Shaft of Steel," *Architectural Forum* 113 (November 1960): 120.

15 C. Wright Mills, *White Collar: The American Middle Classes* (New York: Oxford University Press, 1951), 189–212.

16 On flexibility and the "organization man" in the postwar office building, see Martin, *The Organizational Complex,* chapter 3, "The Physiognomy of the Office," 80–121.

17 Hugh D. Menzies, "Union Carbide Raises Its Voice," *Fortune* 98, no. 6 (25 September 1978): 86.

18 Ibid., 86–87.

19 Kevin Roche, as quoted by Kunio Kudo, "World Headquarters, Union Carbide Corporation," in "Kevin Roche: Seven Headquarters," *Office Age* special edition 01 (1990): 112.

20 Kevin Roche, "Design Process, World Headquarters, Union Carbide Corporation" in "Kevin Roche: Seven Headquarters," 115–19.

21 On the use of mainframe and personal computers in architectural offices as design and production tools in the early 1980s, see for example "Computers in Architecture," *Progressive Architecture* 65, no. 5 (May 1984), a special issue on the subject. See also Joseph Giovannini, "Architecture of Information," *Architecture and Planning* (Winter 1982), 2–7.

22 Roche, "Design Process, World Headquarters, Union Carbide Corporation," 132.

23 Ibid., 135.

24 Foucault, *The Birth of Biopolitics*, 219–33.

25 Warren M. Anderson, Chairman, and Alex Flamm, President, "To Our Stockholders," *Union Carbide: Putting Technology to Work*, Annual report, 1981.

26 A variety of sources list the official government count at 1,754, including the International Campaign for Justice in Bhopal, http://www.bhopal.net. Surviving Bhopal: A Fact Finding Mission, http://www.bhopalffm.org; and Dominique LaPierre and Javier Moro, *Five Past Midnight in Bhopal* (New York: Warner Books, 2002), 375.

27 Amnesty International, *Clouds of Injustice: Bhopal Disaster 20 Years On* (London: Amnesty International Publications, 2004), 10–12.

28 Bridget Hanna, personal communication with the author, 10 January 2006. Hanna maintains the Web site for the Bhopal Memory Project, http://bhopal.bard.edu, is a coeditor of *The Bhopal Reader*, and has worked with victims' advocacy groups in Bhopal.

29 LaPierre and Moro, *Five Past Midnight in Bhopal*, 380. The article cited by LaPierre and Moro is Douglas J. Besharov and Peter Reuter, "Averting a Bhopal Legal Disaster," *Wall Street Journal*, 16 May 1985, 32.

30 Bridget Hanna, personal communication with the author, 10 January 2006. See also Veena Das, "Moral Orientations to Suffering: Power, Legitimacy, and Healing," in *The Bhopal Reader*, ed. B. Hanna, S. Sarangi, W. Morehouse (New York: Apex Press, 2005), 54–59; and H. Rajan Sharma, "Catastrophe and the Dilemma of Law," in *The Bhopal Reader*, 65–70.

31 Bridget Hanna, personal communication with the author, 10 January 2006. According to Hanna, "activists have tried over the years to create alternate counts to interrupt official numbers. In one particularly important move, the group that has evolved into the Sambhavna Trust Clinic and Documentation Center began to do 'verbal autopsies' in 1996, coming up with a set of questions through which they could determine if a death was the result of gas exposure, and therefore try to affect the official count." See also Bridget Hanna, "Bhopal: Unending Disaster, Enduring Resistance," in *Nongovernmental Politics*, ed. Michel Feher with Gaëlle Krikorian and Yates McKee (New York: Zone, 2007), 488–521.

32 Bridget Hanna, "Bhopal as Planned," C-Lab File 3, *Volume* 4 (2005), 22–25.

33 "Carbide Plans Sale of Headquarters Site for $340 Million," *Wall Street Journal*, 7 November 1986, 58; and "Carbide Closes Sale of Headquarters," *Wall Street Journal*, 2 January 1987, 5. Five days before the sale was announced, the *New York Times* reported, "The Indian Government is urging a district court to restrain the Union Carbide Corporation from selling any more of its assets, saying such sales could reduce any eventual settlement of the 1984 gas tragedy." Sanjoy Hazarika, "India Fighting Sales of Union Carbide Assets," *New York Times*, 2 November 1986, 6.

34 James N. Barton, Director, General Services, Union Carbide Corporation, interviewed by Kunio Kudo in "Kevin Roche: Seven Headquarters," 147.

35 Asked by Francesco Dal Co about the generous use of mirrors on the interiors of many of his firm's office buildings, Roche replied, "The interesting thing about mirror is that it is very inexpensive, almost as inexpensive as paint. Most interior surfaces are static, unchanging: if painted, the paint remains the same until it fades. The marvelous thing that happens with mirror, if used in a certain way, is that it is constantly alive, constantly alive as one moves. It becomes a kinetic surface, a kinetic experience of light. It picks up reflections, sparkle. Dark spots, a constant painting where the real world is reflected in a painterly way. A tremendous decorative effect from what exists, always changing, always moving." Roche, "Kevin Roche on Design and Building," 85.

36 Manfredo Tafuri and Francesco Dal Co, *Modern Architecture* vol. 2, trans. Robert Erich Wolf (New York: Electa / Rizzoli, 1979), 314.

37 Roche, "Design Process, World Headquarters, Union Carbide Corporation," 134.

38 Kracauer, "The Mass Ornament," 75.

39 Agamben, *Homo Sacer*.

40 On the "life that does not deserve to live," see Agamben, *Homo Sacer*, 136–43. On "the distribution of the sensible" see Rancière, *The Politics of Aesthetics*, 7–45. Rancière defines "the distribution of the sensible" as "the system of self-evident facts of sense perception that simultaneously discloses the existence of something in common and the delimitations that define the respective parts and positions within it," 12. As such, this "primary aesthetics" contains a division of labor whereby the power to designate parts and positions is also apportioned. Notably, Rancière offers a dual definition of utopia under these conditions: first, as "the unacceptable, a no-place, the extreme point of a polemical reconfiguration of the sensible, which breaks down the categories that define what is considered to be obvious;" but also as "the configuration of a proper place, a non-polemical distribution of the sensible universe where what one sees, what one says, and what one makes or does are rigorously adapted to one another," 40.

41 Deleuze, "Postscript on Control Societies," 180.

42 Kracauer, "The Mass Ornament," 78.

43 Ibid., 76.

44 Foucault, *The Birth of Biopolitics*, 226. Lecturing in 1979 (immediately prior to the developments we have been following), Foucault also speculates on the economic dimensions of a biotechnologically customizable genetic makeup in constituting a type of "human capital" that he calls an "abilities-machine," 227–29.

45 The quotation from an unnamed woman protesting the court's decision is recorded in Veena Das, "Moral Orientations to Suffering: Legitimation, Power, and Healing," in *Health and Social Change in International Perspective*, ed. Lincoln C. Chen, Arthur Kleinman, and Norma C. Ware (Cambridge, Mass.: Harvard School of Public Health and Harvard University Press, 1994), 161. Das's article is reprinted in abbreviated form in Hanna et al., *The Bhopal Reader*, 51–59. I am also alluding here to Gayatri Chakravorty Spivak, "Can the Subaltern Speak?" in *Marxism and the Interpretation of Culture*, ed. Cary Nelson and Lawrence Grossberg (Urbana: University of Illinois Press, 1988), 271–313

7. Architecture

1 The "housing question" generated by large-scale migration to the newly industrialized cities was much debated in Germany in the late nineteenth century. In 1872 Friedrich Engels issued his famous response to Proudhonism, a type of reformist socialism influential at the time that advocated for home ownership for workers on an agrarian model. For Engels, this attachment to "hearth and home" was regressive, as it prevented the formation of a revolutionary urban proletariat necessarily uprooted from tradition. In that sense, the transformation of housing has long been seen as linked to the transformation of society. See Engels, *The Housing Question*, ed. C. P. Dutt (New York: International Publishers, 1935). I refer to these debates also because one of the outcomes of the perceived failure of public housing (or social housing) since the 1970s was the worldwide incorporation of ideologies of home ownership into public policy at both the municipal and national levels.

2 There is an extensive literature on architecture and the utopian imagination, particularly in relation to Enlightenment thought. Especially relevant here are Tafuri, *Architecture and Utopia*; Anthony Vidler, *Claude-Nicolas Ledoux: Architecture and Social Reform at the End of the Ancien Régime* (Cambridge, Mass.: MIT Press, 1990) and Vidler, *Claude-Nicolas Ledoux: Architecture and Utopia in the Era of the French Revolution* (Bäsel/Boston: Birkhäuser, 2006); Georges Teyssot, *Città e utopia nell illuminismo inglese: George Dance il giovane* (Roma: Offina, 1974); and Françoise Choay, *L'urbanisme: Utopies et réalités* (Paris: Éditions du Seuil, 1965). An alternative perspective is supplied by Antoine Picon, who emphasizes the "triumph of the engineers" over the aesthetic idealism of the "revolutionary architects," in *French Architects and Engineers in the Age of Enlightenment*, trans. Martin Thom (New York: Cambridge University Press, 1992). An important early reference is Emil Kaufmann, *Von Ledoux bis Le Corbusier: Ursprung und Entwicklung der Autonomen Architektur* (Wien/Liepzig: Verlag Dr. Rolf Passer, 1933), as well as Kaufmann, *Three Revolutionary Architects: Boullée, Ledoux, and Lequeu* (Philadelphia: American Philosophical Society, 1952). See also Fredric Jameson, *Archaeologies of the Future*; Phillip E. Wegner, *Imaginary Communities: Utopia, The Nation, and the Spatial Histories of Modernity* (Berkeley: University of Cali-

fornia Press, 2002); and Marianne DeKoven, *Utopia Limited: The Sixties and the Emergence of the Postmodern* (Durham, N.C.: Duke University Press, 2004).

3 Lyotard, *The Postmodern Condition.*

4 Tafuri, *The Sphere and the Labyrinth*; and Tafuri, *Architecture and Utopia.*

5 On the "knight's moves" attempted by the historical avant-gardes, see Tafuri, *The Sphere and the Labyrinth*, 8, 16.

6 Erwin Panofsky, *Perspective as Symbolic Form*, trans. Christopher S. Wood (New York: Zone Books, 1991).

7 Derrida, *Specters of Marx.* Derrida opens with the problem of "learning to live with ghosts" in the Exordium (xviii) and develops it throughout. In the sense that a utopian "spirit" can, in principle, be found anywhere, I am also referring more indirectly to the work of Ernst Bloch, especially *The Spirit of Utopia*, trans. Anthony A. Nassar (Stanford: Stanford University Press, 2000), though without fully sharing Bloch's convictions regarding Expressionism.

8 Correspondingly, Mark Wigley has argued that Derrida's earlier references to ghosts and to haunting are always-already architectural. See Wigley, *The Architecture of Deconstruction: Derrida's Haunt* (Cambridge, Mass.: MIT Press, 1993), 162–74.

9 Tafuri, "The Ashes of Jefferson," 298. See also Tafuri, "L'architecture dans le boudoir," 267–90.

10 Portoghesi, *Postmodern*, 7.

11 Karl Marx and Friedrich Engels, *Manifesto of the Communist Party* (New York: International Publishers, 1948), 8.

12 On postmodern architecture and *posthistoire* thought, see Vidler, *Histories of the Immediate Present*, chapter 5, "Postmodern or *Posthistoire?*" 191–200.

13 Jencks, *The Language of Post-Modern Architecture*, 2d rev. ed., 80.

14 Charles Jencks, *Critical Modernism: Where Is Post-Modernism Going?* (Hoboken, N.J.: John Wiley, 2007), 205–8.

15 See Alan Colquhoun, "Democratic Monument: Neue Staatsgalerie, Stuttgart," *Architectural Review* 176, no. 1054 (December 1984): 19–22, and William J. R. Curtis, "Virtuosity around a Void," *Architectural Review* 176, no. 1054 (December 1984): 41–47. Both authors refer to the competition requirement to include a path through the building (which Curtis describes as "a common demand in German architectural competitions"), and Curtis refers to the route through Stirling's building as a "'democratic' path," 41.

16 In 2001, Ungers completed an addition to the same museum that is unrelated to the earlier competition entry.

17 Georg Lukács, *Theory of the Novel: A Historico-Philosophical Essay on the Forms of Great Epic Literature*, trans. Anna Bostock (Cambridge, Mass.: MIT Press, 1971), 61.

18 Tafuri, "'European Graffiti,'" 47. Tafuri is in fact referring to Peter Eisenman's early houses. See also Tafuri, *The Sphere and the Labyrinth*, chapter 9, "The Ashes of Jefferson," 291–303.

19 Kevin Roche, in conversation with Michael Graves, in *The Charlottesville Tapes:*

Transcript of the Conference at the University of Virginia School of Architecture, Charlottesville, Virginia, November 12 and 13, 1982 (New York: Rizzoli, 1985), 167.

20 Jameson, "The Brick and the Balloon."

21 Jencks implies that "Late-Modernism," in the form of Kenneth Frampton's "critical regionalism," appropriated from "Post-Modernism" a concern for "local traditions." Jencks, *The Language of Post-Modern Architecture*, 4th rev. ed., 6.

22 See Liselotte and Oswald Mathias Ungers, "Utopische Kommunen in Amerika 1800–1900. Die Community von Oneida," *Werk* 57 (July 1970): 475–78; "Utopische Kommunen in Amerika 1800–1900. Die Amana-Community," *Werk* 57 (August 1970): 543–46; "Utopische Kommunen in Amerika 1800–1900. Die Hutterschen Brüder," *Werk* 58 (June 1971): 417–20; Liselotte and O. M. Ungers, "Utopische Kommunen in Amerika 1800–1900. Fouriersche Phalanxen in Amerika," *Werk* 58 (April 1971): 272–76; Oswald and Lisolette Ungers, "Early Communes in the USA," *Architectural Design* 42 (August 1972): 502–12; and *Kommunen in der Neuen Welt 1740–1971* (Cologne: Kiepenheuer & Witsch, 1972).

23 On the Internationale Bauausstellung (IBA) in Berlin, see Josef P. Kleihues and Heinrich Klotz, eds., *International Building Exhibition Berlin 1987: Examples of New Architecture*, trans. Ian Robson (New York: Rizzoli, 1986).

24 John Hejduk, *Mask of Medusa: Works 1947–1983* (New York: Rizzoli, 1985).

25 Marin, *Utopics*.

26 Philipp Oswalt, ed. *Shrinking Cities*, vol. 1, *International Research* (Ostfildern-Ruit: Hatje Cantz, 2005). Oswald Mathias Ungers et al., "Cities within the City," *Lotus International* 19 (June 1978): 82–97. See also Pier Vittorio Aureli, "Toward the Archipelago," *Log* 11 (Winter 2008): 91–119.

27 Ungers et al., "Cities within the City," 96.

28 Jameson, *Archaeologies of the Future*, 218–21.

29 See, for example, Josep Ramoneda and Eyal Weizman, eds., *Arxipèlag d' excepcions: Sobiranies de l' extraterritorialitat* (Barcelona: Centre de Cultura Contemporània de Barcelona, 2007).

30 For documentation of Taillibert's plan, see "Centre 300: Nouveau parlement européen à Luxembourg," *Architecture d'aujourd'hui* 200 (December 1978): 23–24.

31 For documentation of Krier's project, see Léon Krier, *Léon Krier: Architecture and Urbanism*, ed. Richard Economakis (London: Academy Editions, 1992), 88–101.

32 For an elaboration of a number of the aporias inherent in the transformation of Europe after decolonization, including the internal apartheid of "immigration recolonized," see Étienne Balibar, *We the People of Europe? Reflections on Transnational Citizenship*, trans. James Swenson (Princeton: Princeton University Press, 2004), especially "*Droit de cite* or Apartheid," 31–50. On Speer, see *Albert Speer: Architecture 1932–1942* (Brussels: Archives d'architecture moderne, 1985), which was published under Krier's direction, as well as Léon Krier, "Krier on Speer," *Architectual Review* 173, no. 1032 (February 1983): 33–38; and Léon Krier, "An Architecture of Desire," *Architectural Design* 56, no. 4 (1986): 30–37.

33 Alberti, *On the Art of Building in Ten Books*, 23.

PUBLICATION HISTORY

An earlier version of chapter 2 was published as "The Last War: Architecture and Post-modernism, Again," *New German Critique* 99 (Fall 2006): 63–82. Excerpts of chapter 2 were also included in "Atrocities, or Curtain Wall as Mass Medium," *Perspecta* 32 (2001): 66–75.

An earlier version of chapter 3 was published as "Environment, c. 1973," *Grey Room* 14 (Winter 2004): 78–101.

An earlier version of chapter 4 was published as "Architecture's Image Problem: Have We Ever Been Postmodern?" *Grey Room* 22 (Winter 2006): 6–29. This was translated into German as "Das Bildproblem der Architektur: Waren wire je postmodern?" in *Authentizität: Diskussion eines ästhetischen Begriffs*, ed. Susanne Knaller and Harro Müller (Frankfurt am Main: Suhrkamp Taschenbuch Wissenschaft, 2006), 289–315. Parts of chapter 4 were published in both English and German as "Postmodern Precision? The Science of Images," in *Precisions: Architecture between Sciences and the Arts*, ed. Ákos Moravánsky and O. W. Fischer (Zurich: Birkhauser, 2008), 82–111.

A portion of chapter 5 was published as "Liquidity: Architecture and Oil," in *Philip Johnson and the Constancy of Change*, ed. Emmanuel Petit (New Haven: Yale University Press, 2008), 110–19; reprinted by permission of Yale University Press. Another section of chapter 5 was published in German translation as "Spiegelglas," *Arch+* 191–192 (2009): 103–9.

A version of chapter 6 was published as "Mass Customization: Architecture and the 'End' of Politics," in *Communities of Sense: Rethinking Aesthetics in Practice*, ed. Beth Hinderliter et al. (Durham, N.C.: Duke University Press, 2009), 172–93; all rights reserved; reprinted by permission of Duke University Press.

INDEX

Abbe, Charles, 111

Abramovitz, Max, 111, 114

Adorno, Theodor, 6, 37, 145, 186n.15, 199n.3–5, 200n.33; on capitalist growth, 81; critique of Heideggerian existentialism, 70; on pseudo-personalization, 127

aesthetic judgment, normalization of, 6

aesthetic populism, 73, 74

aesthetics: economics and, 95–97, 109; primary, 207n.40; technology and, 48, 88

Afghanistan, post-9/11 conflict in, 30

African-Americans in Pruitt-Igoe housing development 14

Agamben, Giorgio, xvi, 12, 176, 187n.28, 188n.34–36, 207n.39–40; camp-as-paradigm thesis, 13; diagrams showing movement toward "state of exception," 19–20; examples of provisional (yet increasingly permanent) zones d'attentes, 13, 188n.35; homo sacer of, 11, 19, 141; topologies of exception, 11, 12–13

AIDS research, controversies over, 84

Alberti, Leon Battista, 8, 177, 187n.21, 210n.33

Alcoa Building in Pittsburgh, 111, 115

Alessi tea service (Lynn), 128

Alexander, Christopher, 3, 56

Alfonzo, Juan Pablo Pérez, 101, 203n.28

alienation, mirror stage and psychic, 124

Allen, James Sloan, 199n.12

Allied Bank Plaza in Houston, 111

Altes Museum in Berlin, 100

American Institute of Architects, 116

American pragmatism, 54

Amnesty International, 206n.27

Amon Carter Museum in Fort Worth, 95

Anderson, Perry, 181n.1, 185n.7, 193n.37

Anderson, Warren M., 137, 138, 206n.15

antinomy: double-sided norm with gated communities and slums on either side of, 24–25, 190n.65; of the modern, 24–25

antipollution program, Nixon's, 50; See also environment

Apple Computer, 1

Arbusto Energy, 97

Archigram, 3

archipelago: Cities within the City project for reurbanization of West Berlin, 173–76; Jameson's political model of federated, 174–75; Krier's "city-within-a-city" archipelago model for Luxembourg, 176–77; See also island(s)

Architectural Forum, 39–40

architecture, 147–79; as avatar of postmodernism, xii; axis of production, 11–19; axis of representation, 4–11; as both an object and frame or mediating instrument, 124; as cipher encoded with virtual universe of production and consumption, xi; of circulation, 154–63; collective neurosis and foundational insecurity in, xviii; crisis in, 39, 42–43; derealization through mediation of, 147; existence under postmodernity, question of, xviii–xx; as form of "immaterial production" fully materialized, xvi; immanence of, xiii–xiv, 4, 50, 106, 129; projection, question of, 147–51; *See also* autonomy of architecture

Architecture 2000: Predictions and Methods (Jencks), 79–81

Architecture and Utopia (Tafuri), 28

architecture-as-language, 79–80, 197n.41; Eisenman's theory of, 59, 66, 67

Architecture magazine, 116

"Architecture of Complexity, The" (Simon), 9

Architecture of the École des Beaux-Arts, The (1975 exhibition at Museum of Modern Art, New York), 181n.2

Architecture of the Postindustrial Society, The (Portoghesi), 151, 153

Architecture of the Well-Tempered Environment, The (Banham), 56

Architettura della Città (Rossi), 2, 6, 7–8; Eisenman's introduction to English version, 8, 11–12

architettura radicale, 3, 148

Arnheim, Rudolph, 55

Arthur Anderson, 98

Arts of the Environment (Kepes), 52

artwork, architecture as autonomous, xix–xx, 37, 43; crutches obscuring, 98–100

"Ashes of Jefferson, The" (Tafuri), 27, 30, 31–32, 191n.1

Atrocity Exhibition, The (Ballard), 41–42, 43

AT&T building (Johnson/Burgee), Chippendale roof atop, 101

aura: Benjamin's reflections on decline of, 70, 73; of image, 73

Aureli, Pier Vittorio, 184n.3, 210n.26

authenticity: of decoration on Guild House, 72, 73; jargon of, 70

autonomy of architecture, xiv, xvii, xix–xx, 40, 60, 98, 128, 129, 164; as condition for immanence, 50; Rossi's project for, 7–8, 9; Venturi's path toward, 9–11

avant-garde: exhaustion of avant-garde project, 27; projected control of future in avant-garde project, 28–29; revolutionary "languages of battle" characteristic of, 30; Tafuri on, 31–32, 63

Badiou, Alain, 1

Baird, George, 192n.12, 205n.13

Balibar, Étienne, 210n.32

Ballard, J. G., 41–42, 43, 91, 113, 193n.30

Banham, Reyner, 3, 56

banlieux, French, 13

Barry, Charles, 112

Barton, James N., 207n.33

Baudrillard, Jean, 111

Bauman, Zygmunt, 188n.35–36

Beauregard, Robert A., 189n.39

Beck, Ulrich, 43–44, 51–52, 193n.24, 194n.5, 201n.53

behaviorist precepts, reshaping of urban space according to, 116

Belden, Marva Robins, 184n.1

Belden, Thomas Graham, 184n.1

Bell, Daniel, 1, 80, 184n.2

Bell Laboratories in Holmdel, New Jersey, 119, 139, 140

Benhabib, Seyla, 2, 185n.7

Benjamin, Walter, xx, 70, 73, 102, 120, 145, 163, 170, 183n.13, 199n.4, 199n.6

Berlin, Germany: Altes Museum in, 100; Cities within the City project for reurbanization of West Berlin, 173–76; Hotel Berlin (Ungers) in, 169; as a kind of split island, in Hejduk's Berlin

Hood, Raymond, 110
Horkheimer, Max, 6, 81, 186n.15, 200n.33
Hôtel Arcades in Roissy, as *zone d'attente*, 188n.35
Hotel Berlin (Ungers), 169
house-as-city, Albertian formula of, 8–9
housing: enclaves as diagrams of inclusive exclusion, 13; in late nineteenth century Germany, 208n.1; Pruitt-Igoe housing development in St. Louis, 14–19, 20, 26, 147; public, 26, 147; tabula rasa spatial configuration of modern enclaves, 13
Houston, Texas: Allied Bank Plaza in, 111; network of buildings and tunnels in, 102, 109; Pennzoil Place in, 93–94, 95, 97–101, 102, 104, 108–9, 119, 120, 202n.18; Republic Bank Center in, 102; Roche Dinkeloo project of twinned towers in, 120–21; Transco Tower in, 102, 109–11, 119
Houstoun, Lawrence, Jr., 116, 204n.54
Hudnut, Joseph, 181n.2
Hudson Institute, 34, 81
human capital, 137, 189n.52
humanism of Chomsky, centered on notion of linguistic creativity based in human nature, 63–64
human relations, Union Carbide headquarters designs and influence of, 131, 133
human scale, displacement of, 164
Huntington, Samuel P., 47, 194n.44
Huxley, Julian, 80
Huyssen, Andreas, xviii, xxi, 2, 31, 182n.3, 183n.11, 184n.17, 185n.7, 187n.15
hypermodernism, 30, 190n.60

IBM. *See* Internationale Business Machines (IBM)
Iconography and Electronics upon a Generic Architecture (Venturi), 9
ideology as language, 70
Illinois Institute of Technology, 100

image(s), 69–92; architecture's entry into agonistic field of postmodern science as an, 88; assimilation of proliferation of images into ecological model, 78, 79; aura of, 73; authentic, 73; imaging of science, 83–92; Jencks's radical eclecticism and, 76–83, 91, 92, 154; problem of taking into account architecture-as-image, 90–91; unequivocal fact of real images, xxv
Image of the City (Lynch), 55, 73
immaterial materiality, 105–6, 119
immaterial production, xvi, 184n.1
India: Bhopal catastrophe (1984), 137–39, 141, 143, 145, 206n.26–31; chemically enhanced "green revolution" of, 142
informe of consumerism, 10
inside and outside: problems of, xxiii, xxiv, xxv; production of new inside-outsides, 11–19, 188n.35
interdisciplinary knowledge, NEPA and use of, 52
International Bauausstellung (IBA), 169–70, 181n.2
International Business Machines (IBM), 1, 184n.1
Investors Diversified Services (IDS) Center, 99, 104–6; Crystal Court atrium, 104–6; inside-out mirrored corners at, 104–6, 108
invisibility: of deindividuated Bhopal victims, 141, 143; perceptual paradox of certain visible, 125; tendency toward, accompanying global growth, 131
"Invisible Environment: The Future of Erosion, The" (McLuhan), 60–61
invisible hand, 44
Iraq, post-9/11 conflict in, 30
island(s), xvi; archipelago of built, 173–77; as basic unit of postmodern city, 21; island-space diagrammed by Agamben, 19; networks and, 4, 184n.3; thematic of, xxv

island, Utopia as, 21–25, 169–73; in
Disneyland, 22–24; geography of
More's Utopia, 21–22, 23; island
form, 21–22, 23; island function, 169,
171–73; Jameson's analysis of, 21
Italian *architettura radicale*, 3, 148
Italian exurban housing estates, 13
Izenour, Steven, 2, 184n.4, 185n.12,
192n.24, 199n.7

Jacobs, Brian, 204n.50
Jameson, Fredric, xv, xvii, xviii, xxii,
2, 5, 25, 29, 31, 38, 41, 43–44, 67,
106–8, 181n.3, 182n.5, 183n.11,
185n.7, 185n.8, 191n.66, 193n.26–37,
199n.1–2, 199n.62, 200n.31, 201n.3–4,
201n.55, 202n.6, 204n.44, 204n.64,
209n.2, 210n.20, 210n.28; analogies
between psychoanalytically oriented
film theory and imagistic preoccupations of postmodern architecture,
205n.3; analysis of Utopia's island
form, 21; on antinomies of postmodernity, 190n.65; on architecture
lining Strada Novissima, 165; assembling minimal "units" of architectural
grammar, 36; on cognitive mapping,
73–74, 169; on "colonization of the
future," 81; on commercialized vs.
oppositional "populism," 185n.11;
defense of postmodern architecture,
69; on Gehry, 36, 83, 190n.54; identification of largely Hegelian posthistory
with postmodernism, 45; on Jencks,
82–83; on mediations between the
economic and the aesthetic, 95–97;
on periodization, 44; political model
of federated archipelago suggested
by, 174–75; postmodernity found
in certain authors of science fiction
by, 91; postmodern sublime of, 145;
reproduction of Latour's 1984 list of
sardonic synonyms for "the modern
world," 83; on spatialization of the

temporal, 91; on suffocating totality
or closure of postmodern system
of images, 79; version of crisis of
historical materialism, 109; on Westin
Bonaventure Hotel, 74, 75–76, 106–7,
108
jargon of authenticity, 70
Jefferson, Thomas, 31–32; attempted
synthesis of modern technology and
postrevolutionary aesthetics, 32
Jencks, Charles, 2, 16, 48, 76–83, 96,
125, 181n.2, 189n.42, 199n.11,
200n.26, 200n.30, 200n.33, 205n.6–7,
209n.13–14, 210n.21; assimilation of
proliferation of images into ecological
model, 78, 79; on critical evolution, 79–80; "evolutionary tree" of
architectural styles, 76–78, 81–82, 90,
91, 154; faux-historical "timeline" of
postmodernism of, 154; futurology of,
76–78, 79, 81, 82; ideological association of new forms of production with
global consumerism, 127; Jameson's
treatment of, 82–83; on Portman's
Westin Bonaventure Hotel, 76; radical
eclecticism, 76–83, 91, 92, 154; on
regionalism as one of postmodernism
defining features, 166; six architectural traditions diagrammed by,
81–82; target of postmodernist revolt
codified by, 86, 88; three systems
of architectural production, 78; on
Venturi and Scott Brown's communicative, aesthetic populism, 73
John Hancock Center, 115
Johnson, Lyndon B., 195n.10
Johnson, Philip, 37, 94, 95, 96–97,
202n.14–15, 203n.23, 204n.45; on
diverse forms of fetishism (crutches)
characteristic of modern architecture,
98–100; as instance of something like
absolute immanence, 106; as medium
and mediator, 97; New Canaan estate
of, 99

mimesis: mirrors and, 106; to the second degree, 124

Minimal art, corner detail on Pennzoil Place as ghost of, 101

Minneapolis, IDS Center in, 99, 104–6, 108

mirrors, xxiv, 103–14, 207n.35; circular and tautological seriality created by, 108–9; concealing the outside, 114; as feedback loop, 106; Harvey's hypothesis of underpinnings of postmodernity as "economics with mirrors," 103; inside-out, 145; on interior of Union Carbide's Danbury headquarters, 139–40, 144; looking at rather than into, 108, 114; mystique of, 117–19; network of, unfolding, 111; as paradigmatic device for production of interior/exterior threshold, 203n.36; reference to stone, 110, 112, 113, 117, 118; rereflection technique with, 104–6, 114; ubiquity of, 104, 106, 109

mirror stage, 124

Modena, Italy, San Cataldo Cemetery in, 171–73, 177

modernism: as avatar of modernization, 10–11; Gray/White debate as stylistic legacy of, 27, 29–30; learning to live with ghosts of, 150–51; modernist visual techniques, Kepes on, 55; postwar, 37, 39; problematization of, as unified category, xx–xxi; Pruitt-Igoe demolition and ruination of modernist utopian enterprise, 15; rationalization of everyday life in large-scale and primarily state-sponsored housing estates defining, 13; renewed interest in early, 198n.43; roots of Jencks's architectural theory in, 73; as statistical aberration outside norms of Levittown and Las Vegas, 6; Venturi and Scott Brown's communicative, aesthetic populism as inversion of, 73

modernity: balancing of environmental and ontological risk as hallmark of new, self-correcting "reflexive", 43–44, 48; utopia and camp as poles of antinomy of the modern, 24–25

"Modernity—An Incomplete Project" (Habermas), 2

modernization: modernism as avatar of, 10–11; Tafuri's allegory of, 22; war in Vietnam as war of, 47

Moholy-Nagy, László, 54

Moore, Charles, xx, 22–24, 26, 40, 66, 160–63, 190n.62, 193n.28; competition entry for mixed-use development in Tegel Harbor district of West Berlin, 169; condominium complex in Los Angeles by, 160–63; on Disneyland, 22–24; house-within-a-house of, 167; predilection for "leaky" space, 161; revolution test, 23; as self-appointed maker of "places" in opposition to non-places of modernism, 160

Moore, Rogger, Hofflander Condominium, Los Angeles, 160–63

More, Thomas, 19, 21–22, 23, 190n.53

Morgan Bank Headquarters in New York, 121–22

Moro, Javier, 206n.26, 206n.29

Morris, Charles W., 54, 57–58, 73, 197n.34, 199n.12

Muller, Edward K., 204n.53

multinational capital: networks of, passing through hole in Disneyland, 24; predatory expansion of, 141

multinational corporations: as "main phenomenal form of capital," Mandel on, xvii; monumentalized by Union Carbide's Park Avenue headquarters, 129

multinaturalism, 89–90

Mumbai, juxtaposition of gated community with walled-in favelas (slums) in, 12 myth, Disneyland as "degenerate Utopia" and, 24

Mies, 38–39; *See also* curtain walls of corporate architecture; *specific office buildings*

O'Gorman, Marcel, 204n.43

oikos, or home, 78; origins of economy and ecology in, 53, 62, 64, 88, 90, 92; split into two houses of parliament in Latour's model, 89–90

oil: architecture and circulation of oil money, 94–103; corrupting promise of, 101; as fetish, 97, 101, 122, 202n.10; as hybrid plurality of actual objects, 97; OPEC oil embargo, 64

oil crisis (1973), 117

On Photography (Sontag), 79

OPEC oil embargo, 64

Operation Igloo White, 46, 194n.43

"organizational complex," systems-based organicism of, 37–38

organization man: functional adaptability demanded of, 131; made visible by architecture of buildings, 131

Oswalt, Philipp, 210n.25

Ovaska, Arthur, 174, 175

Panofsky, Erwin, 149, 209n.6

Papademetriou, Peter, 202n.13

Pareto, Vilfedo, 195n.15

"parliament of things," Latour's, 84–85, 88, 89–90

Parmet, Herbert S., 202n.12

Parsons, Talcott, 53, 195n.15

Pastier, John, 202n.15, 203n.27

pattern recognition: architecture as both instrument and object of, 64; McLuhan on necessity of, 60–61, 62

Patterson, John Henry, 184n.1

Payette Associates, 86, 87

Pei, I. M., 55, 111

Peirce, C. S., 54

Pennzoil Place in Houston (Johnson/Burgee), 93–95, 97–101, 104, 119, 202n.18; corner detail of, 100–101, 108–9; description of, 93–94; influence on

Roche Dinkeloo's project for two office towers, 120; as "monument to liquidity," 102; network of subterranean tunnels under Houston fed from basement level of, 102; "pretty plan" of, 98–99; reliance on crutches, 98–100; temple form, 101

perception: perceptual denaturalization, 140–41; perceptual paradox of certain visible invisibility, 125; retraining of, 124–25; Rowe and Slutzky's relativized perceptual system, 55–56, 58

periodicity: asynchronic, 45, 46, 193n.38; self-reflexive cycles of, 44

Perspecta 11, 60, 198n.43

Perspecta 12, Eisenman's review of, 59–60

Perspecta 13–14, 55, 59

perspective, Panofsky's essay on, 149

petrifaction, 113, 117

petroviolence, 101

Philadelphia, Pennsylvania: Guild House in, 71–73, 87; Venturi's house museum for Benjamin Franklin in, 168

Piazza d'Italia in New Orleans, xx, 23

Picon, Antoine, 208n.2

Piranesi, 31, 38, 161

Piranesian space, 161

Pittsburgh, Pennsylvania: Alcoa Building in, 111, 115; dematerialization into "post-steel," 116, 117; Golden Triangle commercial development, 111, 114–15; Market Square renovation, 116; PPG Place in, 111–17, 119; "Renaissance II" urban revitalization project, 115–16; U.S. Steel Building in, 111, 115; Urban Redevelopment Authority (URA), 114

"Planning Man's Physical Environment" (conference at Princeton University), 55

Plan Voisin for central Paris, Le Corbusier's, xviii

playfulness, replacement of professional melancholy with, 148–49

policy think tanks, risk/reward calculations underwriting, 36
political ecology: of Latour, 89–90;
politics of, 92
politics of language, 65
popular culture (culture industry), 6; dual
meaning within term, into 1980s,
187n.15; postmodern erasure of
distinctions between high art and, xix
populism, 4–6; aesthetic, 73, 74; as a
biopolitical practice, 5; commercialized vs. oppositional, 185n.11; duality
of meaning, 187n.15; free-market,
124; as measurement or calibration in
relation to perceived norm, 5
Portland Building (Graves), 164
Portman, John, 21, 36, 38, 74, 75–76,
83, 91, 169, 204n.44; See also Westin
Bonaventure Hotel in Los Angeles
Portoghesi, Paolo, 151–52, 153, 165,
181n.2, 209n.10
positivism, Vienna Circle of logical, 54
post-criticality, metaphysical, 128,
205n.12
post-Fordism. See postmodernism
Postmodern Condition, The (Lyotard), 69
postmodernism: ambiguous genealogy
in architecture, 181n.2; aperiodicity
of, xiii; asynchronicity of, xi; central
role of process and reproduction in,
107–8; coordinates of institutionalized, 2; counterintuitive authenticity
of, 76; cultural, 147; faux-historical
"timeline" of, 154; literary, 41; new
naturalizations of, 44; power/knowl-
edge nexus, xiii; power redefined as
control/self-control in, xiv; preemptive, exuberant embrace of status quo
by, xiv; problem of distinguishing
the real from the unreal as central to,
4; reference to architecture made in
accounts of cultural, xviii; Utopia as
name for the unthinkable in, xiv, 1, 3

postmodernism, architectural: benchmark year (1984) of, xii; circular
(videographic) temporality of, 29;
control over history relinquished
by, 29; crisis of projection associated with emergence of, 149; as
discursive formation, xii–xiii, xiv,
xv; exile of Utopia in, xvi–xvii, xxi;
globalization and, xxi–xxii; outsides or
underarticulated reality as backdrops
to, xiii; socioeconomic arrangement
and, xxiv; theoretical moves toward
rappel à l'ordre, 3–4; transformation
of "environment" as epistemological
category and emergence of, 49
Postmodernism (Jameson), 79, 83
postmodern space, 169
postmodern sublime, 76, 107–8, 145;
environment as type of, 49
Post-Modern Visions (1984 exhibition,
Deutsches Architekturmuseum in
Frankfurt), 2, 181n.2
postwar modernism, 37, 39
poverty, structural, 124
power: nested character of, xxii; redefined as control/self-control in postmodernism, xiv; role for architectural
thought in analysis, interpretation,
and critique of, xiii–xiv
PPG Industries Plaza and Tower, or PPG
Place, in Pittsburgh, 111–17, 119; as
project of reenchantment or revitalization, 115; source material for,
112–13; as urban enclave configured
as mirrored interior, 113
pragmatism, American, 54
"Presence of the Past, The" (1980 Biennale in Venice), 152, 181n.2
pretty drawing, or "pretty plan," crutch
of, 98–99
primary aesthetics, 207n.40
primary decipherment, principle of, 51
Princeton University, Lewis Thomas

Laboratory for Molecular Biology at, 86–88

production: immaterial, xvi, 184n.1; Jencks's three systems of architectural, 78

production, architecture's axis of, xvi–xvii, 4, 11–19; Agamben's topologies of exception, 11, 12–13; new segmentations, 11

Progressive Architecture (journal), 186n.13

projection, 147–51; need for new forms of, 169; persistence or afterimage of specific form of modernist vision within postmodernism, 150–51; professionalization of, 148; project (ideological phantasm) as distinct from, 149; rules of, 149–50; transformation of (modernist) crisis of representation into crisis of, 149; utopian, 148

promenade architecturale, 154–56, 162; "democratic" path, 156, 160; figural role played by, 154–55, 162; of Stirling's Neue Staatsgalerie, ambiguous anticlimax of, 155–56

Proudhonism, 208n.1

Pruitt-Igoe housing development in St. Louis, 14–19, 20, 26, 147; demolition of, 15, 16; as icon of modern architecture's presumed failures in social reform, 14–15; as instrument of environmental reform, 15–19; physical boundaries encouraging "territoriality" in, 16

pseudo-personalization, 127

psychoanalysis, 204n.43; Eisenman's "psychological man" as subject of, 8; Lacanian, 124; underlying spatiality of, 205n.3

psychology: environmental, 8–9, 187n.23; Gestalt, 55–56, 73

public housing, 26; as emblematic of allegedly failed modernist utopia, 147;

Pruitt-Igoe housing development, 14–19, 20, 26, 147

public/private partnerships, politico-economic model based on, 115–16, 117

Pulsa, 195n.9

pure visibility, 183n.14

Rabinbach, Anson, 194n.38

racism, Foucault on, 116–17

radical eclecticism, Jencks's, 48, 76–83, 91, 92, 154; unspoken anxiety encoded in, 79–80

Rainwater, Lee, 189n.40

Ramoneda, Josep, 210n.29

Rancière, Jacques, 128, 205n.1, 205n.13, 207n.40; notion of "distribution of the sensible," 123, 141, 207n.40

RAND Corporation, 34, 46

Rational Architecture (1973 Milan Triennale exhibition), 181n.2

Rause, Vince, 204n.52

Reagan, Ronald, 193n.34

Reaganomics, 103

reflexivity, risk-based paradigm and its feedback loops as models of, 43–44

regionalism, 166; critical, 182n.4, 199n.6, 210n.21

Related Companies, 139

Renaissance II urban revitalization of Pittsburgh, 115–16

repoliticization of vanguardist architectural discourse, 128

representation, architecture's axis of, xv, xvi–xvii, 4–11; populism and problem of representation, 4–6; question of how to represent unity, 10; Rossi and problem of representation, 7–9, 10; Venturi and problem of representation, 9–11

reproduction: in name of postpolitical multiplicity, 144; without original, 113, 120; privileging of, over putative original, 107–8

REINHOLD MARTIN is associate professor of architecture in the Graduate School of Architecture, Planning, and Preservation at Columbia University, where he directs the PhD program in architecture and the Temple Hoyne Buell Center for the Study of American Architecture. He is a founding coeditor of the journal *Grey Room,* author of *The Organizational Complex: Architecture, Media, and Corporate Space,* and coauthor of *Multi-National City: Architectural Itineraries.*